FIGHTING FIRES AND EATING SMOKE

FIGHTING FIRES AND EATING SMOKE

A London Fireman's Story of Infernos and Rescues

Allan Grice

Book Guild Publishing

Sussex, England

First published in Great Britain in 2009 by
The Book Guild Ltd
Pavilion View
19 New Road
Brighton, BN1 1UF

Typesetting in Times by
YHT Ltd, London

Printed in Great Britain by
CPI Antony Rowe

A catalogue record for this book is available from
The British Library.

ISBN 978 1 84624 332 5

To all within the 'Big Smoke' who, in being touched by fire and emergency, inspired me to write these accounts

Contents

Introduction

This book is an account of some of the most memorable fires, rescues and other non-fire emergency calls to which I and my colleagues responded in a near 20 years with the London Fire Brigade.

As a former Fireman in West Yorkshire, I had satisfied an ambition to become a member of one of the world's biggest and busiest fire brigades, by transferring to the capital in the 1970s.

Having had my appetite for emergency work whetted by my early career in the north, the thought of the extra challenges and experience potential within the capital strongly appealed to my nature.

In addition it was the case in those days that the gaining of a solid practical experience in fire and rescue work was a prerequisite for advancement. Accordingly, I sought out some of the capital's busiest fire stations from an early stage.

To me it was a privilege to have served in the sharpest of 'sharp end' stations within some of the highest fire risk districts in the world and to be part of a force that contained some fine characters, unparalleled in courage and leadership.

Regarding practical experience, I was fortunate to have worked within London during what were, with hindsight, some of its busiest operational years in terms of 'working jobs'.

My motives for writing have been twofold. Firstly, it has been the case over the years that upon learning of my occupation many people have shown a genuine interest in what it was really like to be a Fireman in those busy years.

I use the term Fireman, because that is what we were known as until the early 1980s when the first women entered front-line operational service and the term Firefighter was coined.

Interestingly, I have been quizzed about the sights I have seen and the emotions I have experienced by almost as many women as men.

All wanted to learn more about what it was actually like to 'turn out' to emergency calls in such a large and well-known city. A city crammed with buildings and with people of many nationalities, ethnic origins and cultural differences, and in which the potential for human drama is so high at any second of every day of every year.

Many people seemed particularly interested in the emergency responses made in the dead of night, while most people are asleep, and oblivious to the peril of fire and smoke.

For example, they wanted to know what it was like to race up to the rapidly spreading inferno of a burning house in the small hours. Our feelings on witnessing someone with their clothes alight from head to foot, someone who had leapt desperately from four floors up only to impale themselves on the sharp iron railings below, something I had seen on more than one occasion.

Many showed a fascination with the East End territory of Jack the Ripper and the Kray twins when I revealed that a large portion of my time with the London Fire Brigade had been spent within those mean and moody streets.

Others wanted to know how in those days, before health and safety legislation exerted its grip, we managed to enter burning flats, houses and commercial premises without breathing apparatus, crawling on our bellies to locate a missing child or the source of a deep-seated smoky fire.

Some of those asking questions wanted to know more about our attendance at the non-fire emergencies. How we dealt with someone threatening to jump from a tall building. How we coped when faced with having to crawl under a tube train to recover the remains of a suicide, or what it had been like to deal with the horrific aftermath of such carnage as the dreadful Moorgate tube disaster of 1975, where I had spent four days as a young officer deep under the capital's streets.

More recently, I had been asked about 7/7 and how that would have compared with the Moorgate tragedy, and the part our fire services will have to play in this new age of global terrorism.

The UK fire and rescue services have been, over the years, an essentially modest and 'silent' service. Television programmes have partly helped to publicise the work, but there have been very few personal accounts available of what it was really like to have been there, at the 'sharp end' during such operationally hectic years.

The second motive for writing was to provide something of a social record of a period that has now gone, yet which was integral to the high regard in which today's fire and rescue crews are now held.

It is also important to mention that although times and equipment and operational strategies have by necessity changed, what will hopefully never alter is the spirit, attitude and courage of all dedicated fire and rescue workers. These are the heavy ballast of consistency in an ever shifting world.

Although the actual number of emergency responses received today has increased in many cases compared with the earlier years of these accounts, the ratio of calls that turn out to be 'working fires and rescues', is far smaller today than was the case in the periods of most of the accounts.

These reductions in regular serious fire and rescue jobs are a consequence of progressive fire safety and building regulation advancements and a far greater focus upon fire prevention.

So the accounts within this book contain and record a good deal of what was often firefighting in the raw, during which you were measured as a 'good hand' by your ability to 'get into fires' and by your willingness to 'eat smoke', the term used to describe working without breathing apparatus, before every crew member was provided with this vital protection in later years.

Given the very high numbers of emergencies attended, I have had to be very selective in the accounts chosen. However, those depicted embrace such incidents as fires caused by the once deadly paraffin heater, by cigarettes, by arsonists, along with some of the most notable non-fire emergencies of the time.

The accounts also record the sterling part played by the wooden-wheeled escape ladder and the precariously poised hook ladder in the annals of rescue and firefighting within the capital, up to their withdrawal in the early 1980s.

It is probably correct to say that most visitors to London associate far more with its West End than with its East End. But many of the most serious incidents over the years involved what used to be termed 'The London in the East', including the blitz raids of the early 1940s. Author Geoffrey Fletcher entitled one of his books *The London Nobody Knows*, and that description could apply to some of the locations of some of the incidents depicted in these accounts.

The East End has a rich history of human life and struggle, and since the 1980s it has witnessed a great deal of change. The 2012

Olympics will see The London in the East, or at least its outer periphery, developed in a fashion that few of us would have ever envisaged when we charged on fire engines through those grey streets to the east of Tower Bridge.

London undoubtedly holds a fascination and attraction for visitors from across the planet and many return time and time again as it has depths that can never be properly plumbed by a thousand visits.

The fascination for the capital overall, which I had first experienced as a young man from the north, and which was no doubt heightened by my being from outside its environs, still holds me in its thrall today.

The comprehensive experiences I was privileged to acquire from the challenging business of fire and rescue in this teeming metropolis have consolidated those feelings as I look back on them from the standpoint of today.

As I have mentioned, the book was penned for those two major reasons and I hope that some of the questions asked of me will be answered satisfactorily, and that what was an historic era in the Brigade's fine and noble history will have been recorded from the perspective of those who kept that ceaseless vigil on the front line.

If I have been successful in my task, it is likely that the next time you see those red Pumps, ladders and rescue units charging through the thronging streets amidst the haunting wail and blare of sirens and the spinning whirl of beacons, you will be seeing them with a new eye and a deeper insight.

Chapter One

Deadbolts

It's just after two in the morning when the urgent clarion call of the turn out bell signals an emergency somewhere out there in this highly populated and high-fire-risk district.

A few men leap up from their chairs in front of the television on which a spaghetti western has bored them for the last hour. Others spring up from their dormitory bunks or from their seats around the mess room table where they were sipping mugs of tea.

The doors to the pole house are pushed open with a crash. With a metallic-sounding squeal, men plunge down the brass pole, landing with a cushioned thump on the circular mat of the appliance room floor.

'Smoke Issuing Hoxton Street N1 – Pump Escape and Pump,' the duty man calls out as he reads the cryptic message hammered out by the teleprinter keys. He gives copies to the Station Officer and Sub Officer. They mount the gleaming red Pumps, which always stand, cab doors ajar, poised, ever-ready for that rapid response to someone's shout for help.

The huge red doors to the station rumble upwards. They have barely halted as the two machines roar out into the Shoreditch night, the rotating blue arcs of their beacons reflecting in the windows of adjoining premises. On with helmet, neckerchief, boots, leggings, tunic. Finally axe and belt as the eight tons of Pump Escape, the Pump hard on its tail, accelerates away, the motion causing the huge, red, wooden-spoked wheels of the escape ladder to spin.

As the driver makes a squealing left turn into Hoxton Street, a unique odour comes through the half-open cab window. It is the unmistakable smell of a burning building. A pungent, sharp smell that indicates this call is not another false alarm. It is a pulse-

1

quickening signal to the crew that here is a working fire, and that at this early hour it is likely that persons will be involved.

The blue beacons of the Pump from the neighbouring station of Kingsland Road can be seen a hundred metres ahead. In the yellow light of the street lamps the crouched silhouette of a Fireman can be seen unrolling a length of hose, usually a good indication that something urgent is 'on'.

'Looks like they've got something,' shouts out Mike Deveen above the engines' drone.

'Do you want BA, Guv?' asks Leading Fireman Andy Carlisle.

'Let's wait a minute and see exactly what's what,' he replies as the two appliances hiss to a halt. As Station Officer Tuke alights, Kingsland's Sub Officer runs over to him. 'Guv, we've got a fire in a second-floor flat. It's smoke-logged and neighbours say that an old woman lives there on her own,' he blurts out in a breathless voice. 'We're hauling a hose line up on to the balcony before forcing an entry,' he goes on.

'OK, Sub, got it. Transmit a *"Persons Reported"* and then follow that with an informative from me at this address: *"Flat on second floor of residential block smoke-logged, one person believed involved, efforts being made to gain entry."'*

The Sub Officer turns on his heel to get his driver to transmit these messages, and Station Officer Tuke's voice follows him: 'Sub, make sure the rear of the block is checked and let me know the score – my fellas will rig in BA now.'

'Got you, Guv,' he shouts back.

The heavy rhythmic thump of a 14-pound sledgehammer is echoing in the morning air as we access the balcony. It has transpired that the flat door, like so many others in this locality, is secured with deadbolts as it has failed to yield to the kicks from firemen's boots.

Within the inner city, where the fear of crime is high, people, especially the elderly, cannot be criticised for feeling the need to be protected by strong steel deadbolts, which lock the heavy front door into the heavy frame. Although fire emergencies occur more often in heavily populated areas, its threat is not perceived with the same fear as burglary or assault. But when fire does occur, forcing an entry to rescue those overcome can cost valuable time, which can spell the difference between life and death.

Time is of the essence in firefighting. Especially when persons are involved who may be gasping the last portion of air remaining in the smoke-logged flat as we beaver away urgently.

The music hall jokes about sliding poles belie the vital importance of the saving of seconds once a call for help has been received, and no quicker method of accessing the appliances than that provided by the polished pole exists. The area around Shoreditch is mainly high-fire-risk territory. All calls to building fires will, in normal circumstances, result in two pumping appliances being on scene within five minutes with a third one arriving within eight.

From the first clamour of the bells at Shoreditch our progress is aided by the sliding pole, and by the overall swiftness of crews turning out in under a minute. We are also assisted at this incident by the relative quietness of the streets at this early hour. But unless we can force the flat door soon, this time advantage will be lost.

Station Officer Tuke has over 25 years service. The bulk spent in and around Shoreditch and London's East End, on whose boundary stands Hoxton, once one of the poorest areas of the country. He has seen it all before and his coolness is legendary. Had he kept a record over the years he might have noted that his involvement at fires in these huge redbrick tenements would run into many hundreds.

With that finely honed instinct for danger, only achieved via practical hands-on experience of similar incidents, he knows that there is not a second to lose, and that the forcing of the door is taking too long.

'We're going in through the window. Take out a pane,' he shouts to Fireman Johnny Carre.

Fireman Carre has been around years also. With a skill honed by having done it many times before, he removes his axe from its pouch in almost a single movement. With the flat side of the blade he makes a small hole in the kitchen window from which a malevolent looking cloud of yellow smoke races out and up the front of the building. The yellow indicates the presence of sulphur. One of the constituents of that deadly cocktail of smoke, which arises from a bottled-up fire. It awaits only the right proportion of oxygen before it explodes in a flashover of flame and searing heat. Just as it had done when two Chelsea firemen had died following severe burns received during early morning firefighting operations inside a King's Road restaurant.

The release of this smoke could play its part in improving the conditions for whoever might be inside. But by this stage they would normally be in no state to know the difference and a 'snatch' rescue would have to be attempted.

BA wearers are rigging, ready to enter via the doors with their hose line already charged. But the bulk of their BA sets won't facilitate a quick entry via the small window. It is this certain knowledge, informed by years of experience, that causes the Station Officer to order the window to be broken and opened.

Knowing how hot conditions would be inside, John Carre pulls his tunic sleeve over his left hand to protect it from the heat of the window's metal handle. Twists it and slowly opens the casement to vent even more of that evil smoke.

There is no time to waste now because the external air could cause the whole flat to 'light up', and without further ado Station Officer Tuke instructs me to follow him as he climbs into the kitchen.

'For God's sake get that door open,' I shout out, as I too pull myself up and over the narrow window opening into the kitchen. To know that the door has been forced means that the Station Officer and myself will be able to grab anyone inside. Pull them out to fresh air without fumbling in these vile and lung-bursting conditions for the deadbolts and securing chains of the door. It is such thoughts that provide the impetus to make that extra push to locate and retrieve the casualty in what is termed a snatch rescue.

I lower myself slowly into the flat. Placing my feet cautiously. Trying to establish if anyone is under my feet. It is not unusual to find casualties below windows or behind doors. These are the positions often reached by them in their desperate efforts to escape to the outside air.

Above the thump of the sledgehammer I can hear a running tap close by. But so thick is the smoke that it is impossible to see more than a few inches, and its brown thickness along with the great heat bottled up is already causing me to feel light-headed. There isn't a second to waste. If the occupant hasn't already succumbed to the smoke, their death must be perilously close.

The plan is to carry out a crawling search, the arms doing a sweeping motion, not unlike a swimmer's breaststroke, and feeling, all the time feeling for a victim.

Firstly around the perimeters. Then diagonally across the floor. It is vital to feel under beds. On top of them. On and around sofas and chairs. Even to look inside wardrobes, broom cupboards and into filled baths as people have been known to try anything to escape the smoke and heat of fire. Children have even been known to climb inside a chest of drawers, sliding them shut.

Without a BA set, it is vital to keep as close to the floor as possible. If there is any breathable air remaining, it will be there. A life-saving draught of oxygen, a half inch below the toxic 'cosh' of carbon monoxide, which lurks with such deadly intent inside the thick, acrid, hot blanket of smoke. Like a mugger's lead pipe wrapped in a woollen sock, awaiting its opportunity to knock you into unconsciousness from behind. A smoke that can start a coughing fit, which, with each convulsion, draws in more of its deadly stew. A smoke that is sometimes so high in temperature that the sensitive skin of the ears begins to tingle, ringing the warning bell of withdrawal. All experienced firemen, in those days before full face-mask BA sets covered the ears and muted this signal of great heat, knew that such a tingling could be a precursor to the flashover, one of the Firefighter's most lethal enemies. That tingling provides an early warning that conditions are getting too hot. Firefighters are human beings with the same skin, lungs and senses of other people.

No matter how well trained, it is not humanly possible to remain inside buildings where the heat is about ready to peel the skin on the ears, especially when not protected by BA. Our ears are tingling at this fire. Myself and the 'Guvnor' instinctively know that we must locate the occupant quickly and make good our escape with an even greater urgency before the whole apartment erupts in a ball of searing flame, which could reduce us both to charred hulks.

I am flat on the floor of what is the kitchen to this council-owned dwelling. My mouth is closed. I am breathing as steadily as possible through the 'filter' of the nostrils, thus limiting the amount of toxic smoke inhaled. I am, in fact, 'eating smoke'. It is a foul tasting dish, which stings the lining of the nose, mouth and throat. But at least I am not as yet coughing and vomiting up its foul content, which often results when too much smoke from a smouldering fire is ingested.

I can feel the relative coolness of the thin life-preserving channel of air, a fraction of an inch above the floor linoleum, which now feels more than a little hot. I can feel the moistness of tears running down my hot cheeks as the hot smoke pricks my eyeballs as I search every inch of my side of the kitchen.

My right hand brushes against and then grasps the polished smoothness of a tubular steel table leg. I feel under and around but can feel no human form. I raise the same hand above and feel if the woman is slumped on top of the table but there's no one there. While running my hand over the table I am contorting my body so as to keep my nose near that air channel at the floor. It is good that this invisible lifeline now feels a little stronger from the external cool morning air entering via the broken and partly open window. It is not good to hear the heavy thumps of the sledgehammer, indicating that those dreaded deadbolts are still holding the front door, and I inwardly curse.

I can hear the rasping cough of Station Officer Tuke as he searches the other half of the floor. We can't have been inside the building more than a minute but it already feels ten times longer. Even though Ben Tuke is only a few feet away the thick shroud of smoke has rendered visibility to virtually zero. Only his coughing, the scrape of his leather fireboots as he moves around, and the soft swish of sweeping arms indicating his presence.

The plan is, as a last resort, for me to locate the door, if still unforced, and release its frustrating security devices to allow the BA crews to enter. But at almost the same time, Station Officer Tuke croaks out, 'She's here, I've got her.'

I crawl towards his voice, sensing the increasing lightness in my head. My hands land on the limp, hot skin, slippery with perspiration. In the yellow fog of smoke my lamp can just discern a woman's face.

'Let's lift her up, Guv, and pass her through the window,' I cough out, and with that we grasp her clammy hot form.

Although she only weighs about eight stone, the heat of the fire has made her perspire so much that it is like trying to grip a bar of wet soap, and the toxic fumes have weakened us both to the extent that the lifting of her is not as easy as it might seem.

It is perhaps inevitable that a 25-year history of fighting fires in the busiest stations in the highest fire risk areas of the East End could sometimes catch up with a man. Even one whose reputation for eating smoke is legendary could succumb at some fires if the conditions are right. Too many nights of sudden change from inertia to the hard conditions like in this fire can exert a heavy physical toll. And the Guvnor was now nearer 50 than 40 years of age.

I sense that the smoke has got to him more than me. Perhaps it is that he has a quarter of a century on me, and that my own frame has not been exposed to his years of punishment. Whatever it is, his efforts to lift the woman, notwithstanding her diminutive size, are proving a struggle. Time is not on her side. We have to get her out now!

My own head now feels lighter still so it is now or never. I push my left hand and arm under the victim's back, and the right under the thin thighs, the skin of which is hot and clammy to the touch. 'Grasp my hands, Guv,' I cough out. He does, his thick fingers dwarfing mine, and we slowly lift the unconscious slumped form. As we stumble on to our knees the heat encased within that viscous brown wool-like shawl of smoke stings the face and ears like a thousand hot knitting needles. It stings even more as we raise her higher through this baking oven of rolling smoke, which races towards the open window.

With a joint heave, I push hard on her left calf and feel something come away in my hand. It is a sliver of skin, cooked by her earlier involvement in whatever fire had caused this dense, acrid smoke, now so thick that I can almost chew it.

With head reeling and almost on the point of collapse, we push her small frame up to the strong hands at the window and she is out, and the same hands assist the pair of us back to the outside. There we stoop, coughing and retching, and feeling the recuperative effect of the never so sweet taste of the London air.

Through running and puffed-up eyes, and with mucus hanging from the nose like icicles and caking our lips and chin, we can see the limp form of an elderly woman. She is lying face upwards. Her frail, hot body laid in an undignified, legs splayed position atop a rapidly pulled off fire tunic, placed to insulate her from the cold concrete balcony.

Her flimsy flower-patterned nightdress clings to her still perspiring form. There is a raw pink patch on her left calf, clearly a burn, and from her left nostril a bubble of mucus and blood has issued. Fireman Carre is crouched over her now, applying mouth to mouth resuscitation through the filter of his black silk neckerchief. He continues diligently until the ambulance crew take over and administer oxygen before speeding her away to the London Hospital at Whitechapel.

'It was bleedin' hot in there – and those poxy deadbolts are the death,' snarls the Station Officer to no one in particular as he begins to recover from the smoke and heat. His back, like mine, is propped up by the external wall of the flat and our legs are stretched out in front. Our tunics are unbuttoned to release the perspiring body heat caused by our exertions and by the heat of the burning apartment.

'John,' calls out Station Officer Tuke to Fireman Carre, who only a few minutes earlier had been crouched over the rescued woman applying mouth to mouth resuscitation, 'Send a "Stop" will yeh?'

John Carre pulls his notepad and stub pencil from the inside tunic pocket. 'What do you want sending, Guv?' he queries, licking the lead point of his pencil briefly.

'From me, at this address – *three-roomed flat on second floor, ten per cent damaged by fire, remainder damaged by smoke and heat. One elderly female rescued from kitchen at front of flat, overcome removed, one hose reel jet, breathing apparatus,*' instructs the Station Officer.

Almost simultaneous with the rescue, the front door has finally yielded. Two BA men, equipped with a hose reel, have soon located the fire's source. They ventilate the remaining smoke by opening the sash windows, two thirds open at the top, one third the bottom. This piece of good practical firemanship ensuring the most efficient release of pent-up smoke and heat.

In a back bedroom where sepia-tinted photographs of a young man garbed in the uniform of the British Army stand on a bedside cabinet, the scorched and burned bedding points to the culprit. An electric underblanket, probably not serviced for years, has overheated and caused this fire, and the resulting flames have begun to burn a veneered wardrobe, hence the acrid smoke.

There is little doubt that the burning to the victim's calf was caused by this heat. She must have awoken, already half dazed by the smoke, and, sensing the pain and the fire, crawled from the bed and into the kitchen to get water, which would explain the running cold tap.

But those deadly fumes overpowered her with their hot breath, and deadly they were because we learn an hour or so later that she was dead on arrival at the London Hospital in nearby Whitechapel.

Death can never be a stranger to those whose daily business is that of firefighting and rescuing people from the calamities and emergencies that can strike without notice at any time, and no more is this so than in the larger towns and cities.

Death leaves its calling card captioned 'fire' all too often. Annually, across the globe thousands perish or are injured by its searing flames and fiery toxic fumes, which can extinguish a human life as rapidly as a breath can snuff out a candle flame. Included within these casualties are those Firefighters who made the supreme sacrifice with their lives that others might live, or their properties be saved.

Entering into situations where the natural human reaction is to flee, lies at the heart of this occupation. It is a tribute to Firefighters' training, experience and calm in the face of what are often extreme hazards that the ratio of Firefighter death and serious injuries is low relative to the thousands of incidents responded to every year. But it is because their primary goal is to preserve life that such a sense of failure can accompany such incidents as this in which, in spite of valiant efforts, a life is lost.

Recuperated by the cold fresh air, we are soon back inside the flat, carefully checking to ensure that the fire has been fully extinguished. Station Officer Ben Tuke senses that the woman won't survive and, in anticipating the coroner's inquest, requests the brigade photographer to record the scene, firstly ensuring that nothing is unduly disturbed.

As officer in charge it is his responsibility to attempt to accurately pinpoint the cause of the fire. A close examination later reveals that the underblanket had overheated and that the fuse was inappropriate for the equipment. It is likely that the overheated and poorly insulated circuitry had ignited the bedding, and all of these facts are recorded in the Station Officer's small beige-coloured notebook. I stand alongside Ben Tuke as he makes his notes and look around the flat, which has been the home of the 79-year-old woman. It is a typical dwelling, one of thousands to be found throughout what was then the Greater London Council area.

Across inner London there were scores of blocks of flats of this type. The same design as those seen by all who had ever watched cricket matches at the Oval at Kennington. The large redbrick blocks with access balconies overlooked the ground, and it is on one of those balconies that the woman rescued is first laid, and it is in such a block that she had lived the last years of her life.

In the living room is an old oak sideboard with brass-handled doors either side of a central cupboard. On top of this there is a porcelain salad dish within a polished rosewood bowl, itself edged with brass. It is the sort of prize given in the 1930s and 1940s for sporting success, and a small brass shield, its inscription now almost disappeared from years of weekly polishing, is affixed to the front. By the side of this bowl is a sepia-tinted photograph. It shows a

9

muscular young man, in his mid-twenties. He has a head of thick dark hair and is standing, in a boxer's pose, wearing a white singlet, black shorts and tall black boots, which reach the lower calf.

I walk out on to the balcony where several elderly neighbours are now gathered, shocked and tearful at the drama that has taken place so close to home. I discover that the woman did indeed live on her own. Her husband had been killed in the Second World War at Arnhem, and he had been the boxer on the sideboard photograph. She had never remarried, had no children and kept herself largely to herself. Decades on your own, I think. Old, frail and with only the frozen-in-time photographs of happier days past to glance at along with memories to sustain the soul in the early dark hours of a life which has ended so sadly in this austere hard brick block of a tenement dwelling.

In due course we clamber back into the Pump to begin the mile drive back to Shoreditch, and as the appliance traverses the deserted streets, I look around at the great diversity of commercial and residential property, which makes up this area, and can't help but reflect upon the irony of the national fire risk categorisation system.

In this inner city location, which at the time of this incident had some of the highest levels of fire risk, occupants of houses and flats, no matter what their social or financial status, were virtually guaranteed two fire appliances inside of five minutes from the making of an emergency call.

By contrast, those residents of most parts of the outer suburbs, including those owners of some of the most expensive properties at the pinnacle of green belt suburban affluence, would, in many cases, not see a fire crew inside double that time.

I can't help but ponder as to whether the frail old woman, seeing out her final years in her run-down estate with its high crime rate and general shabbiness, would have traded the speed of the fire service attendance for the chance to live in the relative peace and cleanliness of the green belt.

But it is a futile thought, I conclude. Not only has our promptness not saved her life, but she, like the vast majority of the population, would have no inkling that such a risk categorisation existed.

Fires and emergencies 'always happen to others' is the usual way in which the public perceive things. I feel sure that even though there have been many, many incidents at which the swift arrivals have

10

saved countless lives and properties, this perception that 'fires only happen to others', means that most residents of the outer suburbs are blissfully unaware that they have to wait longer for the fire service to arrive at their burning homes.

I articulate these thoughts around the mess room table on our return, and it leads to a lively debate.

'So if you think that, why is it that whenever the Brigade publishes proposals to close a local station in the sticks, there's such a hoo hah made by local residents?' asks Mike Deveen, a stocky 33-year-old with ten years service, and one of the more forthright members of the watch.

'Well, that's just it ain't it, nobody gives two hoots about such things until they are about to lose everything,' responds Niall Pointer, a 24-year-old thin young man with a footballing gift that has led to him having trials with a prominent London side.

'Look at that job on North Kensington's ground last year when they got four kids out of that tenement, and the third floor collapsed a few seconds afterwards. If that had happened out in the sticks, it could have been four dead,' he continues, with a rising passion in his voice.

'Suppose it all comes down to if you're a rich geezer in a posh mansion in say Totteridge, you have to accept that you might cop it. Or you have to wait longer to be rescued than if you live around 'ere,' pipes in Jim Pile, a keen angler, whose placid temperament reflects the relaxing nature of his hobby, but belies his abilities as one of the most experienced and capable men on the station.

'Yeah, maybe that's true, but most deaths and injuries happen much more in the sharp end of the Brigade, usually in the most run down areas for a variety of social, economic and political reasons,' injects Jim Peating, a former schoolteacher with a degree in economics.

'Oh hark at brainbox here,' half jokes our chef and mess manager, Fireman George Joynt.

'Well, Jim's not wrong is he, and let's not forget the Home Office risk categorisation scheme is about the most effective use of public money in the way Pumps are sited within the locations of highest fire risks,' says Station Officer Tuke from his position at the top of the mess table, where we have gathered for our post incident mug of tea.

'I reckon that in the future it won't be the number of Pumps on stations that will be the only thing. It will be fire prevention involvement by us as well,' remarks Jim Peating.

'You can stuff that for a game of soldiers, Jim, I came into this job to put fires out. If we prevent 'em too much, we'll be out of a job,' retorts Niall Pointer, who is never slow to give his opinion.

'Faulty thinking, Niall,' responds Jim Peating. 'In the future politicians will be all for prevention rather than cure,' pontificates the ex-schoolteacher.

'Trouble with you, Jim mate, is that you have read too much crap,' Niall digs back smartly.

'You will see, mate, you will see,' says Jim, giving his head a sideways shake, as if to register his impatience with those incapable of a bit of lateral thinking or sense of vision.

'It's getting too heavy for me is all this, especially at half four in the morning. I'm off to my pit,' shrugs Jim Pile.

'Changing the subject, Guv,' chips in Dec Mayo, the watch probationer, a heavily built 22-year-old whose prematurely greying hair makes him look a lot older than he is. 'When are the Brigade going to get us a decent bit of gear for forcing our way into buildings? Those deadbolts were a right problem earlier.'

'New breaking-in tool, young man,' challenges the Guvnor. 'Some of you want to get some extra fitness training in. I've got a 15-year-old boy who could have got into that flat in half the time you lot took,' he glowers with only a little bit of tongue in his fleshy cheek.

But then our Station Officer was not a man to hand out praise easily. He was of that school of management that likes to maintain control and authority by creating an impression that one could always do better. He was the 'old sweat' who knew that too much praise could create complacency, or cause his men to think that he was becoming soft. Ben Tuke was a product of a tough heritage.

Chapter Two

Firedogs and Fire Risks

Perhaps the philosophy of our Station Officer was not surprising, given that when he had joined the Brigade there were quite a few men who had enrolled before the war, and returned to it after active military service.

Then the nation's mood was one of a confidence in the no-nonsense, pugnacious approach that had helped vanquish a foreign foe. He also had worked with those who had remained with the National Fire Service and endured the huge conflagrations caused by the nightly blitz raids on the capital. The massive casualties in two world wars within a quarter of a century had also sensitised the country to the need to preserve life, not destroy it. It was perhaps such an awareness of the sanctity of human life that consolidated the Brigade's traditional life-saving ethos and its heritage of modest, unassuming bravery.

In his early career he had worked with many tough old 'firedogs', most of whom had once crewed the open-bodied Pumps, which had no protection from the elements. Many was the occasion when they, soaked to the skin after a fire, would return to their stations in the early hours. Frozen by the icy draught whistling through their ill-protected frames, and with ungloved hands almost welded to the brass handrails in freezing winter temperatures.

Like many veterans who tend to scoff at the relative comforts of the new generation who follow them, they would have perceived the 'new breed' of recruit as soft and ill-disciplined. These experiences had forged his own attitudes and philosophies, which were themselves further tempered by the strict discipline code applicable to the British Fire Service by way of the national disciplinary regulations.

In Ben Tuke's early career orders were still orders. It was rare in

13

those more deferential times for even the loquacious citizens of the capital to seriously question the orders of the junior ranked officers in charge of stations, and certainly not those holding senior ranks.

London has always had relatively more employment prospects than in the provinces, and some who had enrolled with the Brigade, but couldn't 'cut the mustard' of a disciplined service, left to take up a less demanding occupation. But for those within, its reputation as one of the world's most respected firefighting forces, allied to the no-nonsense semi-military style of man-management, created an efficient and effective emergency service. An efficiency gained from passing on to future generations of Firefighters the hard-won practical skills of firemanship within the capital city.

True, Ben Tuke had moved along with the times to a fair degree. His two teenage children saw to that. But his basic attitudes and instincts were moulded in those early years, and by the hot anvil of the inner city fireground, on which he had witnessed all too often the ravages of fire on property and the human frame. It was these factors that had convinced him that managing men in such a potentially hazardous public service needed a fair mind, but a firm, unyielding countenance, so as to ensure that they reacted immediately to his commands.

He reasoned that this would lead to the highest levels of efficiency in terms of effective rescue and firefighting, as well as acting as a safeguard to their own skins. The alternative sloppy, liberalised approach was not something Ben Tuke would ever countenance. He saw that as a danger to both the men under his command and the public whom they were employed to protect from fire and emergency in this huge city.

Whenever a boss and worker situation exists, there will always be those who will try to exploit any perceived weakness in those holding the mantle of Officer in Charge. It is a fact that some, born and bred within the centres of large metropolitan cities, can develop a code of craftiness and guile by which they live their lives. 'Dog eat dog' can more often than not be the rule within the asphalt and brick jungle.

Nowhere is the potential for such exploitation greater than when men are in a group, and outnumbered are those who have taken on that mantle of responsibility. Then, as now, on some watches on some stations, it only needed the Guvnor to drop their guard by not asserting their authority, for the left hook of dissent and backchat to land with a bang. It was only a short walk from that point before a weak Guvnor could be beaten into submission by the tail wagging the dog. Always a potential where the collective security of 'the pack' can provide a louder and more persistent bark than the dog on its own.

No one knew this fact better than men like Ben Tuke. He had been born and raised within the mean streets of the inner city. He had spent a lifetime within that environment in which the art of surviving in a hard, cold world had been instilled in him. He was the very antithesis of the sort who have their head in the clouds and fail to see the sucker punch. Above all though, he was a man's man, who had been raised and mentored throughout his life by those of a similar inclination.

Officers like Ben Tuke knew that the safety of the public and his Firefighters, along with the effectiveness of operational strategies, relied upon the firm and decisive hand of leadership. Under such experienced and strong characters was the fine reputation of the Brigade built.

The foundations of that construction were solid, and the aggregate within its building blocks was an unquestioning discipline and a high courage, which derived from a great respect for human life.

It was hard for most of his younger firemen to come to terms with their guvnor's philosophy. A philosophy that was in sharp contrast to the permissiveness and liberalism of the times. Getting his Firefighters to appreciate that in his day the donning of breathing apparatus at every fire was considered almost a sign of weakness, even a form of being effete by some officers and men, was almost impossible.

In those days, before the advent of health and safety legislation, which, in due course would have a major bearing upon the strategies adopted at fires and other emergencies, firemen were expected to be able to withstand the punishment from the smoke and heat of fires without outwardly flinching.

The somewhat masochistic practice of enduring thick smoke was known as smoke eating. In those days it was often seen as a mark of toughness and resolve amongst firemen. There was, of course, little option because the luxury of a breathing apparatus set for every crew member did not exist until some years later. Only two or three sets existed on selected fire engines, and for the large and smoky fires the specialist Emergency Tender would be be requested and this had a crew specifically geared and trained in advanced BA procedures.

15

In any event, the self-contained oxygen BA set was a far more complicated piece of equipment than the compressed air apparatus of today. Not only did it take several minutes to don and start up, but after use at a fire it required a long-winded cleaning, servicing and testing procedure before it could be used again. Thus, for all of these reasons, it became the custom to 'eat smoke' and cough one's lungs up, but not complain, at least not over-much.

At that period there were few pressures and safety lobbies to hinder these masochistic practices. Or to warn of the potential for lung disease in later life, and these raw practices became the norm. Indeed, in relative terms of safety, compared to the hazards faced by many firemen during the war, the prospect of a future illness as a consequence of fighting fire was not necessarily viewed as a major concern by fit young men. In any event, it was a chance that would be taken, given the long-term security of employment provided.

Given the thousands of emergencies responded to annually by the Brigade, the numbers of Firefighter deaths and serious injuries have always been relatively low. But these relatively low figures mask the extremely diverse range of fire hazards existing across the capital, and the ever present risk to life and limb that such hazards create.

Hoxton, the scene of our earlier fire, and only a short distance from Shoreditch, is said by those who have studied the capital's history, to be the real gateway from north and west London to the East End. A district that is historically famous and infamous.

Within and around these streets, many barely changed from the Victorian era, were hundreds of commercial concerns and many dwellings, all of which posed varying levels of fire risk. Printers and lithographers, furniture makers, timber and veneer yards, garment manufacturers, gold and silversmiths, coffee, tea and spice merchants, glue and paint factories, handbag and umbrella makers stood shoulder to shoulder with huge warehouses. Many on the waterfront of the Thames. Some in quaintly named streets such as Frying Pan Alley, Flower and Dean, Bell Lane, Fournier, Heneage, Chicksand and Goulston.

In such streets, seldom visited by the millions of tourists who visit the capital each year (and hundreds of others from the West End to the capital's suburbs), the noble history of London Fire Brigade has been written. If those buildings could speak, they would tell a tale of smoke. Thin at first, then gradually thickening to blot out the yellow glow of lamp standards. Of a faint ruddy glow behind windows,

16

which grew into massive tongues of orange flame with frightening speed, to shatter glazing and to burst through a roof high above the pavements and courtyards below.

They would also tell of those occasions when human life was imperilled. When the form of a man or woman, boy or girl, might be silhouetted by the raging fire about them. And they would tell that without fail, above the crash and noise of fire and the sometime cries for help, would come the urgent and insistent clamour of a bell or siren, echoing in the streets all around, and heralding the imminent arrival of the Brigade.

A Brigade made up of individuals trained to work as an effective team, who would flinch at nothing in their quest to save life and property. Often they would succeed. Sometimes they would be too late, and sometimes they would pay the ultimate sacrifice. As was the case at such incidents as Smithfield in 1958, King's Road in 1967, Dudgeons Wharf in 1969, Maida Vale in 1975 and King's Cross in 1987 to name but a few.

This is an account not only of some of the fires and emergencies attended within the boundaries of the East End, and in other parts of the capital, but of the underlying spirit, attitudes and motivations of those called to confront them.

Chapter Three

Mean Streets

In the area of the London Fire Brigade, it has often been the case that a high proportion of what are termed 'working fires' and rescues, occur in the suburbs. A working fire or working job is one in which crews are fully committed with fighting a serious fire and/or involved in the search for 'persons reported', or rescuing either via internal staircases or by Brigade ladders or aerial platforms.

Where a district has a high immigrant population, it is usually the case, as it is in other world cities, that many are housed in substandard accommodation, where the fire safety is often poor or non-existent. In any large city there are always areas of social deprivation, and, as a general rule, more fire fatalities occur here than in the more salubrious districts.

During the period to which these chapters relate such fire station grounds as Paddington, North Kensington, Brixton, Shoreditch, Stoke Newington, Whitechapel, Islington and Holloway recorded high numbers of working fires and multiple fatalities and rescues on a regular basis.

Many if not most of these incidents involved domestic dwellings, but within these areas there was a high number of commercial premises. The combined effect of this was that the level of fire hazard and its corollary of fire risk was very high, and accordingly those serving on such stations could be assured that they would have little rest from the clamour of the call out bell.

By way of example, Holloway fire station is one of these inner-city suburban stations. On my first ever journey to London by road, I had entered the capital from the north via the Archway and Holloway Roads. I can well recall my own sense that the streets here had seen more than a little activity by the firemen of that district, and that the level of attendance to fires was probably as high as ever. When I was eventually fortunate enough to work within this area, my instincts proved correct.

When I served at a later stage in most of those other inner city districts, I discovered that these fire stations were equally active.

As a place name, Holloway is said to have derived from the 'hollow way', the name given to a trench-like route along which cattle droves were herded to the market area at Smithfield, before the expansion of the capital and the construction of those roads which became the vital arteries, carrying London's lifeblood. Holloway Road is in fact the southern end of the A1 Great North Road. Beginning in the City of London, it travels to Highbury Corner just above Islington fire station on Upper Street, after which this teeming broad highway travels mainly in a straight line. After Highbury Corner the road passes a magistrates court, council flats, garages, department stores and shops of all sizes plus the inevitable pubs, clubs, cafes and take away outlets. It then climbs to Archway and the Archway Road, not far from the huge general hospital named after London's one time mayor Richard Whittington. Thereafter it unfolds passing through ten English counties on its route northwards to Edinburgh.

Many will have travelled along the mighty Holloway Road. Many newcomers from the north will have seen that vast vista of the coming capital below them as they descend the Archway Road. Some, like myself, will have realised, as the size and density of buildings increase, that here is the beginning of the real inner suburbs. Many will have travelled along the Holloway Road but few will have been aware that within those often bleak streets, many of the capital's 'bread and butter' working fires and rescues have taken place over the years. During the earlier part of the period in question, more than a small portion of streets that fell within the boundaries of Shoreditch, Stoke Newington and Islington were very shabby, unkempt and down-at-heel. It certainly would have been difficult to envisage then that many of Islington's streets would witness a process of 'gentrification' such that the country's prime minister would eventually live there.

But it was precisely because the district had areas that were low rent rather than high that the fire stations' logbooks showed such a high percentage of turnouts. From the early 1950s, Holloway was a settling ground for a good proportion of Irish men and women. They came over to take advantage of the work prospects created by an expanding post-war economy. The men in the fields of building construction, civil engineering and public transport, while many of the women supplied a high proportion of the demand for nursing staff in the hospitals and infirmaries across the area.

In addition, a steady stream of immigrants from Malta, Cyprus, Greece and Turkey began to arrive in London. They began to occupy the relatively cheap accommodation in such districts as Finsbury Park, Camden Town, Holloway and Islington. Similar to other parts of the capital such as North Kensington, Paddington, Hammersmith, Brixton and Camberwell, and not too dissimilar to the Lower East Side of Manhattan or the Bronx and Harlem, a cosmopolitan melting pot of languages, traditions and native cultures.

It is within such a heady brew of humanity that the inner-city Firefighter is often a first-hand witness to life in the raw. A witness to scenes of tragedy and triumph, disaster and success as they carry out their unceasing vigil. A vigil by day and in the long watches of the night.

Chapter Four

Perilous Paraffin

During the 60s and 70s, particularly in those areas that had a pre-ponderance of large Victorian houses, many of which were converted into flats, or had the older tenement type dwellings, the Brigade witnessed many serious fires caused by paraffin heaters, and these regularly resulted in death and injury.

During this period, such stations as North Kensington, Brixton, Harlesden, Paddington, Holloway and Islington responded regularly to fires in such premises, which were usually in the more socially deprived parts of London boroughs, and which often involved immigrants to these shores.

In the often icy winter months, and in properties without central heating, it was customary to make use of the portable paraffin heater to try to counter the cold. A cold that would be more acutely felt by those whose origins were in warmer climes, and by the elderly population in general. Paraffin was a cheap form of heating and was readily available from dispensing pumps at the 'open all hours' corner shop, or at the local petrol filling station.

Any portable heater has an inherent fire risk. This risk is magnified when flammable liquids are used as fuel, particularly when no auto-matic cut off to the supply is provided, which was the case until regulations were introduced to remedy this potentially lethal omission.

The shrill teleprinter indication bell had barely begun its ring when it was followed by the much louder urgent clamour of the call bells and by the automatic switching on of the lights, which bathed the semi-darkened station with their yellow glow. It was just after 1.30 a.m. on a freezing cold Saturday in January and up to this time the tour of six-until-nine night duty had been relatively uneventful.

23

On every watch there was one Fireman who acted as the mess manager. His task was to prepare the suppers and breakfasts on night duties when no civilian cook was employed, and to buy in the food and provisions for all the meals on the tour of duty. Geoff Joynt was the chef on our watch. He was a medium height man of 33 with a deadpan expression, which belied his creative mind and his skills as a photographer. To supplement his fire department salary he made use of his talents with the camera at weddings, a service he would soon be taking part in himself, after his long-term fiancée had finally agreed to become his wife. On this freezing night he had made a spicy Indian curry to stave off the cold.

At 7.20 p.m., the call bells had tolled and sent us to 'persons shut in a lift' in the tower block just a few streets away. Something that always seemed to happen over the weekend. Difficulty in gaining entry to the lift motor room had turned a 20-minute incident into almost an hour, and by the time we returned, the evening meal wasn't on the table until half past eight.

'It sure smells great, Geoff,' said Andy Carlisle, licking his lips in anticipation and forking up a chunk of highly spiced chicken breast, and blowing out air as the high octane curry powder met his taste buds. 'This curry is … ' Andy's words were cut off by the harsh ringing of the bell as another call came in, and we all leaped up and headed towards the pole drop. 'Fire in rubbish skip – Pump only,' shouted out the duty man for the shift, Niall Pointer.

At least the Pump Escapes crew could enjoy the curry, I thought, as my feet thumped on to the rubber mat at the foot of the sliding pole.

With a roar and hee-haw of siren, we charged out into the already icy night air to travel the half mile to the burning skip. It was only a small fire on the surface of waste deposited by builders renovating a nearby house and in ten minutes the hose reel tubing had done its job and we returned, via the 'back doubles' of shabby, down-at-heel streets to the station, to polish off the curry followed by some cooling vanilla ice cream.

Prior to the call out bell sounding at 1.30 a.m., two of the watch were lying on their bunks, the atmosphere fuggy from the heat of the radiators. Three were watching the end of the midnight movie. One was studying for a forthcoming promotion exam, and the rest were sitting in the darkened watch room, which housed the teleprinter and duty man's bed. It was here that all incoming emergency calls and other administrative messages were received. It was positioned at the front of the station adjacent a main traffic route, and allowed a clear view of the drunken revellers, slewing their way homewards from the many pubs, clubs and dance halls of this area.

The watch room was suddenly illuminated as the bells rang out and the founts of the teleprinter began their metallic chatter, darting quickly on their carriage across the teleprinter roll and then springing back, rather like Saturday's televised football results, which were printed using a similar machine.

'*Fire in-house, multiple calls being received,*' was the message that mobilised our two pumps, plus the next nearest pump from an adjacent station.

Multiple calls meant that more than one 999 call had been received, which would result in Control automatically despatching a fourth appliance. Multiple calls also indicated that this could be a working fire, and the early hour of the morning, along with the sub-zero temperature, did not bode well, especially as the street we had been called to was infamous for its serious house fires over the years.

Right out of the station, left at the traffic lights, right again, third right, the drivers could almost get there blindfolded, so familiar was this location. I could feel the bitter cold of the morning quickly numbing my exposed left arm next to the half open rear crew cab window before sliding the arm into the cloth sleeve, still slightly damp from the water used on that earlier skip fire.

The street to which we had been called was a gradually sloping avenue of Victorian redbrick terrace houses from three to five storeys in height. All had stone steps leading up to a front door. Some had dormer attics 50 feet above the ground, and many had basements. Like so many similar streets throughout this huge city, cars, vans and small trucks were parked nose to tail, especially in the early hours. This dense parking could be a source of problems when positioning ladders during firefighting and rescue operations.

The lead Pump Escape, by tradition the principal life-saving ladder, and always first away from the station, made an arcing turn into the street, and this caused a gallon or so of water from the onboard tank to cascade on to the freezing road and turn immediately to ice. The Pump followed suit and we could see that a browny-grey fog of smoke had already blotted out many of the street lamps, and in the air was that pungent and unmistakable odour of burning wood, plaster, rubber fabric and paint.

Any doubts we might have had that this was a serious fire were rapidly removed as we noticed that on our left angry orange, crimson and yellow flames were leaping out from the ground, first and second floor windows of a four-storey terrace. The ruddiness reflecting on the thick pall of brown smoke.

'Fuck me, it's going like a torch, have we got a goer here?' shouted Andy Carlisle above the blasts of the two-tone, and the roar of the diesel engine.

Even at such an early hour, and in spite of the cold, there was a small crowd of onlookers. Mostly neighbours, some with overcoats pulled over their night-clothes, others returning from a night on the town. Some were pointing upwards. Several of the women had their hands flattened over their mouths in shock, noticing, through the smoky haze, three people trapped by this fierce blaze at a second-floor window, waving frantically and screaming for help.

The Pump Escape squealed to a halt about 40 feet past the house to allow room for the huge ladder to be slipped and positioned, whilst the Pump shuddered to a stop some 40 feet to its rear.

'Slip and pitch to the second floor, and get a covering jet to work pronto,' shouted the Station Officer. The bulk of his tall frame and 17-stone bodyweight accentuated by the comb atop his white helmet, and by the drawing-in effect of his belt, which exaggerated his barn door shoulders even further.

The rescue procedure ordered was a bread and butter action for inner London stations, and was practised almost every day, making it almost an automatic reaction to perform. Similar to the way in which a soldier will provide covering fire whilst others advance across an exposed position, the 'covering jet' was a powerful water jet and spray from a large hose. It provided some protection to rescuers and rescued working on a ladder above the fire from the flames, smoke and heat shooting out from below, and assisted also in providing a more breathable atmosphere.

As the 'escape' was pitched, others grabbed a delivery hose from lockers and slung it along the road where it rapidly unrolled with a sharp slap against the icy tarmac. To the female coupling at its end another man connected a branch pipe to provide the high velocity covering jet.

Geoff, the Pump Escape's driver, had coupled the other end of the

26

hose coupling into the delivery of the rear pump. He spun open the wheeled valve to send the 300 gallons in the onboard tank surging along to fatten the flat hose line to emerge with a throaty hiss and crack, looking like a silver lance, which rammed into the wall before cascading from the red hot brick heated by the searing flames, which were leaping up from the lower windows.

It was at such scenarios as this, with the congestion of parked vehicles obstructing our closer approach, that the almost one ton weight escape came into its own. Its ability, because of this weight and stability, to be positioned over the tops of parked cars, and over front entrances, was such that it was one of the most effective rescue ladders around, its solidity making it almost like a staircase.

Jim Pile was extending the ladder like a man possessed. Within half a minute its head was resting on the hot wall in the lee of the flame and smoke. Just to the side of the second-floor window where two women and a small boy were trapped, the main stairway being rendered impassable by the heavy body of fire, which was roaring up it as if the stairs were a chimney.

Almost before the top section of the ladder halted, Andy Carlisle was ascending it like a circus monkey running up a pole. Andy Carlisle, whose rugged good looks had earned him the nickname Steve McQueen, was a well-built man of 33 who liked the women and kept fit by swimming and weight training. A disciplined, neat man whose uniform was always immaculate, Andy was one of the most respected firefighters in the district, let alone the station or watch. If there was anybody equipped to excel in the hard business of firefighting and rescue it was the twinkling blue-eyed and brown-haired Andy, a transferee into the Brigade from the Midlands seven years earlier.

I had laid out a second line from the Pump ready to start knocking the fire down at ground level whilst the BA wearers rigged. I inwardly praised Geoff for already having connected up to a street hydrant to provide a limitless supply of water, knowing that the onboard supply lasted only a few minutes when using large diameter hose lines. As the water sped along towards me, crouched low outside the front entrance, I could hear the loudspeaker of the Pump's radio repeating the Station Officer's message, and in the distance, the siren and bells of reinforcing appliances.

'*Received from Station Officer Tuke – Make Pumps 4 – persons reported.*'

The request for the extra Pump was academic because every call to this high risk locale guaranteed three Pumps, and the repeat 999 calls received meant that Control would automatically despatch an additional Pump, and that would be well en route by now. '*Persons reported*' indicated persons trapped and an ambulance would now be on its way to provide first aid and rapid transportation to hospital if required.

During a visit to New York City, where I had ridden to fires with their fire department, I had noted some of the differences between the radio messages sent from fires by the officer in charge to our own in London. For example, 'All hands working'. This informed chiefs and men on surrounding fire houses that those in attendance were all fully engaged with fire suppression, ventilation and/or rescues. In the City of New York, such a transmission was often the prelude to a serious request for extra appliances and crews, and it was a signal to firefighters nearby that soon they might be rolling too.

'All hands' were certainly working here, and the two other crews, now speeding up the slope towards us, would be vital to our endeavours.

'Sub, get yourself around the back and check the situation and report back to me,' shouted Ben Tuke to the Sub Officer just arrived on the first reinforcing Pump.

Although events at the front of the building on fire are usually obvious, those at the rear can be easily overlooked in the frenetic initial activity at a rescue job like this one. Terraced properties create their own problems of accessing the rear, and if the body of fire is such that no access to the back is possible then the quickest way there is through the property next door.

This morning it was a simple matter to get to the rear of the affected house via the immediate neighbours who were themselves out in the street, fearing their own house would be lost. It was an understandable fear, but most houses within inner London of this construction were required to be built with a party wall, which extended above the ridge of the roof, and it was rare for even the most severe house fire to spread to the houses on each side. But, for now, the situation at the rear wasn't my concern. Our efforts were concentrated on knocking down the severe fire at ground floor, which had used the open staircase like a chimney flue to race up and involve upper floors.

With Jim Peating's short but heavy frame humping the hose

behind me I directed the jet firstly to the ceiling of the hallway, and moved it in a continuous sweep. We crouched low as the powerful jet brought down light fittings, wall and ceiling plaster, whose bond had been weakened by the heat of the fire. The jet created a cloud of skin-reddening steam as the water absorbed the heat of this inferno. A raging mass of orange, crimson and yellow, veiled by a semi-transparent fog of acrid brown smoke, which seemed to sear into the eyeballs and produce instant running as the tear ducts tried to protect them.

Fortunately for us, not protected by breathing apparatus, most of the smoke was rapidly venting out of the windows whose glazing had been shattered by the heat and rolling flames. Even crouched so low that we were almost prone, the heat was intense. I could feel rivulets of perspiration running down my back and legs. I winced as a piece of hot ember found its way past my neckerchief on to the back of my shoulders, rapidly blistering the skin.

I swirled the nozzle around and aimed the water stream at the ceiling of the stair landing, then at the walls of the stairway. A door to a room off the stairs was open so I directed the jet on to the ceiling of that room, and, inching slowly forwards with Jim Peating humping the heavy hose line, rotated the jet round and round, soaking the room's walls and lower levels. The jet had always to be kept in motion. This enabled as much of the burning materials as possible to be extinguished via the actual knock-down force of the stream, at the same time as cooling the burning mass. Such is the heat at fires like this that a flame will be knocked down, only to leap back as soon as the jet is taken away. It is therefore a running battle of water against the fire triangle of fuel, oxygen and heat. This is why it is called firefighting.

After a few minutes we had cautiously ascended to the first-floor landing, and with each extra foot gained in height, the hotter became our surroundings. We moved tentatively, in case the severe fire had weakened the staircase to the point of failure and collapse.

As we gingerly progressed ever upwards, hauling up the heavy hose line, I couldn't help but recall a photograph I had seen years earlier. It was in a book about the history of the London Fire Brigade, and, in its own small way, had helped inspire me to become a part of the capital's firefighting force. For some reason it had lodged itself in my mind. It was a black and white image of two firemen slumped against a wall with their helmets removed. Their faces were white, shocked, soot-stained and grimacing with pain. It was captioned 'The firemen injured when a staircase collapsed during firefighting operations at Upper Thames Street ... '

Amidst the noise of the fire and the hissing and crashing created by the jet, we could feel the staircase slightly vibrating. I began to worry that we too would end up in that same predicament. I need not have done, as I realised that the vibration was caused by the bulk of Station Officer Ben Tuke ascending, whose huge form was suddenly crouching at my shoulder. 'How are you doing, men?' he asked.

'OK, but it's bloody hot, isn't it?' I replied.

'Certainly is, son, which is why a couple of BA men are about to relieve the pair of you. You've done well to get this far in this heat. The ADO's come on and he's made Pumps six and ordered a set of ladders.'

'OK, Guv, we'll keep pushing upwards until relieved. How many persons are involved?'

'Not sure but neighbours say the house is divided into flats and bed-sits, could be ten or twenty or more,' he replied.

Three miles away ADO Tom Monsal, a veteran of over 30 years, had been using the early quiet hours to complete a report when Control advised him that repeat calls were being received for this fire. He switched on the receiver monitor, which allowed him to listen to all radio traffic across the whole Brigade area, and within a few minutes had intercepted the '*Make Pumps 4 – persons reported*' message.

He had been a Station Officer himself in the area of this fire and knew from first-hand experience the number of serious, sometimes fatal, jobs, which had occurred there all too often over the years.

It was Brigade policy for the duty ADO to go on to all '*persons reported*' jobs, but Tom Monsal had been around a long time, and knew that too prompt an attendance could cause those officers below him to think that they were not to be trusted. Accordingly, he decided to wait to hear the first informative message from the incident.

He didn't have to wait more than a couple of minutes to hear '*... Terraced house of four floors, approximately 30 feet (width) by 50 feet (depth), seventy-five per cent of ground floor, fifty per cent of first and second floors, and staircase from ground to top floor alight, unknown number of persons involved, building being searched by BA crews, escape ladder and covering jet in use.*'

30

The message painted a clear picture of a serious fire and one that could develop further, and he had no doubts that it was his duty to go on and take overall responsibility for operations, and within minutes his staff car was en route. He was on scene within ten minutes. After being briefed by Station Officer Tuke, he formally took over command. His long experience enabled his decisions to be informed and soundly executed and he had sent a *'Make Pumps 6 – Turntable ladder required' radio message.*

Although a party wall at ridge level would help prevent the fire spreading to adjacent houses were it to burn through the roof, it was not unknown for persons trapped above such a severe fire to make their way to the attic and try to break through the slates, or a sky-light in their frantic efforts to escape from heat and smoke, get on to the roof and hang perilously over the slope hoping to be rescued. Were this to happen here then at the least there would be a tall enough ladder on scene to better facilitate their rescue.

Although it seemed ages, Jim Peating and I had only been inside the house 15 minutes before being relieved by the BA crew. We could have pressed on. But why suffer unnecessarily, having already inhaled enough heat and smoke to weaken us, when the BA-protected team could ascend to the highest and hottest levels of the house with relative impunity.

After the sauna-like heat of the staircase, going back out into the sub-zero air was like taking a plunge into an icy pool. But the freezing sharpness of the night was recuperative and we stopped to look back at the scene, our perspiring bodies steaming like two horses that had just finished the Grand National.

The ambulance, automatically mobilised on receipt of a 'persons reported' message, was parked in the centre of the street, its rear doors flung back. Its stark interior light revealed three persons in the back, draped in the official red blankets of the London Ambulance Service.

Andy Carlisle hadn't had time to worry about the fire and smoke belching out of the windows as he put into life or death reality a drill evolution, which was familiar to so many firefighters. Slipping and pitching the escape ladder and getting a covering jet to work was a basic manoeuvre taught from the earliest weeks of basic training and polished to perfection thereafter.

It wasn't the first time that he had been in this position of rescue, but he remembered that first time. It had been a severe blaze, in which three had died in a similar house to this. Before then he had often tried to imagine what it must be like to be trapped in a burning building with your escape route shut off by searing flame and poisonous smoke. Especially in the small hours when few people were around to hear your cries for help, even in the centre of this, one of the biggest cities in the world.

How welcome, he thought, must the distant note of horns be, almost calling out to those trapped to 'Hold on – Hold on,' and how welcome the throaty roar of engines and sight of those spinning blue beacons. Heralding the salvation that they must surely have prayed for from the skin-blistering flames and heat, held back now by only the room's timber floor and flimsy, ill-fitting door. Andy was at the head of the ladder in seconds and locked himself on to it by pushing a foot and leg through one round (rung) and then wedging it under the round below.

Through the smoke and steam coming up from the belching fire below his position, he could see that two of the occupants of the room were women, probably in their fifties or sixties, and the other was a boy of about twelve or thirteen.

One woman was plump, clad in only a green cotton nightdress. The other noticeably skinny even with the bulkiness of a towelling housecoat. The boy had on a pair of red pyjamas with a Dennis the Menace print on the jacket front, and all of their faces, but especially the small boy's, had that transfixed look of petrified fear.

They were straining their heads and upper bodies out of the open sash window in an effort to escape the pungent brown smoke, which had seeped under the door and through gaps in the timber floorboards. Sinister, searing heat-filled smoke, which was now harassing and intimidating them with its cloying, clinging presence.

Andy knew that the floor might be weakened by the intense fire below. So much so that it could collapse at any time. Or that the bedroom door, their last line of defence from the fire and heat, might be about to give, consuming the room and its three victims in a flash of exploding flame.

There was no time to lose. 'Right, I'm here and will get you all down but do everything I say,' he shouted above the crackle and crash of the blaze, and the drone of the fire pump some 30 feet below.

The ladder vibrated with the thud of boots. 'Andy, I'm right below you, mate, pass 'em to me when you are ready.' Jim Pile who had a few minutes earlier hauled the ladder to its present position had mounted it and ascended to a few rungs below Andy to provide those vital extra hands needed to safely bring the three down.

'What's your name, old son?' Andy asked the shivering and petrified boy.

'Peter,' he half sobbed.

'Right, Peter, you'll be down in a jiffy, just stay there, I'm coming in,' and with that he released his leg lock and in a bound was into the hot, smoky furnace of the room. He could see the thick smoke pushing up around the skirting boards. It looked just like a slowly moving roll of hot, brown cotton wool. With each second it grew more dense, and the timber floor felt springy. The tongues of searing flame below, curling their red-hot forked tongues around and into the ceiling laths, floor joists and old floorboards of this Victorian house.

Jim Pile was now at the ladder's head and, in a flash, Andy picked up the small boy.

'Don't worry, Peter, I'm passing you to Jim on the ladder, hang on to him tight and do as he says, right?'

Jim Pile's outstretched hands and arms gripped the boy with all the strength he could muster. For a fleeting few seconds, he pictured his own 14-year-old son now safely tucked up in his bed back in the family council flat in East London, and gripped the scared little boy even tighter.

'Put your arms around me, son, grip tight and don't let go until we are down, yeah?'

The boy grunted OK and his own instinct to survive ensured he did as he was told. In a minute Jim had descended sure-footedly in spite of the heat and smoke issuing from below, and grateful for the spray from the covering jet, handed the young lad down to outstretched hands at the heel of the ladder.

Thirty feet up on the second floor Andy was inwardly concerned at the fire-weakened floor on which much of their fate depended but he couldn't show it. Suddenly the housecoated woman let out a shriek. 'Oh God, the fire's coming through the floor.' Sure enough curling red tongues of flame, tinged with yellow, were licking six inches or so up on a far corner.

'It's going to be all right, we'll be out in a tick,' said Andy, 'trust me.' He moved a yard to his right and was heartened to see Jim Pile ascending at a run. 'Jim, be ready, I'm going to put them out one after the other, the floor's iffy and we've little time.'

'Ready when you are,' he coughed back as a pungent wave of smoke rolled out of the window.

Andy had got both women to the right-hand side of the window near the white painted head of the ladder. The plumpest one would be the first to go out. Then, if it seemed that the floor was going to go, Andy reasoned that he could sit astride the sill and hold the skinny woman around her waist, and grab the head of the ladder, and bale themselves out if it came to it.

'Oh, Holy Mother of Mary, help me,' the plump woman cried out in an Irish brogue as broad as the River Shannon, as she looked down at the hard pavement below and saw the fire smoke and steam.

'Get hold of the ladder here,' said Jim Pile, gripping her plump bare left upper arm to steady her as she did, his strong fingers sinking into the doughy, white goose-pimpled flesh.

'Now get your leg over the sill and put your foot on the ladder – I'll guide you.' Andy secured her from the room side by her right arm, and with a pull she was on the ladder. 'I'm right behind you, love, just keep your hands holding on tight and I'll guide your feet, take it easy, nice and easy,' reassured Jim, noticing the tremor in her calf as she stepped down.

'Oh my God, oh my God, save me, save me,' she sobbed. Jim Pile was directly below her small slippered feet, and as the combination of fear and relief hit her nervous system, the stream of hot urine hit him across the face. Then she was down, and covered with a red blanket by the ambulance attendant and assisted to the waiting vehicle.

Andy, in spite of the critical nature of the situation, had managed to establish that the skinny woman was called Carmel, and in those tense moments, as he anxiously eyed the creeping fire, had got her to sit astride the sill where he had now positioned himself, his left arm around her and his right hand gripping the ladder's head.

Should the burning floor fail before Jim Pile came back up he would grab her and knew he had the strength and power to hold her and pull them both on to the ladder. He felt as if he had been in the room for ages, but no more than five or so minutes had elapsed since he had first run up the ladder to them.

Breathing hard now with the exertion of carrying down the boy and assisting the first woman, Jim's emerged again from the smoky atmosphere. In a few seconds Carmel was slowly being guided down to the ground.

As Andy Carlisle mounted the ladder himself the flames had now burned through about six square feet of floor. Even though the two and three quarter inch hose now at work on the ground floor had begun to knock down the fire, it was too late to prevent the floor from collapsing. It did so with a thump and a crash, the hot draught from which sent a torrent of smoke and sparks up the front of the house. 'That was a bleedin' close shave,' Andy muttered to himself, as he prepared to descend.

The last woman to have been rescued was being assisted to the ambulance to join the other two. They were all draped in red blankets. Their throats and mouths were parched by the smoke, and their faces were covered in an oily grime, mixed with that clammy perspiration that is the hallmark of shock and relief.

Andy descended to the street, his foot and hands moving in a smooth synchronisation, and, looking down at his feet to ensure he didn't slip on the overlaps of the chunky ladder's extensions, he reflected how very much different things might have turned out had they arrived a few minutes later.

'Ace piece of work there, Andy and Jim. A first-class rescue above a real goer of a fire,' praised Station Officer Tuke.

'Cheers, Guv, but it's what we're paid for ain't it, although it don't half prove the value of regular drilling on the basics.'

After Jim Peating and I had been relieved, we went around the rear of the house via next door to see if any help was needed there before reporting back to the front. Large flames had been curling out of top-floor windows but this was quickly dying down. The grey smoke was turning to steam as the BA men who had relieved us started to knock down the remaining fire with the large diameter hose, its huge gallonage delivered every minute rapidly absorbing heat and cooling red-hot walls, floors and ceilings.

We saw no occupants shouting for help from the rear, but that didn't prove that no one was there. They could be now lying unconscious below the window. Behind a door. On or under a bed or settee. Prostrate on a staircase, landing or hallway, or overcome in an attic space as they tried in desperation to break through the roof to escape the malevolent monster beneath and around them.

We returned to the street to report back to our own Station Officer, and as we came opposite the front entrance, the heavy thump and scrape of fireboots and a dragging sound came from the staircase. Two BA men, part of the reinforcing crews who had been detailed to make a floor-by-floor search for the persons reported, emerged from the smoking, steaming and fire-charred hallway. They were pulling a heavily built male by his armpits and on his back down the remaining few stairs. He was about 15-stone and over 6 feet tall, clad only in a string vest and Y-fronts, and had the dead weight of unconsciousness.

The BA crew from Station 23 had located him behind the door of a bed-sitter on the top floor. There was no time for the niceties of rescue techniques as they allowed his weight to assist the humping slide down the now passable stairway, dragging him over the still smouldering plaster and charred wood and floor coverings. Any bruising or lacerations from this was the price to pay if a quick retrieval to the outside air could help save his life. The first could be repaired whilst the second was irreversible.

We rushed up to grab an arm and a leg to assist the BA men, spent from bringing this heavy victim down 50 feet of stairs, and drained by the heat within the hot chimney of the stairway. We placed him on the freezing pavement, which contrasted with his skin, hot and perspiring from the heat of the fire.

Niall Pointer's excellent work with the covering jet was now over and in a flash he was at the man's side, his thin fingers trying to locate a pulse in the folds of flesh in the man's bull neck.

'Can't feel anything, and I think his lips are blue,' he said, shining his lamp on to the man's grey complexion.

A green canvas salvage sheet appeared as if from thin air, and in a second the strong arms of four firemen had lifted the prostrate form up enough for the sheet to insulate him from the icy ground. Niall whipped off his black neckerchief, provided to all firemen as a basic protection from the hot embers and hot water present at fires, and put it to its other unofficial use, as a 'germ filter'. He placed it over the man's mouth before beginning oral resuscitation, his tilted head observing the rise and fall of the unconscious man's chest as he forced his life-giving breath down his windpipe. A second ambulance was now on scene and they augmented Niall's efforts, continuing them on the high-speed rush to hospital.

The ADO and our own Station Officer had been able to verify from neighbours that normally there were five occupants, and unless they had visitors at the time of the fire, there was only one person still unaccounted for.

Every inch of a fire building has got to be searched. Even if no one has indicated that there are people still inside, a precautionary search is made. But where there are 'persons reported', the searching assumes a greater criticality. It calls for experience, patience, skill and persistence if victims are not to be missed.

Sadly the search did not take long. The conditions within the burned house, completely untenable only 30 minutes earlier, had now improved where it was possible to work without BA. The venting of the huge body of fire and heat and the associated products of smoke and poisonous fumes had created breathable, if not pleasant, conditions. The upper floors still felt like the inside of an oven, and the familiar pungent odour of a burned building remained.

Rising above this familiar smell of scorched plaster and brick, charred timber, soaked now with water, and producing that unique whiff of steam, was a sickly sweet smell. However infrequently it entered the nostrils in a career fighting fire, it was an odour that was unforgettable. It was the smell of burned human flesh present somewhere in the top floor room.

Even in the world's busiest fire departments, where death and injury from fire occur regularly, it is certainly not every day that firefighters witness death, and it is quite possible for a Firefighter to go a long period and not be around when such incidents occur.

But whether death from fire has been experienced a little or a lot, firefighters never become accustomed to it, and its finality can stamp images in the mind that are not easily, if ever, forgotten.

This is not to suggest that Firefighters, like police officers and nurses, for example, do not become case-hardened by the fatal situations they experience over the years. It would not be psychologically possible to continue in such occupations without a numbing of the senses when actually confronted with death. However, it is unlikely that a man or woman of normal sensibilities, no matter how many raw sights they witness, will become totally immune. Many will never completely forget those incidents in which people perished in fires and other emergencies they attended and witnessed.

For those whose primary objective is the saving of life, any death occurring in connection with an emergency situation to which they have responded is the opposite of all they set out to achieve. In that regard, fire deaths can seem to be a double blow.

And so it was on this icy morning in the streets of inner London, where the freezing temperature was in marked contrast to the flesh-searing heat and asphyxiating smoke that had wreaked their havoc on person and property once more.

Station Officer Tuke's powerful box lamp swept its white beam across the fire-weakened floor of a rear bedroom on the top floor. It highlighted the foot or so of charred debris, which included the remnants of a double bed with only a blackened iron frame and the coiled steel springs of a one-time mattress as a reminder of what it once had been.

The sweet smell was strongest near the foot of a sash window. In the increased light of a tripod-mounted searchlight, a pile of debris about 5 feet in length, and gently steaming, was clearly illuminated. Yes it was debris all right, but not that of the burned wood, incinerated contents and spalled plaster of the house, but that of a human.

To the inexperienced, untrained eye, it would be difficult, if not impossible, save for the peculiar smell, to distinguish the two. But those who had this experience, born out of responding to hundreds of fires over time, could discern that what appeared to be a baulk of charred roof joist, roasted, blackened and serrated by great heat, was the remains of a human body.

The effect of severe fire and heat upon the structure of the human limbs is often such that the fists and arms are fixed in the foetal position. It is almost as if, at this terrible ending of life, the body returns back to the position it once occupied inside its mother, before first emerging into the light of day and life.

Here, now, was the dark of night and sudden death. But we could be sure that in the majority of such fatalities, the victim would mercifully have been rendered unconscious and asphyxiated by the smoke and fumes before being burned.

This sudden death shifted responsibility from the fire service to the police and coroner, but it was the Brigade's task to ensure that the scene was undisturbed. None of those present could know at this stage whether the death was a result of arson, accident or whether a murder had taken place and the fire set in an attempt to destroy the evidence.

Now that all five occupants had been accounted for and that a fastidious searching of all parts of the property and the piles of debris had not discovered any more victims, the ADO felt confident that he could send the 'Stop' message to Control.

At just before 0300 hours the following message was received in both Area and Brigade controls from ADO Monsal:

'Stop (no further reinforcing appliances or equipment needed) for [address]. *House of four floors, approximately 35 feet by 55 feet. Eighty per cent of ground floor, 90 per cent of first, second and third floors, and staircase from ground to top floor damaged by fire and smoke. Two women and one boy rescued by Brigade from front room at second floor via escape ladder, suffering from the effects of smoke. One man rescued by BA wearers from rear room on top floor via internal staircase, overcome – all removed by ambulance. One man found in rear room on top floor apparently dead awaiting removal. Three jets, two hose reels, breathing apparatus.'*

The ADO was now free to go, and handed the reins back to our Station Officer, congratulating him on the good work carried out in the rescues. We, as the Pumps crew, still had some work to do, but the escape ladder was made up and returned to station because it was the policy to place such life-saving ladders back on to availability as soon as practicable.

Fires of the sort we had just dealt with create a tremendous adrenaline rush, which fuels the energy and strength of all involved. Once the key actions of rescue and firefighting are finished though, this adrenaline evaporates, especially in the small hours when it is the natural human inclination to sleep.

Actions then become far more of an effort but the work required to ensure the fire is fully extinguished is of vital importance as it would be a poor reflection upon the Brigade to be called out later to find the fire had reignited. We would spend the next hour, before being relieved by fresh crews from around the area, cutting away any area of timber that might be hiding fire and heat, and turning over and damping down internal debris save that in the area of the fatality.

One of the biggest hazards is posed by what we called 'bull's eyes'. These are round embers like red, glowing eyes in the dark and have to be cut out as they could otherwise flare into flame at a later stage. Ceiling laths had to be pulled down using a long-handled pole known as a ceiling hook. Plaster had to be stripped away to ensure that no hot sparks or embers lurked unseen behind it, and all the hot debris had to be thoroughly drenched and cooled. It had always to be borne in mind by crews that a gallon of water weighs 10 pounds. A fire-weakened floor, already overloaded by a partially collapsed structure, could be caused to collapse by the weight of water used, and plunge men through several floors.

It was usual then, on the floors above the ground, to shovel charred debris either out of windows or into bins to be carried outside and then thoroughly soaked down. It was also sound fire-manship to replace large diameter hoses with the smaller hose line or to use only the rubber hose reel tubing as soon as the situation permitted it so as to reduce the weight of water used. Whilst this was going on Station Officer Tuke busied himself with the key task of trying to accurately pinpoint how the fire had started.

In due course we were relieved and finally returned to the station at just after 0430. The standby Pump, which had been mobilised to provide fire cover to the area denuded by our hours at this incident, remained until men had got cleaned up. A hot, smoking, working job leaves Firefighters soaked in perspiration and fire gear soaked in water from the firefighting process.

Faces were streaked with carbon black, hair was hot, matted and flattened by the helmet to the head. Eyes were red with smoke and grime, and the mouth and nostrils were caked with dried saliva and mucus, the end product of eating smoke and hard physical graft. How good the hot shower and soap felt, and how pleasant to change from wet, sweaty T-shirt, trousers and socks into the fresh change of clothes kept in our lockers for such occasions.

After this we had to replenish equipment which we had used, service and clean our BA sets, and then, only then could we inform Control that we were back 'on the run' and allow the standby Pump to leave.

By a quarter past five both Pumps were fully operational. Two or three of the watch who were particularly spent by their efforts took the option of resting on their bunks, but the remainder gathered around the mess table for that great rejuvenator, the mug of hot, sweet tea and a post-incident discussion.

'That was a bit of a goer, fellows, wasn't it?' said Dec Mayo, the watch probationer.

'Nah, you haven't seen nuffing yet, mate,' quipped Geoff Joynt in that good-natured put down, which was part of the unwritten process of preventing inexperienced newcomers becoming too cocky, and was something akin to the armed forces jibe pertaining to length of service – 'Get some in'.

'Actually, young Dec, it was going well, and I would wager that if the fire weren't deliberately started using some flammable material, there must have been paraffin heaters involved again. Every fire involving buildings I have attended, which spread as rapidly as this one, was either as a result of accelerant use by arsonists, or was in a factory in which flammable materials were present.'

'You're probably right, Geoff, the way that the fire went up the staircase like a rocket and the degree of plaster spalled away along with the depth of timber charring does point to that,' chimed in Jim Peating.

'It certainly was hot in there working the large diameter hose up the stairs, and the way that the "stiff" was charred indicates great heat as well.'

'Andy and Jim did a great job with the rescue above all of that heat and flame,' said Geoff, who had been instrumental in getting that vital water supply coupled up so rapidly.

'I'll be blushing in a minute', said Andy, 'won't we, Jim? But we all did a good job, and without you getting into the hydrant so fast, Geoff, to supply Niall on the covering jet and the others entering from the front, our position would have been very iffy.'

'I'll second all of that,' said Jim Pile, 'and the escape can't be beaten for this type of job in a street with lots of parked vehicles.'

'Yeah, maybe so, but the Brigade will soon have to get rid of it on grounds of maintenance and repair costs,' remarked Sub Officer Ray.

'Then they should have looked at the alloy constructed escape,' countered Niall Pointer.

'Aye why not?' said Jim Crowther in his flat northern voice, and who had seen service in a large northern brigade before transferring to the capital. 'My owd outfit used to have a couple of alloy escapes, they wur as fast as wooden uns, and a bloody lot lighter to 'andle,' he said.

'Yeah, Jim, old mate, but up in the effing frozen north it don't matter what you use, all that there is to catch fire are hayricks,' chuckled George, and all but Jim broke into laughter.

'Look I shan't be baited by you lot – ye know I'm right,' he replied.

'By gum, there's trouble at mill again tha knaws,' chuckled Niall Pointer.

41

With that Jim's broad face broke into a creased grin. 'OK, OK, when in Rome do as the cockneys do, I give in,' he laughed.

Such banter was par for the course, and arguments could be had with impunity amongst all on a watch whose very effectiveness and personal safety depended on each other.

The good-natured frivolity and gentle teasing was also an effective antidote to the stresses and strains of the previous few hours, a few hours that had seen rescues carried out in the best traditions of the Brigade, but which had also seen fire claim yet another victim.

All fires attended required a variety of reports and forms to be completed by the officer in charge of the incident, and every fire involving a structure necessitated the filling in of a Home Office report, and of particular importance on it was the section headed 'Supposed Cause'.

Chapter Five

Fire Investigation

The actual cause of a fire is important for a number of reasons, and this importance is magnified whenever there have been fatalities, injuries and rescues. It is magnified even more should there be suspicions that the blaze might have been ignited maliciously.

In addition to the coroner's inquest, which exists to determine the cause of a sudden death, and which normally would result in the officer in charge and the firemen discovering a body giving evidence, there could be an attendance many months ahead in a higher court, either in respect of criminal or civil law proceedings.

The whole outcome of such cases could rely very heavily indeed upon what the officer in charge had concluded to be the cause of the fire in question. In cases involving litigation against individuals, companies, or the fire authority itself, the contents of the fire report, associated statements, photographs, and the all-important 'real time' recorded radio telephone messages from incidents, could be crucial to outcomes.

In addition to these 'judicial' and 'semi-judicial' reasons, the causes of fire also play an important part in the public educational process in respect of fire prevention and fire safety. If the source and cause of fires can be accurately pinpointed, then the resulting publicity can be all that much more precise in its targeting of intended audiences.

Although fire brigade officers were aware of their responsibility to try to ascertain the cause, the heading 'Supposed Cause' was not always as helpful as a more precise one might have been. 'Supposed' had ramifications of an educated guess. It encouraged a cause to be entered, which, whilst possible, was not necessarily probable.

Where crews had spent several gruelling hours absorbing heat, swallowing thick smoke and becoming soaked to the skin, it was not too hard to adopt only a cursory approach to the fire cause investigative process. Firemen could be extremely persuasive about getting back to a station for a shower and change into dry clothes. At such times a Station Officer needed to have a strong personality and adopt a professional approach. If not he would end up looking for evidence to try to support a particular theory as to how the fire had started, rather than remaining objective.

It was possible also to enter 'Unknown', and with a rising number of arson incidents, the former imprecise process of investigation began to be replaced by a much more forensic approach, especially in the busier metropolitan fire authorities. Such was the development by the fire services, working in conjunction with the police and scientific forensic services, that eventually 'Unknown' would be quite a rare entry on the Home Office fire report.

Not only would this increased accuracy in determining the causes of fires have beneficial effects upon fire safety drives, but it also assisted in the detection of arsonists, lessened potential insurance fraud, and helped bring perpetrators to justice.

Within the London Fire Brigade and an increasing number of provincial brigades, specialised and dedicated Fire Investigation Units were introduced and staffed by experienced officers. These possessed an aptitude and interest in this branch of work, and they brought all of their previous experience in firefighting and rescue, and applied that knowledge.

This difficult task was aided by the use of a range of equipment such as highly sensitive accelerant detectors, even 'sniffer' dogs to assist the officer in charge to arrive at an accurate assessment of how a fire had begun, and how it had spread.

In attempting to find out what had caused the fatal fire that we had been called to on that freezing cold morning, Station Officer Tuke didn't have the luxury of a sensitive device to 'sniff' the scent of petrol, paraffin or other accelerants. Accordingly, he had to rely upon his own nose and eyes, drawing on his considerable experience of previous fires and of the tell-tale signs as to not only where the source or sources of the fire might be, but also whether it had developed slowly or quickly.

In the former instance, he would be noticing whether any window glazing or internal mirrors, not shattered by the fire or by firefighting operations, were heavily sooted or smoke-stained. This indicated a slow, smouldering fire, which had produced heavy smoke over a long period.

In the latter instance he would be looking for an absence of smoke staining and for clean breaks of glass, which could point to a rapid build up of heat, as was the case if accelerants had been used.

Such flammable liquids, poured on to floors and stairways, even through letter-boxes, would produce on ignition a rapid fire with a high temperature of flame and superheated smoke. These high temperatures would lead to deep charring of wood, and could cause wall plaster to spall away, and, in the area of initial ignition, produce a definite lightening of exposed brickwork, as well as a pattern of burning.

Arsonists often would start fires in more than one part of a building in their quest to ensure certainty of damage and spread, and more than one fire seat was and is one of the clearest indications of deliberate ignition.

All of these developed skills and empirical fireground experiences were in the forefront of the Station Officer's mind as he set about the tedious process of investigation. Conscientious by instinct and developed practice, he applied as much diligence and tenacity in attempting to locate the actual cause of fires as a keen police sleuth would apply in finding out who had committed a murder.

He had made a mental note immediately on our arrival several hours earlier of the rapidity with which the fire was developing. The colour of the smoke, and the speed and force with which flames and smoke were issuing from windows at nearly every floor.

Later, when providing reassurance to myself and Jim Peating working the jet up the stairs, he had felt the great heat and the springiness of the floors and stairs, pointing to structural weakening caused by very hot flames.

Now, as he checked the blackened, steaming interior from top to bottom, he could see little smoke staining on dressing-table and wall mirrors, but noticed how much plaster had come away, particularly in the area of the ground-floor hallway, and along the whole walls of the staircase from top to bottom.

In his notepad he recorded that a wall clock in the kitchen had stopped at 0135, roughly the time of our arrival. He noted that in the understairs cupboard all of the fuses to the electrical supply were intact and of the correct amperage rating for power and lighting circuits respectively.

He had spoken to the immediate next door neighbours earlier and they had confirmed that paraffin heaters were used in the house, especially during the icy cold currently being experienced as Britain felt the freezing blast of a cold front from Siberia.

In the hundreds of house fires that he had attended over the years, many of them involving the paraffin stove, he had seen far more times than he could remember fires started by heaters placed either at the bottom of the stairs or in hallways and landings. He had even been to several fires in which the occupants had placed the smaller stoves under their beds!

He therefore concentrated his efforts in the ground-floor hallway, about six feet away from the start of the dog-legged staircase. An area in which he had already observed much spalling of plaster, deep charring of the staircase treads and risers, and a section of exposed brick on the right-hand wall, which was the party wall between this and the neighbouring house.

Rising from the blackened and still steaming pile of debris adjacent, there was a definite outline of a jagged shape. This mirrored what had been a flame. Hot enough to cause the plaster to come away, and which had turned the red brick to a whitish salmon pink.

Station Officer Tuke knelt in front of this debris, his burly form hunched over as he gently probed into the charred pile, a searchlight illuminating the scene. The small spade he was using so gently touched something metallic about five inches below the black detritus of the fire. He stopped his gentle probe, put down the spade and felt around. His fingers felt what was a round edge of a cylinder, lying on its side. Uncovering more of the debris he felt and saw a thin wire handle, then the mica plastic window of what was clearly a paraffin stove.

The Brigade photographer had finished his recording of the body and fire scene as required by the Station Officer some 20 minutes earlier, and was soon taking further shots of the heater and immediate surroundings.

Three further paraffin heaters were found, one on the first floor landing, another on the second floor landing, and the third outside the room in which the fatality had occurred on the top floor.

Later on, Ben Tuke was able to confirm from those fortunate to have been rescued that the owner of the house lived in the flat at the very top of the property, and had regularly placed paraffin heaters in the locations in which they were discovered. He was also able to

46

establish that the owner had two cats, which roamed freely about the place.

In due course he was able to complete the 'supposed cause' section of the Home Office report in respect of this tragic blaze.

Filled and ignited paraffin heater placed in hallway near foot of stairs knocked over, probably by domestic cats, causing contents to spill and ignite stair carpeting and surroundings including contents of three further paraffin heaters on first, second and third floor landings.

A month later, Station Officer Tuke, and the Station 23 BA-wearer who had discovered the victim, attended the St Pancras coroner's court inquest where a verdict of accidental death was recorded.

The two cats were never seen again. They probably escaped by leaping from an open window and roamed about as wild cats or were taken in by someone somewhere, with whatever remained of their nine lives.

Their keeper, the landlord in the small top-floor bed-sit had only one life. That ended on an icy morning in north London, yet another victim of the far too many fires caused by paraffin heaters in London and elsewhere during this period.

Chapter Six

The Good Hand

After working in the north of England, I had joined the London Fire Brigade to satisfy a long-held ambition of working within the capital city. I eventually found myself serving at Islington fire station, then, unlike the modern station of today, a redbrick Victorian structure on Upper Street, only a few hundred yards from the teeming Holloway Road.

I always liked to get to the station a good half hour or so before the roll-call was taken. This allowed me to spruce up the fire gear of helmet, tunic, belt, axe and pouch, and the black calf-length leather fire boots over which leggings of a rubberised black fabric were fitted.

During the period in question, it was considered very important within the UK Fire Service in general, and the capital's Brigade in particular, for career ambitious personnel to have gained an extremely solid practical operational grounding. 'Ops experience' was the watchword. Both on the watch of fire stations and in the minds of senior-ranked officers who sat on promotion interview boards. At that period, the percentage of higher ranked officers with very solid operational backgrounds was far higher than those who had managed to ascend the promotion ladder without such a pedigree of practical experience. In later years this situation would be reversed in more than a few instances. Then 'style' would be viewed as of greater importance than substance. Form would supercede function. But those days were a good few years ahead when I reported one cold January morning for a promotion board interview.

In a fire authority that had experienced those catastrophic conflagrations caused by the Luftwaffe's bombing blitzes, and which had, in peacetime, had to deal successfully with some of the nation's largest blazes, it was natural that practical competence on the fire-ground would be the order of the day (and more often the night!).

Theoretical knowledge was essential to pass the written parts of promotion exams, but woe betide any would-be junior officer who, in those days where operational experience and fireground competence was vital, had not gained himself a solid practical pedigree before arriving to command a crew or a watch on any of the 'sharp end' stations.

On those busiest inner London fire stations, some of which were responding even then to over 3,000 calls per year, many being solid 'working fires', the efficiency and personal safety of firemen relied upon an officer in charge being 'a good hand'. To be known as a 'good hand' carried great weight and provided a credibility based on practical abilities of coolness under pressure and the ability to exercise sound judgement in the firefighting tactics employed.

The 'bookman', the 'paper officer', the officer who panicked when persons were screaming for help four floors above the street with heavy fire would be ridiculed and condemned as an incompetent. In short, that sort of man would, on the sharp end stations, be eaten up for breakfast and then spat out!

To avoid such a personal embarrassment and the risk of attracting a derogatory label, which could stick with them throughout their entire career, prudent firemen with aspirations to command, did all they could to earn and win their spurs. They built a solid reputation on the foundations of their coolness, courage, operational competence and the ability to handle men.

As such they would be known as a 'good hand'. A qualification that would precede their arrival at any new posting by way of the Brigade's 'tom-toms', which had a strength and clarity capable of relaying signals across the entire capital.

My interview was at Brigade Headquarters on the Albert Embankment at Lambeth. It was an impressive building of nine storeys with a seven-bayed appliance room, all overlooking Old Father Thames. To my impressionable young eyes, this 1937 building, with its commanding position with the Houses of Parliament in full view, appeared to be everything that a fire brigade headquarters in one of the world's most famous cities should be.

I was shown to a side room, one of many on the second floor where large, dark, polished wood doors and wooden wall panels were in abundance. There was a good 15 minutes before my interview so I tried to relax by looking at an impressive display of photographs of some of London's most notable fires over its long and proud history. There were images from the 1930s of brass-helmeted men fighting a docklands warehouse fire in temperatures so low that huge icicles were hanging from warehouse walls and Brigade ladders. From the 1960s, there were dramatic shots of a rescue by hook ladder from a tall building within the 'Square Mile', from where grey rolls of smoke, looking like roughly wound balls of knitting wool, issued.

There were images of major fires in the affluent West End, and, by contrast, there was a grim photograph of a fire-bombed minicab office in the East End's Hackney, with barely recognisable blackened bodies. The terrible aftermath of a period when the famous London hackney carriage trade was feeling threatened by the inception of the private hire vehicle, 'Come,' shouted the booming voice following my knock on the large polished door, which bore the shiny brass plate of one of the Brigade's upper echelon officers. I marched over to the far end of a cavernous office. Behind a large green leather-topped desk sat the two who would grill me for the next 15 or 20 minutes. Their backs were facing the Thames on which I could see tugs and lighters bobbing past.

'Sit down please,' commanded the officer in a rasping voice, which sounded as if his vocal cords had been cured in the thick smoke of too many fires. Behind his gold-rimmed reading glasses, the dark eyes were set in cavities around which were weathered brown pouches, an outward hallmark of the effects of long years of running, smarting eyes in those cruel seas of smoke. I could almost imagine that if those brown bags under the eyes were pierced, smoke remnants would ooze from a thousand inner London fires.

Both officers had cast their critical gaze over my shiny black shoes, and the razor sharp creases of my uniform. But as important as a smart appearance is to a disciplined service, they were far more interested in what you knew.

Operational experience and recommendation reports, which recorded that a man seeking promotion was up to the highly responsible task of commanding crews safely (and up to the job of protecting the capital's buildings and its populace), were what they were looking for in those days.

I must have successfully fielded the difficult 'googlies' – the complicated fireground scenario questions bowled at me during the

51

interview – because, a month later my name was placed on the year's panel from which promotions to Leading Fireman would be made, but for now it was back to being a Fireman at the sharp end. Back to Islington, where I was serving at the time, with its numerous calls to street after street of houses, tenements and factories. Its underground stations of Essex Road, Angel, Highbury and Islington, and the neighbouring high-fire-risk areas of such places as Holloway, Stoke Newington and Shoreditch, had provided me with some first-class operational experiences.

After this I transferred to other stations in and around the East End, and was able to augment my experiences with numerous others, turning out on some stations more than a dozen times a night, seeing and fighting fires in a diverse range of commercial and domestic premises.

I had no doubts that it was the high level of anticipation, the not knowing what the next emergency call might be on the busiest stations, that was such a large part of the motivation to serve on them.

In addition, the high number of calls and working jobs meant that the many hours of drills and simulated scenarios were undertaken with the sure knowledge that within a tour of duty the potential for putting into play those procedures on the real life stage of emergencies was far more likely to arise than on the far quieter stations in the outer suburbs.

The words printed on the cover of a national Sunday newspaper of the time – 'All human life is here' – applied there, and to the environs of the most active inner city stations.

Several years after first inhaling that pungent odour of stale fire smoke, which seemed to then permanently permeate the fire tunics hanging in the gear room at such places as Islington, Whitechapel, Holloway and Shoreditch, I began to admit that the buzz gained when first stepping into the inner-city firefighting environment, and which I had at first thought to be the initial thrill of a newcomer, had a permanence that time, or a thousand emergency responses, would never still.

Over many years the London Fire Brigade's image had become, in countless black and white press photographs, synonymous with the traditional fire gear of black helmets, black double-breasted tunics, boots and leggings. Those black items of protective apparel contrasted with the scrubbed, clean white ash-wood shaft of the axe, the scrubbed white coiled line attached to the belt, and the white combed helmets denoting ranks of Station Officer and above.

National and international photographic archives display these piano keyboard contrasts of uniform at thousands of fires and emergency scenes across the capital city. They evoke a thousand memories and stand as a strong reminder of the Brigade's history and its presence to not only those who have spent time within its ranks during its busiest years, but to those who had either lived and worked in London or visited its bustling streets and quiet, secretive backwaters over the periods in question.

Nowhere have such images been more poignant than those which illustrate those major fires in which firemen were killed. At such notable incidents as Covent Garden, Smithfield Meat Market, Dudgeons Wharf, Clifton Gardens, Maida Vale, the black helmeted heads contrast with the strained white faces of men, which reflect the sadness of their loss in streets shrouded in funereal wreaths of life-taking smoke.

With my own fire gear now prepared for the roll call, I carried it up to the appliance room. At just before half past five permission was given for me to relieve one of the day watch, and I went into the watch room to ensure that the duty man entered the change of rider in the station logbook.

The watch room was the place where the teleprinter was located. The place where the card indexes showing the routes to all streets were filed. On its wall was a large map showing the whole of the station's ground, and on the wall above the teleprinter, a large brown clock showed that there were some fifteen minutes left of the nine-hour day duty.

Most watch rooms faced the street and, during the last half hour of a duty, it was customary, even though Brigade orders forbade it, for men to congregate and amuse themselves watching the passing scene, and to be the first in line to collar an oncoming man so as to get off early.

'Bloody hell, mate, you're keen ain't ya? There ain't a night goes by without you relieve some fucker – what's up, mate, has her indoors kicked you out?' asked 'Motormouth' Ricky Tong, with a sneer, as he nonchalantly rocked back the tubular steel chair on which he was sitting adjacent the large street-facing window.

'Something like that, Ricky, but you'll have noticed that I never relieve you,' I responded with a half grin, knowing well that to reveal that one of the main reasons for my coming on duty early, to try to get a larger slice of the action, would be a passport to constant ribbing.

However, it was the case that such accusations only tended to demonstrate the irony of the situation. If the real truth were known, probably a good three quarters of every watch, certainly on the busy inner-city stations, were equally passionate about their work. But they liked to assume an air of indifference and to wear the 'old green waistcoat' to disguise the fact to their watch-mates, certainly during station stand-down hours.

Where such men did show their enthusiasm though was out on the fireground. I had never forgotten that during my time in the East End there had been one man who, to all intents and purposes, was Mr Cynicism personified. His whole attitude and demeanour when not involved in an emergency response was negative. He grumbled about the Brigade's principal officers. He was always moaning about appliances and equipment, and he tried to convey a disinterest in his work. However, come the urgent clamour of the call bells, he underwent a Dr Jekyll transformation. First to the appliance. Fully rigged in his gear before most of us had our boots on, and at fires he was unbeatable in getting his hands on the nozzle.

I remembered a fire one Saturday lunchtime. It was in one of those mean streets near a point where the boundaries of Shoreditch and Whitechapel overlap, and involved one of those tall Victorian terraced houses, so typical of inner London.

A child was reported trapped. His mother was screaming hysterically for her young son to be saved, and she was surrounded by a small crowd, their necks craning up to the top-floor window from which thick clouds of that ugly, yellowy-brown smoke were billowing, as the Pump Escape and Pump roared urgently into the wide street. The ever gleaming red of their bodywork, the blue, white, red and gold livery of the London Fire Brigade crest, and the whirling electric-blue arcs of beacons contrasting with the seedy drabness of buildings in this shabby, run-down district.

As was mentioned earlier, getting rigged in the oxygen BA set with its nose clips, aqualung-type mouthpiece and buckled body straps was a slow business. When persons were involved, many firemen just slung the set over their shoulders, jammed in the mouthpiece and got into the building to begin a search.

'Mr Cynicism' didn't even look at a BA set. He ran straight in. Straight up the stairs. He ducked under the dense smoke and fast rising heat as he made his way to the top floor where the boy was reported to be. A long corridor ran off the top landing. He dropped flat. His nose just above a grubby, threadbare, trammelled carpet, sniffing out that thin layer of breathable air.

He saw a glow. A red torch of flame made a dim orange by the masking filter of the choking, rough-edged smoke, which would soon overcome him if he didn't find the boy and get out fast.

He pulled himself with his arms and elbows down the long corridor, like an SAS soldier crawling under the nose of the enemy barrels. His head was spinning as he reached the bedroom door. Crawled across the floor until his hand found the leg of an iron-framed bed. Felt on top. No one there. Felt under the left-hand side. No one there. Then he heard the soft whimper of a sobbing child. Felt further around under the bed totally blinded by the brown smoke, which now had the heat of a furnace within its layers. Felt on the right side and his large, rough hand brushed the soft smooth skin of a young child. In a second he had the boy in his grasp, pulling him by the wrist across the floor. His strength was almost gone now. Sapped by the debilitating, life-taking veil of fire fumes. He knew he wouldn't make it back down the stairs. His mind raced as the black shutter of a coming unconsciousness began to fall.

He was in the centre of the room. Then into his fast receding consciousness he heard the pure cockney accent of his old 'firedog' instructor at Southwark Recruit Training Centre 15 years ago. 'If yer lost in smoke, stop. Find a wall. Work ararned it to find a door or window.' A life-saving tip of good firemanship, which he now struggled to implement.

Across the floor, pulling the now unconscious small form. Hand hit a skirting board. Brushed an electric power point, then the long drape of curtains around a window. Felt up and reached the wooden inner sill. Knelt up, still grasping the boy's wrist. Daren't let it go. Might not locate him in this horrible, hot, lethal fog. Then on his knees. Left hand unstudded his personal axe pouch. Left hand grasped the steel blade. Out with axe. Fierce swings at the glazing with the flat of the blade. Shattering glass. Fast rushing smoke out into the street. Further blows with axe as the smoke temporarily thinned and the sweet light of day and life appeared. He pulled the limp form of the lad up and held his head out into the life-giving

London air. Within seconds the escape ladder was crashing into the wall below the window and strong hands took the boy to the ground and a waiting ambulance and a waiting mother, whilst he hung out of the same window pulling in lungfuls of oxygen, vaguely aware that the worst was now over before his colleagues brought him down to safety.

Never again, I thought after witnessing that heroism, would I make assumptions based on limited information. That man had been the kind who, when the chips aren't down, delights in running against the grain, but who, when they are, like on that Saturday, come into their own, defying all predictions as to their actions. That man was indeed a 'good hand' and was deservedly awarded a commendation for his sterling efforts carried out like so many in those days without the protection of breathing apparatus so as to save those precious seconds, which can spell the difference between this world and the next. As it did for that boy who thankfully survived because of his rescuer's selfless actions.

There was no extra 'action' for me on this occasion in those 20 minutes or so before I paraded with my watch. Following the routine handover checks of appliances and their inventories, and the checks of breathing apparatus, we sat down to the mug of hot, sweet tea, a Brigade-wide tradition, before starting on the evening routine, which tonight was the continuation of the technical lecture, interrupted by a call the previous day.

The subdued ring of the bell, which sounded whenever the teleprinter started to clatter out its message, mingled with the babble of conversation around the mess room table.

Although the printer conveyed a number of routine items of information, such as the lists of out duties for the next night shift to cover station crews depleted by sickness, its alerting bell was also the usual prelude to the clamour of the large red call out bell on the mess room wall. As a consequence, the subdued tringing caused us to instinctively tense, cocking ears and placing senses on alert should an emergency call be coming in. After about 20 seconds, we would normally assume that the message was of an administrative nature.

'It'll be the out duties for ...' Johnny Carre's voice was drowned by the urgent clamour of the callout bell. 'Bleeding hell, that was a delay,' shouted out Mike Deveen, as he and the rest of us sprang up, pushing back our tubular steel chairs with a collective scrape and rumble on the polished wooden floor, as we briskly but calmly headed for the pole house and the 20-foot drop to the appliance room below.

Chapter Seven

Jumpers

She cannot have been more than 18 years old, and her ginger-red, punk-styled, spiked hair was already sodden with the steady persistent spray of drizzle falling over the capital on this early March evening. The Pump had been called to 'Person Threatening to Jump', an emergency known to the London fireman as a 'jumper'. The venue was one well known to both ourselves and the residents of this district, as a spot from which more than a few people had chosen to commit suicide.

She was standing on the outside railings of a cast-iron bridge. This stood above a busy major road. Along this route the headlamps of the late evening traffic reflected with the shiny black surface of the wet road. Traffic which included the so familiar red London Routemaster buses as well as the ubiquitous black taxi-cab, plying their trade in this thick sea of vehicles. The young woman had been seen climbing over the railing by an elderly resident of a nearby flat. She had called the police, who, in turn, had called for the Brigade.

A short, squat Inspector was waiting at the roadside, his black raincoat glistening with rain under the yellow light of the tall lamp standard directly above him. In an accent as broad as the River Clyde he said, 'It's a young lassie. She's threatening to jump and she'll need more than an aspirin if she does. It must be seventy feet down to the road,' he remarked in the dour manner, and with the deadpan expression of the case-hardened copper, who has seen more of human drama in his 20 years with the Met than many of us would see in two lifetimes.

It certainly was a long way down. If she did jump there was the obvious threat to others below and it was becoming clear that the shut down of the carriageway directly below would be a prudent decision.

'I've tried to talk to her but she told me to eff off,' said the Inspector. 'She's asked to speak to a female PC, so I've requested one,' he went on, and as he spoke, a small white car pulled up. A tall, youngish looking woman got out and the inspector trundled his heavy frame along to speak to her out of earshot of the young girl.

'Geoff,' said Station Officer Tuke, 'request a Turntable Ladder and send an informative: "*One female threatening to jump from road bridge – police in attendance*" Geoff repeated it all and transmitted it to Control.

The Turntable Ladder could be extended up to where the girl was, and, hopefully she could be persuaded, notwithstanding her agitated state of mind, to get on to it and make the assisted descent down over 80 feet of hard metal rungs or be helped back on to the roadway.

The Inspector returned and informed our Station Officer that he had instructed that the incoming carriageway be closed, and that the WPC would try to reason with the girl.

'Do you think that's wise to risk your colleague's life going over on to such an exposed position especially with how greasy it will be on those cast-iron supports?' enquired our Station Officer.

'But she said she wanted to speak to a woman,' the Inspector replied.

'Yeah, and I understand that. But I think that one of my men, who are used to working at heights, ought to get down to her first and try to reason with her; you never know but she might be OK talking to a Fireman.'

'Very well then, perhaps we'll try your way. You never know,' said the Inspector with an air of resignation, but tinged with a grudging respect for the work that the Brigade carried out.

'Right. I want a volunteer to put on a safety line and get out to try to reason with her, and persuade her that she has to allow us to assist her,' said Station Officer Ben Tuke, quietly.

'I'll do it, Guv,' called out Mike Deveen, 'You know the ladies can't resist me.'

'Typical effing Mike, he'll do anything to pull a bird,' quipped Niall Pointer.

'The only pulling I want is her back up here on terra firma,' grunted the Guvnor with a grin that belied his concerns for both the girl and Mike.

The rescue line was 130 feet long. At its end were two adjustable legs into which normally just one person would be secured. The ultimate plan if she wouldn't return the way she had gone was to extend the Turntable Ladder and persuade her to get into it and be assisted down to the ground. But if Mike could secure her in the harness, then if she tried to throw herself from the stanchion, she would be safely held. Working swiftly, nimble fingers secured the free end of the line to a suitable stanchion whilst Mike placed one leg of the harness over his head and placed it under his armpits. Pulling it tight, thinking all the time of the standard tests carried out on the rescue lines back at the station only a few days back, and of how the line had passed its test with no signs of weakness.

If ever proof were needed of the validity of such tests, tonight was a prime example. If he managed to persuade the girl to place the sling around her and then she jumped, she might pull them both off. Then the line would really be tested, he thought, given the unconventional procedure adopted.

Before climbing over the bridge railing he took off his helmet. He knew that some people in a very disturbed state can overreact to anyone in uniform. Almost as if the authoritarianism suggested by tunics, caps, buttons and belts comes over to them like a red rag to a bull. So anything that informalises the situation can be of assistance in winning someone over.

Mike Deveen, with the rescue line being held taut by his crew-mates above him, gingerly made his way across to the huge girder on to which the girl had climbed and was precariously perched about 30 feet from him. Far below he saw that the incoming traffic had been stopped and only the northbound lane was open. About a hundred yards along the incoming highway, Mike could see the red of the Turntable Ladder, which was parked discreetly awaiting the instructions by radio from the officer in charge.

'Go away! Leave me alone, I don't want to talk to anyone,' the girl shouted out in the thin, nasal monotone of west Yorkshire, as she suddenly noticed his presence.

She was about five feet three inches tall, very thin and pale and clad only in a pair of tight-fitting denim jeans and a short-sleeved T-shirt, which were thoroughly sodden with the incessant drizzle. The powerful street lamps above were bright enough to reveal the tell-tale scars and scabs on her right arm from countless punctures by needles, where she had searched for a vein to feed her 'mainlining' addiction.

That scrawny arm was now encircling the cold, green, painted, cast-iron stanchion. Apart from a similar girder on which she was standing, shivering with shock and cold, this was the only thing that was keeping her from a sudden frenzied leap on to the unforgiving road so far below her precarious position.

'Eff off!' she screamed, 'one more move and I will jump – what have I to live for now?' she sobbed, her words carrying on a breeze that had risen up from the road far below.

'My name's Mike, what's yours? You can tell me, just take your time. I can help you get down from here, and someone will be able to help sort things for you. It's too wet and cold up here, and whatever you are feeling like now won't be half as bad once you are down and enjoying a nice hot cup of tea. So come on, love, what's your name?'

She remained silent, her teeth chattering, and Mike wondered what depths of despair would lead someone to place themselves in such a situation. Thwarted in love? Deep in debt, grief, anger resentment? Or maybe the malevolent effect of mood-altering drugs, or the irrational thought processes caused by a mental illness?

Mike moved imperceptibly closer to her, pausing often to try to get her to speak, to divert her mind from the suicidal thoughts she was experiencing. 'Tell me what it is that's bothering you. Remember, a problem shared can be a problem halved. Just tell me at your own pace and I promise you I will listen, but please tell me your name,' he went on quietly.

After about 30 seconds, she turned very slowly to face him. Her eyes were puffed up with crying and her teeth chattered from the cold and the shock of her predicament. Then in a tremulous voice she blurted out how she had come down to London after a row at home with her parents at their home in east Leeds. How her dad was a coalminer until a serious accident laid him off work and led to his enforced retirement. Soon afterwards her mother had developed breast cancer, and had to leave her job in the city central markets. They had berated her for failing to hold down a steady job and after a couple of her mates had gone down to the capital, she had traced them and they had allowed her to share their bed-sitter until she got some work. She had got a job serving in a pub in King's Cross where she had met a guy who she had moved in with. He introduced her to drugs. Now she was an addict, and only this week her already collapsed world had plumbed even deeper depths. In the week that her boyfriend had told her to leave, a phone call home had her learn from her sobbing dad that her mother had died a week earlier.

'What's the point of living? I've nothing to live for,' she sobbed, looking down at the wet road 70 or so feet below.

'You might not believe me, but there's plenty to live for, and what about your dad, I reckon he must need you now as much as at any time? What state will he be in right now? And if you were to come to any harm, he'd be devastated,' said Mike quietly. 'Look, all we want to do is help you, it's our job, and there are loads of other people who can help also. Anyway, Yvonne, I'm cold enough with my thick tunic on, you must be frozen solid. Just let me get up to you and I can help,' Mike went on, all the while feeling the tautness of the rescue line from above. 'Come on, Yvonne, let me make you secure with this line, and then we can get you down to the ground and some warm and dry gear and a nice hot drink, yeah?'

The girl didn't say anything for several minutes. Mike knew from past experience that people in her state of despair could in one second lead you to believe that they had listened, and would comply, only in the next second to leap to their death without warning.

She moved her scrawny, scarred and goose-pimpled arm a little higher up the wet iron stanchion. She then half turned her right foot and peered far down to the carriageway below as if contemplating her own fate were she to leap off her footing. Then, she turned her white face with its now sodden spiked red hair towards him and whimpered, 'How can you get me down?'

'No problem, Yvonne, but first let me get up alongside you, yeah?'

'OK, but hurry, I feel sick and faint.'

Mike gave a tug on the line, and looking up could see the Station Officer's white-helmeted head peering over the bridge rails. 'Give us a bit of slack, Guv, I'm moving up alongside.' He felt the line slightly slacken. He slowly edged his way up to the girl, the rest of the crew above following his every inch, ready to take up the slack and hold him should he slip.

Then he was alongside her. 'OK, Yvonne, you are going to be fine. Just do everything I say.'

Mike Deveen's thick fingers gently grasped her right upper arm. He knew that if she tried to jump now, with her puny frame, a quick tightening of his grip should hold her. But he had to get the second webbing sling on to ensure an even more secure situation.

'Yvonne, take this sling in your left hand and while I'm gripping, you put it over your head and push your left arm through. We also want it around your waist and back. Then I will keep hold of you as you put your right arm through. Then we'll pull it tight.' 'Yeah,' she replied, 'but I can't go back on t'road,' she sobbed, a look of terror in her eyes as if pursued by some demon.

Slowly, nervously and with trembling hands and legs, she did as she was instructed. Mike breathed an inward sigh of relief as he tightened the harness, feeling an almost simultaneous tug as the crew above took up the slack line. They were now secure. If she jumped she would have to overcome not only Mike Deveen's vice-like arm-lock around the stanchion, but the massive breaking strain of the rescue line. The very line that his crew-mates had tested only a few days earlier. 'Ladders, Guv, she won't come back over,' he turned and voiced to the Guvnor.

From far below, a diesel engine fired up and the huge set of ladders, which from this height looked like a Dinky toy, moved forward from its stand off position at the roadside. The huge silver-grey sections of the ladder slowly elevated, and then extended, the metallic click of the pawls echoing eerily as if counting down the seconds. Within a half minute the top extension, with a Leading Hand secured on his flip-down foot platform at the head, was slowly extending towards Mike and the young girl. Almost an hour had passed since the Pump had first arrived, and Mike himself was feeling ready to get off this exposed position high up above one of the capital's major arteries on such a wet and cold evening.

'Rest,' the Leading Hand spoke into his microphone, instructing the operator 70 feet below that the ladder was at the correct height. 'Move in towards the bridge about eighteen inches.' 'Eighteen inches it is,' squawked the confirmatory message from below. Very slowly, the ladder came in, and with a superb piece of precision operating, aided by the Leading Hand's instructions, rested no more than an inch from the stanchion on which the rescued and rescuer stood, and at an angle to facilitate the hazardous shift from the bridge stanchion on to the top extension where a strong pair of hands awaited. Both Mike and the Leading Fireman knew that nothing was certain in this sort of incident until the ground was safely reached. Accordingly, the safety line, although slipped from Mike, was kept on the girl and paid out under tension during the slow descent, while he was assisted back on to the roadway by his mates' strong hands.

Mike's arm had been around the girl's shoulders, shielding her as best he could from the drizzle and cold breeze before helping her on to the ladder. But however chilled she was, it wasn't the icy irreversible coldness of death, which could, and unfortunately had, been the outcome witnessed too many times in the past at this location.

Within seconds the wet, black roadway became closer. Then they were down on the welcoming tarmac. Met by an ambulance crew and the policewoman, who had so gallantly offered to go out on that exposed position to reason with the girl. But for now, at the least, the young exile from east Leeds was safe.

About a year later we were on night duty and had just returned from yet another false alarm. It was early summer and still light. I jumped down from the Pump and saw a small, young woman standing nervously on the station forecourt, a few feet from the appliance bay doors.

'Can I help you, you seem lost?' I said, walking across to the doorway. There was something vaguely familiar about the woman, but I couldn't put my finger on it

'I wonder if you can help me find the Fireman who helped me once?' she said quietly in a distinctly northern accent.

'What did he help you with, and do you know his name?' I asked.

'I don't know what he is called, but he helped me with a bad time I was having about a year back'.

'Well, you don't have to tell me if it's a personal thing, but it might help me help you if you could explain things a bit.'

'Oh it wasn't that. I got very down at that time,' she went on, looking down at the ground, as if embarrassed to go on. 'It was on the high bridge up the road, I was really out of my head with a lot of things and I was not bothered what happened and would have jumped off if it hadn't been for that Fireman bloke. He was so nice and understanding, and I really do want to say thanks to him,' she went on, speaking at a fast rate, seemingly glad to at least have blurted out why she had been waiting there.

It was not every day that we got called out to persons threatening to jump off high bridges and I remembered it at once, especially the part played by Mike Deveen on that evening.

As it turned out Mike Deveen had transferred out of the Brigade a few months back. He had met a girl on a walking holiday in the Lake District. She was from Blackpool and he had transferred to a northern brigade to be closer to her. In any event, the personal details of Brigade staff were never given out to anyone, although it was clear that for anyone to have known about the fine details of that incident of a year ago they were likely to be genuine.

I recalled how around the mess table after that job Mike Deveen had filled us in with all the details and that the young woman was originally from Leeds in West Yorkshire.

'Where you from?' I asked of the pale, thin young woman, who looked as if a few solid Yorkshire puddings with potatoes and roast beef wouldn't do her any harm.

'Up north, Leeds ... look do you know this Fireman, can you help me find him?'

'Yes, I do know him, but he has moved on.'

'Do you know where he's gone. Have you got his address?' she enquired. 'It would mean a lot to me to properly thank him as at the time I was so spaced out, what with the drugs and other things.'

'Look, the best thing you can do, if you really want to thank him, is to write to our personnel section at our headquarters at Lambeth. If you do that, they should forward it to him, as I think that they should know where he is.'

'Don't you know where he is? Can't you let me know?'

'I know that he has moved to another fire brigade outside of London, but I don't know his new address. He was a great bloke, but we weren't off-duty buddies or anything. Just hang on a minute and I'll write down the address to write to at Brigade Headquarters.'

'Oh, OK, if that's the only way then that's what I'll have to do. Thanks for helping.'

I handed the Albert Embankment address to the thin young woman. 'I hope that's OK. Sorry there's nothing else I can do to help, and by the way, how are you getting on today?' I asked.

'Things are getting better a bit but I've got some way to go. I live in a hostel at the moment and London can still be very lonely at times,' she replied.

'It sure can, but I was on that call that night and I reckon that the Fireman and others who helped you knew what they were doing and it will be good for you to locate him. So do write to that address and best of luck for the future. I'm sure that things will all come good in the end. Take care of yourself now.'

Yvonne folded the scrap of paper I had given her and placed it in the top pocket of the denim blouson jacket she was wearing. 'Well, I better be off then, and thanks again for your help tonight and also at my bad time last year.'

'That's all right, Yvonne. It's what we're here for. Mind how you go,' and she turned and walked away into the fading light.

A few years after this brief encounter I was at a retirement party for one of the first Station Officers that Mike Deveen and I had served under when at Islington. Like many of the retirements of those days, the respect in which most of the 'good hand' guvnors were held resulted in a large number of colleagues past and present turning up to say their own farewells. Given that Mike Deveen had moved a few hundred miles north, we were all pleasantly surprised to learn that he had found the time to make the trip.

It was good to see him again, and we spent a most enjoyable evening exchanging yarns about the many working jobs we attended in those busy days and nights. Our conversation inevitably included that night, when, high above a north London road, he had used his natural charm and real professionalism to encourage that distraught and unbalanced young girl that she had far more to live for than she was able to envisage at that point.

That young woman must have listened to what I had advised because Mike eventually received a letter from her, and several others over the intervening years. How satisfying to hear that Yvonne had gradually got away from her addiction to drugs and had found new happiness with a guy she had met back in her native Leeds where she eventually returned to be with her dad.

At the last letter Mike said that she was now happily married with two young sons. She had said that her own new life and contentment would never have come about but for the efforts of Mike and those others present on that March night.

The Firefighter's work is such that it is not often that they are able to discover how life turned out for those involved in the wide variety of emergencies and human dramas to which they respond.

How satisfying then to learn of how that shivering young girl, who on that night had been inches away from death, as a result of the distorting prism of addictive drugs, had regained her rationality and rediscovered the will to live, and that the heroic efforts of Mike Deveen had not been in vain.

* * *

'Fire in high-rise – one person jumped from eighth floor ...'

The imprint of a hand was clearly visible on the inside pane of a soot-blackened kitchen window. Eight floors and eighty feet above the frontage of the high-rise tower block, where the lifeless body of a young man was now spread-eagled across the hard concrete. A pool of congealing blood around his head, and his lifeless open eyes, closely resembling those of a cod on the wet fishmonger's slab, staring up to the darkening sky.

We had been called at a little after eight on that late summer evening to 'Fire on eighth floor of high-rise ... one person jumped'.

A thin, grey ribbon of smoke could be seen rising from the top floor area as we neared this large council estate. As the two appliances halted in front of the block, the man's body could be seen. It was about ten or so feet in front of the building. It was clear to even the newest recruit that for this unfortunate person life had ended instantaneously on the cold, hard pavement.

The address to which we had been called was one we turned out to on a regular basis. But those responses were to persons shut in lifts and to fires in the stinking refuse chutes. Not tragedies like this.

Sub Officer Dolan Devine craned his head back until the rear part of his helmet touched his back, as he looked up to the smoke cloud, which was issuing from a top-floor window directly above where we were standing.

'Charge the riser and get the high-rise gear,' instructed Dolan. The soft Irish brogue, still as strong as it was when enrolling with the Brigade many years earlier, following his initial employment as a cable layer with a well-known local Irish company.

We rushed to lockers and took out the hose, branch pipes, lines and the BA sets, which Brigade instructions mandated we use at fires in high-rise dwellings. As we did this Johnny Carre, the driver of the Pump, began to connect the hose into the external coupling of the riser, which allowed us to pump water up a vertical pipe to a valve situated on each landing.

Niall Pointer had already entered the block. He had activated the Fireman's switch, which allowed the Brigade to commandeer the lifts, and speed up our progress to establish a bridgehead on the floor immediately below the fire floor.

'Effing hell, Sub, the lift's fucked,' shouted out Niall to Dolan Devine as he entered the ground-floor lobby.

'Then for sure there's nothing we can do but walk up is there now?' responded Dolan.

'Send an informative – *"Smoke issuing on eighth floor. Lift inoperative. Crews making way to fire floor. Further messages may be delayed. One male apparently jumped from block to ground level – apparently dead. Police attendance required"*,' he instructed to Niall Pointer who sent it at once from the pump.

Our treaded fire boots, four pairs in unison, echoed loudly, along with our laboured breathing, as we lugged the high-rise gear up some seven flights of hard concrete steps and landings. Steps, landings and walls which were daubed with lurid coloured graffiti scrawls. Steps reeking with the stench of urine, and which on some flights were littered with cigarette butts, spent matches, empty fag packets and the odd contraceptive sheath, their grey contents glinting under the weak white lights on the cold brick walls, from which our booted footfalls echoed rhythmically.

Although now five floors and fifty feet above the ground, we could easily hear through the slatted timber ventilation ports the screaming whine of the fire pump. Thrusting the water up the vertical pipe. At sufficient pressure to overcome the frictional resistance of height, and still give us enough hose pressure to fight whatever fire might be present.

On top of this noise, however, another sound rose. It was the rushing, splashing 'shish' of surging water, and as we arrived at the sixth floor landing we were met by a cascade of water racing down the stairs.

'What the hell, some bastard's only had the landing valve away I bet,' snarled Dolan, the droplets of sweat from the effort of the laden climb running down the ruddy complexion of his face and dripping from his sharp nose. 'Jim, get yourself back down. Get John to knock off the water and then fetch up a couple of lengths of the small hose. We'll need to set into the sixth floor valve. But for Christ's sake, be bloody sharp now. We don't know what we have here and the buggered lift has lost us minutes to be sure all right it has.'

On each landing there was a brass valve opened and closed with a hand wheel. In this deprived and vandal-ridden neighbourhood, such an item would be like a glinting jewel to the magpie beaks of some residents, who would earn the price of a good few pints of ale from its exchange at the local scrap metal merchant.

Niall Pointer's exit at the ground coincided with the arrival of the third Pump. In minutes the extra hose had been carried up to the sixth-floor landing. It was connected, and by use of a hose and hand-controlled nozzle, the water would now not reach the missing valve on the floor above.

'Where the fuck have you been?' was the screaming question of a very irate and panicking man of about 25, who was half running and pacing back and forwards outside the eighth-floor flat. 'I fucking called 999 ages ago from a neighbour's phone. My flatmate's inside. Oh my God. I slipped out to the pub. When I got back the frigging flat's ablaze – will he be OK?' he went on in that sequence of rapid, uncoordinated thought and speech that is the product of shock, fear and the uncertainty of not knowing what had happened whilst he had been away.

Whatever fire there had been must have vented itself via the kitchen window because on entering the flat the atmosphere was warm but quite breathable without recourse to BA sets. In the centre of the living room, which had a connecting door to a small kitchen, there was the half-burned remains of an armchair, blackened and still smoking, in thin wisps.

A small pile of what appeared to be burned clothing was on the floor immediately in front of the chair. Other than the inevitable smoke and soot-stained walls and windows, the flat was undamaged.

'It looks to me as if there has been a slow build-up of smoke,' said ADO Tom Monsal. He had decided to come on from Shoreditch after being informed by control of Sub Officer Devine's informative message.

'Dolan, have you had a chance yet to speak to the deceased's flatmate to verify if anyone is a smoker? Looks to me as if the poor sod down on the ground might have fallen asleep in the armchair and somehow set light to a newspaper, and then the clothing or armchair covers,' mused Tom Monsal.

Dolan Devine was about to say that he would go and speak to the flatmate when an anguished cry went up from outside the flat. A police officer had just told the man that the dead body lying outside was his flatmate, whom he thought was still inside the flat.

'Do you know if it is just the two blokes who are occupying the flat, Dolan?' enquired the ADO, his hawk eyes sharpened by years at the sharp end stations, settling on an open sliding-doored wardrobe in the rear bedroom. In that wardrobe there were about 30 pairs of different coloured stiletto-heeled woman's shoes, neatly lined up below rails of skirts and dresses.

'I'm not sure, Guv, at this point. But, just before you got here I had overheard a neighbour saying that a couple of hard-faced women, looking like streetwalkers, were always coming and going at night, along with two men in and out at other times.'

'Maybe the women and the men are the same people,' he suggested.

Tom Monsal's mind contained an extensive mental file of hundreds of fires attended in his long inner-city service. One image sprang up into the forefront of his thoughts. He recalled another fire a few years back, which had involved an arson attack involving a couple of cross-dressers. His old boss had called it a transvestite's tiff, and he pondered if this was a similar incident, or if the women's clothing and shoes were the property of local prostitutes given the flat's proximity to an infamous red light district. It was common knowledge that in the world of vice, violence against prostitutes by their pimps, or by rival vice kings resentful that their own patch was being encroached upon, was an occupational hazard. Arson fires as one form of retribution by these pimps was a possibility that couldn't be discounted.

He then went into the small kitchen and studied the hand imprint on the hinged opening section of the soot-covered window. Through the murky glass he could see far below the revolving blue beacons of the appliances and those of police vehicles. A doctor had certified the man dead, and he could see the scuttling black form of police photographers and others now investigating why and how the young man had ended up on that unforgiving pavement.

After about ten minutes the ADO turned and asked Dolan Devine to come into the kitchen. 'In my opinion, Dolan, I think that the occupier was probably a smoker who has fallen asleep reading a newspaper. The smoking materials have somehow ignited the paper and the resulting flames have ignited the man's clothing and the combustible coverings on the chair. I took a look at the body before I came up and the front of his pullover and trousers appear burned and scorched. The heat and burning might have aroused him. Imagine you're in a heavy doze and wakened by burning. When you come to the room is full of choking smoke so you panic and would be totally shocked and disoriented. He's then instinctively gone into the kitchen for water or to try to get to the window for air. I guess he

71

could have climbed up on to the sink units. In his confusion and panic he climbed half out of the opened bottom bit of the window. He was only a skinny little sod. He could have slipped through and tried to grab the window frame, hence the slurred handprint.'

'It could well be that was the way it was,' replied the Sub Officer.

'Whatever it is, Dolan old son, it's essentially a police matter now. You know the drill. Don't let any of our big-footed fuckers disturb anything and you'll need to make a critical investigation of the fire cause, including getting the Brigade photographer out – yeah?'

'And I'll need your coroner's statements and fire report before you get off,' Tom Monsal went on.

'Yes, OK, Guv. There's no rest for the wicked is there now?'

'At least you are in a lot healthier state than that poor young fella laying cold as a fish on that hard concrete below. I'm away now but keep me posted on things as necessary. I'm keeping an open mind at this stage on this one but I do recall a similar job a few years back. Take it easy, Sub, and I hope that I don't see you again tonight,' his parting words being code for hoping they both had a quieter time in the ten hours of the remaining duty.

Several months later at the inquest which the coroner had previously adjourned to gather more information, an open verdict was recorded. If there were any sinister reasons as to why or how the death occurred they never came to light. Perhaps the theory put forward by Tom Monsal wouldn't have been too far off the truth as to how a young exile from Scotland had met his end on that fateful night in north London. Yet another unfortunate victim of the ravages of fire and smoke.

Chapter Eight

Silent Approach

There must be few adults within the population of the United Kingdom who have never heard of Holloway, the short title of Her Majesty's prison, which is situated on Parkhurst Road in the London postal district N7.

It was at this location that Ruth Ellis, the last woman to be hanged in this country, met her end in 1955, and it is within those walls that many of the nation's most infamous criminals have been detained.

'Fire Holloway Prison Parkhurst Road – Silent Approach' was the cryptic wording hammered out by the teleprinter at just after half past eight on that early summer's evening.

We could count on several calls a month to this location. Some would be false alarms caused by defective automatic fire detectors. Some would be to reports of fire in the prison complex. But, as with any of the emergency calls that come into fire stations, no one ever knew what was behind the clamour of the turn out bell when we were ordered to the prison on a 'silent approach'. The reason for this instruction was that emotionally charged inmates can soon become agitated and the arrival of fire appliances with blaring sirens can induce an excited state. Particularly when a fire has been started as an act of defiance or protest designed to cause disruption to the established scene. So apart from the immediate turn out from the station, when sirens were sounded, the remainder of the run would be without them, and this meant our speed had to be reduced somewhat.

The predetermined attendance of three Pumps and the Turntable Ladder halted near the main gates. A prearranged routine was then put into operation. A routine designed to maintain security and order, whilst still permitting the Brigade to assess the nature of the emergency. A stoutly built female prison officer came through a

73

small wicket-door set in the steel outer door of the prison. She had a large bunch of keys attached to a strong-looking chain attached to a waist belt. 'What's the situation?' Station Officer Pete Revell asked of her.

'I'm not sure at the moment, hinny. We got a call on the internal emergency line saying there was a fire in a cell on floor two. We've not heard anything since, so we better have the usual check with just one crew,' she replied in a lilting accent, which sang of the River Tyne and other north east locations.

'Right, Pumps crew only and bring in a couple of BA sets, one extinguisher and a general purpose line, the usual gear in fact, fellas,' instructed the Station Officer.

Equipped in this way, the Station Officer and the remainder of the pumps crew jogged along a path, which at first was in the open and then went under the prison complex. Only 20 feet above, a crowd of inmates were pushed up to a louvred window. They were braying and cat-calling. They were perhaps enjoying the disruption. They were perhaps thinking whatever thoughts enter the minds of some women, young and not so young, on seeing a crew of fit and mostly young men, especially if they had been starved of male company for a long time. I had been here a fair number of times myself and was always struck by how the new part of the prison seemed more like a hospital than the traditional image of bars and cells.

The security measures here were, of course, far tighter than would be found in any hospital, save those for the criminally insane, and we had to be escorted through another few locked gates before arriving at floor two.

Like hospitals, prisons have their own smells, but they are the odours of humans locked into their small cubicles for a large part of the day, with all the fetid and sickly scents that such conditions can create. Not the antiseptic, well-scrubbed air that most hospitals have.

Pervading these human scents though was the unmistakable odour of burning, and as we turned a corner we were met by a bank of grey eye-stinging smoke, which had mushroomed up to the ceiling and was now all but obscuring the corridor.

'Martin, get a message back to the main gates to let the other two crews in, and haul up a hose reel, it looks like we've got some sort of a fire,' shouted Peter Revell to Leading Fireman Martin Cerclew. He scooted off while we crouched low under the pall, which was coming from a cell at the far end of the corridor.

The door of the cell was half open. Against a wall at the far end a mattress was smouldering, no doubt ignited by one of the inmates who had managed to get hold of matches or a cigarette lighter. Such incidents were not infrequent at Holloway. They were often acts of protest or defiance, or were designed to attract attention to someone's situation or grievance.

Brandishing the water extinguisher, which we had brought in with us, I quickly doused the surface flames and cracked open a louvred window panel to ventilate the pungent smoke. The hose reel wouldn't be needed after all, but it was good firemanship for it to be brought up just in case the fire had been bigger than it was.

Small blaze it might well have been, but the smoke produced in the small dimensions of the cell had been toxic enough to render the cell's resident unconscious. She was just to the right of the cell, a blonde-haired woman, lying face down in the position that the prison officers had placed her after having dragged her away from the smouldering mattress and into the corridor.

The female warders seemed either in shock at the situation, or were acting nonchalantly at the prisoner's dramatic actions. Certainly they were affected by the thick smoke themselves and it was an easy matter to forget that the tensions within their working environment, as high as they were, did not involve them in fire and smoke every day.

Accordingly, the Station Officer quickly sensed the nature of the situation. In a flash he was at the woman's side, helmet now off and kneeling on the cold prison floor, trying to hear sounds of breathing, and with his thick fingers felt for a pulse in her white goose-pimpled neck.

A resident nurse had been sent for and a short, bustling, late middle-aged woman appeared carrying a red box marked 'Oxygen Resuscitator'.

'She ain't breathing and her lips are turning blue,' said Peter Revell as the nurse fumbled with the resuscitation equipment. She was taking too long for his liking, and casting aside any niceties, he said, 'Nurse, let me use it, I'm familiar with this piece of equipment.' She didn't resist and in a second he had connected the transparent face-mask to the oxygen supply tube, and turned the valve on the end of the black and white oxygen cylinder, before tilting the prisoner's limp head back and pressing the mask firmly around her mouth and nose to ensure a good seal.

As I looked down at this unconscious form, whose very life might have been at that moment ebbing away, I couldn't help but wonder what was the background of this prisoner. What crime had she committed that had led to her incarceration within this austere place?

Perhaps she was serving time for the relatively harmless misdemeanour of not paying a fine or for some other relatively innocuous transgression. Perhaps she was serving a life sentence for the premeditated murder of a husband, lover or helpless and frightened child.

Of course it was not our job to make moral judgements, but to simply save life and property. The swift intervention of Peter Revell was doing just that, and doing it successfully. Because only 30 or so seconds after applying the face-mask, and watching the resuscitator automatically filling the woman's lungs to their capacity, in a slow rise and fall of bosom and rib cage, a faint cough became louder as the woman began to recover.

'We've got her – she's coming back,' said the Station Officer with a half grin, and then as if to announce her return to the land of the living, she vomited and the yellow liquid entered a small bypass, provided for such an occurrence at the side of the face-mask. The mask was pulled off and, as she awoke with a dazed start, the nurse took over and placed her in the recovery position.

We got the burned mattress out into a rear courtyard and used our hose reel to drench it thoroughly before being escorted through the three sets of doors and out into the open way to face further jeers and ribald shouts before reaching the appliances and returning to our respective stations.

'We never know who we are assisting when we attend jobs at the prisons do we?' said Mike Deveen as we topped up the hose reel tank.

'No, mate, it's true,' replied Ron Rougier, a burly veteran of over 20 years who had forearms like two legs of prime pork. 'I've been to Pentonville prison down the Cally [Caledonian Road] a fair few times over the years, including attending some riots and cell fires, and you just don't know if the blokes you are helping are helpless, weak old sods in for embezzlement, or half crazed psycopaths and mass killers or child molesters. It's just as well we don't know, ain't it, Mike? Come on, let's see if young Geoff Joynt has got the supper on the table yet.'

76

By the early years of the 1980s, the neutrality of the fire service, so long its mainstay, began to suffer as almost anyone in public service uniform began to be seen as 'enemies' to be stoned and attacked during violent periods of civil unrest, as seen at Brixton and Handsworth.

During the post-war years up to the early eighties fire service personnel could enter most locations and ghettos with relative impunity and indeed the service's apolitical stance was, and is, one of its most significant hallmarks.

Just as medical doctors and nurses see in their daily work how illness, injury and grief are entirely non-discriminating, the members of the fire service witness, all too often, similar scenes. They are scenes and situations that span the whole range of human life from the most blatant financial poverty to the highest reaches of the wealthy.

It is a result of such professional experiences, that the Firefighter is able to value life for what it is. That value cannot be tainted by treating one man, woman or child in a different way to any other. This is why the professional attention given to the unconscious inmate at Holloway was delivered in the same way as any other victim of fire or calamity.

Whatever a person's situation, be they inhabitants of the most expensive house in the most affluent suburb, or occupants of a cockroach- and rat-infested apartment in the meanest part of the inner city, they know that if they call 999 an unquestioning and immediate response will follow every second of every day of every year without fail.

'Ours is not to reason why, only to do, and then to die.'

Chapter Nine

Only to Do and Then to Die

As mentioned earlier, I had once visited New York Fire Department. It was a sobering reminder of the hazards of the Firefighter's calling in that densely populated metropolis, hazards that were then at their peak in such areas as Harlem and the Bronx.

'This could be the night.' Those words, printed on a card, help decorate the wall of some firehouses in the Fire Department of New York City, and are a reminder of a simple but sobering truth: that Firefighters never know if they will return from an emergency response.

Nowhere would that ever present yet repressed thought be more horrifically and tragically illustrated than by the events of 11 September 2001, when more than 300 New York Firefighters failed to return, perishing in one of the most barbaric acts of terrorism the world has ever seen.

Since the inception of the paid New York Fire Department in 1865, there have been, on average, some six or seven operational fatalities each and every year since that date. Every such loss whilst engaged in operational action is a blow to the force's morale. The crushing, numbing shock that as many Firefighters had perished in a few hours on 9/11 as had been lost over any 50 year period cannot be imagined.

Although the thought has to be moved to the back of the mind, the fact that death's calling card has been left so often, and with such chilling regularity over the years means that it is still there to periodically remind us that the business of firefighting and rescue is one of the most hazardous occupations of all. Be it in New York, Chicago, Los Angeles, Paris, London or wherever. September 11 2001 resulted in such a sad and lengthy addition to the names on memorials within New York, which commemorates those who have died as a result of attendance at emergencies. These stand as a solemn testimony to the extremely high levels of hazard that have always existed in that city. A city in which some 8 million people are packed into an area of 300 square miles. A city whose collective heart was numbed on that fateful morning, more than at any time in its proud history.

Three thousand miles way in the foyer of the London Fire Brigade's headquarters on the Albert Embankment within sight of the Houses of Parliament, another memorial records the names of all those who have died within the capital in times of peace and war.

Firefighter fatalities are never in vain. Arising from each and every loss something is hopefully learned to try to improve the safety in such a potentially hazardous profession. After a tragedy, the fire authority and health and safety commissions critically analyse events and, if necessary, produce revised policies and procedures.

Within the London Fire Brigade, post-incident inquiries have resulted in revised operational notes, improved training and other methods designed to ensure that Firefighters are as fully informed as practicable about the nature of the hazards which they are called upon to face.

However, it is often the unpredictable nature of events, coupled with fire's intrinsic hazards, that emphasise and highlight the dangers within the business of firefighting and rescue.

In that regard, the hand of providence must often have played its part, be this in London, New York or elsewhere. It is surely because of this latent danger that Firefighters will never know what fate awaits them behind the urgent clamour of the call out signal.

In Glasgow's Cheapside in 1960, 14 Firemen and 5 members of the Salvage Corps could not have foreseen their fate when a major blaze in a whisky bond exploded with such ferocity that it blew out the heavy stone walls on to those working below. It created the biggest loss of fire service personnel on these shores at a single incident.

In October 1966 on Manhattan's 23rd Street, twelve Firefighters, including a probationer on his first response, perished when the floor of a burning store collapsed without warning. This was for many years the largest life loss at a single incident, until the catastrophic events at the World Trade Centre in September 2001.

In 1969 at Dudgeons Wharf, on London's Isle of Dogs, that 'U'-shaped curve of the Thames, which in 1940 and 1941 had helped the

German bomber crews in identifying the tinderbox of the London docks, hot cutting operations to demolish huge tanks containing a flammable residue went tragically wrong killing five Firemen.

Three years later, Glasgow Fire Service, in a city once called 'the tinderbox of Europe,' suffered yet another tragedy when seven Firemen died during firefighting operations at a cash and carry warehouse in Kilbirnie Street. These, and other Firefighter fatalities, illustrate the potential for danger, which always exists, and which plays its own part in the tension present whenever the emergency response signal sounds.

But Firefighters, wherever they serve, cannot afford to dwell upon the hazards of their work. However, a healthy respect for known risks, along with a professional and developed regime of training, enables them to respond with confidence and skill. Those skills will always be enhanced by the acquisition of sharp-end operational experience. For it is in that empirical environment of fire, heat and smoke, that the Firefighter develops a nose for danger.

They can never be sure, given the fundamental hazard of fire and other risks, whether 'this could be the night'. But gaining extensive hands-on involvement, over time, can better help ensure that it will not be.

Chapter Ten

Taking the Mickey

At just after 0630 whilst most of the watch were lying on their bunks in that half-awake state like that of a dog that always has one ear and eye open, and as Station Officer Tuke tidied up his fire and inquest reports, the bells came in again.

'Fire in factory – Station 27's ground – Pump only,' shouted the duty man, his voice heavy with a sudden awakening from sleep, as the remainder of the watch dropped down the pole, their features pale and eyes bleary with the smoke and energy drain of the earlier rescue.

The Pump weaved through the already building stream of traffic heading from the east into central London, and the radio squawked into life. It was a message from the station officer at 27. '... *no sign of fire, search of premises and area being made.*'

How many times had we raced across the city, keying up to the prospect of whatever was behind the call, only to hear those words, which 30 times out of a hundred were the prelude to the next message, which came just as we were arriving at the factory? *'Stop for [Address] ... false alarm malicious.'*

The white-helmeted figure of Station 27's Station Officer, who was about to climb up into the Pump, gave a two-fingered salute, a friendly signal to tell us we weren't needed, mixed with that annoyed sense of resignation at once more being sent on a wild goose chase.

Andy Carlisle, one of the two men whose sterling work had saved three people from an almost certain death only a few hours earlier when the floor on which he and the rescued had been standing only seconds before, suddenly collapsed, felt an involuntary shudder run up his spine as he sat in the rear of the Pump.

It was a shudder both of relief and anger. A relief born out of the realisation that he and the three persons trapped had escaped, and a suppressed anger at how malicious false alarms such as this could have cost the four of them their lives.

Had both appliances been diverted from that genuine incident because of the foolhardiness of those who got whatever it was they got out of such false calls, those vital seconds could have been fatal.

Fire services in the UK respond to many thousands of false alarms each year, and in the period of this account, approximately 30 per cent of all calls attended resulted from alarms that turned out to be either those made with 'good intent' or those that were 'malicious'.

Firefighters would much prefer any caller who genuinely believes that a fire has broken out to call them using the 999 system, than to not do so. They would much sooner respond to something genuinely reported and, where possible, deal with a small incident, than to have to deal with a conflagration.

'Smoke issuing from roof of factory,' the duty man called out and switched on the green light, which indicated that only the Pump was required, the call being on another station's ground to which our Pump made up the third appliance on the automatic three-machine attendance. We were on scene in five minutes, and the crews from the other two appliances were already reconnoitring the exterior of the factory. Before we could alight the crews were walking back towards us. 'You can go, fellas,' the Station Officer called out. 'Steam issuing from central heating boiler chimney.'

A passer-by had probably seen what he thought was smoke issuing from the roof and called 999. The fact that on arrival the 'smoke' turned out to be steam from a heating vent was appreciated for the public spirit displayed on the part of the caller.

Similarly, residents often call the fire brigade when they see smoke issuing from the vicinity of a neighbour's house, thinking that the property is ablaze, and this may be found to be someone burning garden rubbish.

Some fire stations in London would often receive alarms for fire in the same vicinity on a regular basis over the years. One example was the quite frequent reports via 999 that smoke was issuing from the dome of St Paul's Cathedral, which would send an automatic pre-determined attendance from Cannon Street (Dowgate), and a number of surrounding stations.

On arrival, they would always find that the smoke, which actually did look as if it was coming from the dome of Sir Christopher Wren's masterpiece, was in fact smoke from the chimney of Bankside Power Station on the south bank of the Thames. In certain weather and wind conditions, this would drift across, and in the light of the floodlights used to illuminate the cathedral, the sight was enough to make many a newly promoted officer in charge have palpitations at first glance.

Another 'good intent' alarm involved appliances from Dockhead and Cannon Street racing to the back streets of the south bank to a report of 'thick smoke issuing from warehouse'.

This regularly turned out to be an old established firm of fish curers who smoked haddock, and the venting process again gave callers a genuine reason to believe there was a fire inside.

The point of mentioning just two among hundreds of examples is to highlight the fact that the fire brigade cannot ever adopt a 'cry wolf' complacency, because it can never know whether the next call might be the real thing. There were some calls, however, that were not really the province of the Brigade at all, but served to show that of all the services within the capital, it was the fire service that would be a more certain guarantee of arriving promptly when someone in distress needed aid.

* * *

An Unsettled Mind

She was a well-built woman of about five feet four inches and ten stone and was clad in only a small pair of white pants, which made the coffee colour skin and raven hair of her Asian origins appear even darker. Both hands were firmly clasped around a long-bladed carving knife, which she was holding in front of her naked heavy breasts.

We had been called to a fire in a kitchen, and on arrival had been met by this woman, wild-eyed and screaming at a small balding and bespectacled Indian man to 'Get out, get out and leave me alone.'

A thin blue haze of smoke hung in the air of a kitchen that was accessed directly from the street, and to which the front door was ajar. A strong smell of curry and other oriental spices mingled with the thin smoke.

'Send a priority message requesting urgent attendance of police,' said the Station Officer, without taking his eyes off the knife-brandishing woman for even a second. Gingerly, Station Officer Tuke moved into the kitchen. 'We've been called to a fire here, and I would like to check if everything is OK. Are you able to tell me if the 999 call came from this address please?' he enquired quietly of the man.

The slight Indian eyed the wild-eyed woman warily, as if too afraid to answer. 'I want him out of here,' she screamed out and at the corner of her lips a white saliva could be seen, the sort of fluid that sometimes accompanies a violent screaming rage.

'Please, please, Sunita, there is no need for this, let me come by to talk to the Fireman please,' he pleaded.

'No, no, no, keep away or I will cut you in half,' she yelled, her black eyes glinting with rage.

Whatever the reason for this scene, the woman certainly appeared dangerous. The look in her eyes, the lethal, long-bladed kitchen knife, her half-naked appearance, and her loud threats suggested either a grievous wrong carried out by the man, or a woman whose mental equilibrium was in serious doubt. Our Station Officer had taken a quick look at the gas cooker, and although there were a couple of pans on the rings, there was no sign of overheating, but there was definitely a haze of smoke and a smell of burning in the air.

Station Officer Tuke knew that it was too risky to force his way any further into the house at this stage. There was no obvious sign of fire but a proper check would have to be made before the scene could be left, but at the moment it was simply too fraught. As he con-templated his next move, two policemen appeared at the front door. One was shortish, about five feet eight with carrot-red hair, the other well over six feet, balding, and with a thick paunch redolent of a man who liked his beer.

'What's the score, Guv?' the redhead enquired.

'No idea. We got a call to a fire at this address. There's a bit of smoke and burning smell, but nothing evident. It looks like a domestic squabble,' he replied.

In spite of the seeming danger, the small red-haired Constable went straight into the front room where the woman stood brand-ishing the knife, still staring at the small man opposite. 'Right, listen to me. Put that knife down on the floor now, or I will take it from you, do you understand me?' he inquired in a hard, uncompromising tone. A tone that, in later years, when political correctness placed its restraining hand on instinctive actions, could have seen him accused of racism, when in reality his no-nonsense approach would save the day for all concerned.

'I want him out of this house, he's a filthy dog,' she spat out, but already the venom in her voice was diluting. Perhaps the sight and tone of the policeman was jolting her mind back into a more rational state.

'Just put the knife down now!' came the still insistent voice of the small policeman, his freckled hand moving on to the top of his baton, ready to draw it if she tried to use the carving knife.

'Please do what the officer says,' pleaded the little Indian. 'You know we can sort this mess out.'

Something must have registered in the agitated mind of the woman as she suddenly threw the knife down on to the carpet and began to wail and sob hysterically. The tall policeman placed his huge hands on to her shoulders, the whiteness of his fingers contrasting with the coffee of her skin, and led her to a battered sofa under a window, which was shielded from the street by some shabby net curtains.

'Now tell me what's all this about?' he asked, and as she began to talk, the slight form of the Indian man moved towards the Station Officer.'

'I am so very, very sorry, please let me talk to you in the kitchen,' he said, and still watching the woman, moved into the cramped, seedy kitchen. 'She is sick, you see. She has schizophrenia, and has to have an injection every four weeks to control the worst symptoms. Many times when there is only a few days before the treatment, she gets like this and twists something, which is trivial, into a major crisis, and no matter what I say or do, she simply does not believe anything I say.

'I became very scared when she started to become violent earlier, over nothing at all, and I rang the police but they were taking too long so all I could think of was calling you out. I don't know why I did, but I was so desperate that something made me call the fire brigade.'

'So there has not been a fire then?'

'Oh no, there has been no fire'.

'But the slight smoke and the smell of burning, where is that from?'

'Oh, that is the oil and scent we light and burn for one of our religious rituals, but there has been no fire as such. Will I get into trouble, sir?'

The Station Officer looked the small Indian in the eye before saying, 'I am not happy that you called saying there was a fire when you knew there wasn't any such thing. Someone could have died if a genuine incident had occurred whilst we were here, but I guess you have had a big shock seeing your wife getting so angry and threatening you with that knife, and you panicked because of the police delay in getting here. Taking that into account we will leave it at that, sir, and I hope that things can improve for your wife.'

'Thank you a million times,' said the grateful man, and turned to go back into the lounge to speak to the policemen and his troubled wife. We mounted the appliances from the pavement where we had waited quietly until this 'crisis' was over, and made ourselves ready for whatever else the people and properties of London might throw at us.

* * *

Sprinkler Gong Sounding

The permitted rest period in which Firemen could lie on their dormitory beds and fool themselves that they would have a refreshing few hours ran from midnight to seven. Even on the less busy stations, proper rest was hard to come by for most, as the subconscious anticipation of lights and bells, and the rapid shift from safety to potential hazard, created a silent tension.

On the busiest stations, it had long been argued that the often frequent arousal from sleep, however shallow or fitful it might be, followed by a sudden leap up and a run to the waiting appliances, was likely to be injurious to health in the longer term.

Nonetheless, and especially after a busy evening attending the range of calls possible on busy inner London stations, it was difficult to not sometimes want to lie flat, and, at least try to doze.

The harsh clamour of the bells and the bright white dormitory lights broke through my thin veil of half sleep, and automatically, within a few seconds of the first clang, I was encircling the steel pole with arms and legs, noting through bleary eyes that it was that 'dead' time of 0430, a time when the body is said to be at its lowest ebb.

88

Low ebb or not, the physical and mental arousal of a turn out could be like a bucket of cold water being thrown over you, in the way you were suddenly awake.

'Sprinkler gong actuating Bishopgate,' came the duty man's cry as we glanced up at the indicator lights to see both bulbs illuminated green for the Pump, red for the Pump Ladder.

Fire sprinkler installations have been proving their worth in detecting and attacking incipient fires since the late nineteenth century, and the overall incidence of false alarms arising from these water-driven devices has not, in relative terms, been of a high order. Nonetheless false alarms can occur with such systems, and in the period in question, inner London stations, especially those with the larger departmental stores, factories and warehouses on their grounds would quite regularly receive calls in the early hours and other times to 'Sprinkler gong actuating'. In the event of a fire breaking out, sprinklers rely upon the principle of heat expanding a liquid in a small glass bulb, which is positioned in the sprinkler head. The unbroken bulb holds back the pressure of water.

A fire's heat will cause the bulb to shatter and release the water on to the flames below. A small amount of water is diverted to a small turbine, which in turning, causes a small hammer to strike the iron gong. Some systems were linked into an electronic sensor, which would automatically send a signal to the fire brigade, but many relied upon the loud and distinctive clang of the gong to alert either passers-by or the ears of the patrolling police officer.

We had been called to a large store on this main thoroughfare. Even as we pulled up, the unmistakable slowish clang of the sprinkler gong, sounding like someone intermittently striking steam radiator pipes with a hammer, was echoing along the dark side-streets and passageways.

There was no visible sign of fire or smoke, no smell of burning, but then, sprinklers are designed to check incipient fires not extinguish conflagrations, and sound an alarm in the process.

We had attended quite a few fires in which sprinklers had done their job so effectively that only a lukewarm steam was present when the fire scene was located, and who was to say that here, somewhere in this massive building, the same situation hadn't occurred?

Station Officer Cronine sent an informative: *'Sprinkler gong actuating – no sign of fire, search of premises being made.'* This was timed at 0440. A minute later the night security man appeared from a small side door near to where the large red gong was attached about six or seven feet up on the wall.

The Station Officer walked over to him quickly. 'What you got mate – is there any fire?'

'I ain't seen or smelled anything, Guvnor,' he replied. 'I was doing a patrol and was on the first floor when the gong started up, stopped for a while, and then starts again. I rang in 999 at once, which is what my instructions are.'

'That's fine, you've done the correct thing and we will start a search from top to bottom,' he said, detailing one man to locate the sprinkler stop valve, stay there and ensure no one shut the water supply down.

Because sprinklers are designed to put out small fires, then often only a few glass bulbs would shatter to release water on to the flames, sometimes only one. If the stop valve was closed too soon, before the Brigade had got jets into position, the fire could flare up and get out of control. Turning the water supply back on after the fire had grown could cause so many heads to operate that the system could be overwhelmed, hence the importance of positioning a Fire-fighter at the main valve.

Not all premises with sprinklers have electronic indicator zones to direct Firefighters to that part of the building where sprinklers have actuated, and this store was one of them.

Before the introduction of personal hand-held portable radios, searching for fires in such situations as this was time consuming and relatively inefficient. If crews split up to search individual levels and one team discovered the fire, it could be several minutes before the rest could be advised. The introduction of hand-held radios had greatly improved our communications in such situations.

After about half an hour, the eleven present had searched every part of the store, and there was no sign of any fire, nor was there any outflowing of water from a damaged head, which would also cause the gong to sound.

Once inside the store and when away from the exterior walls near to the gong, the metallic clanging was inaudible. Consequently, when the gong suddenly stopped its rotating clamour, it was only John Lydus, positioned dutifully at the stop valve, who knew. He called up our Station Officer, and 20 minutes later the rest of the watch returned to the ground floor and John was able to confirm how long the gong had been silent.

What had most likely happened was that there had been a short but temporary increase of pressure in the town's mains, which supplied the sprinkler system. Some of the water had entered the supply side of the installation and caused the gong to sound for a time, stop and then start up again. So we had responded to another 'good intent' false alarm, but the number of times that we found ourselves searching premises in respect of actuating sprinkler gongs was very low compared with the increasing number of false alarms arising from electronic detection and alarm devices.

It used to be quite customary for many commercial buildings, be they stores, office blocks, factories, warehouses and so on, to employ night-watchmen or security staff, and the practice still continues in the larger and more prestigious premises. Some commercial concerns, even today, do not have security staff or an automatic fire alarm installation. But developing electronic technology has resulted in more and more premises being fitted with both automatic fire detection and fire warning arrangements. Some of these are routed into permanently staffed private centres, which receive signals and alert the emergency services.

* * *

Alarm Caused by AFA

It was just after 0200 when the bells came in, followed by the printed message: 'Automatic Fire Alarm Actuating Eastern Textile Warehouse.' The call was on our ground.

We were on scene in a few minutes, and the hee-haw of the third Pump's klaxon could already be heard a good mile away.

The warehouse was a four-storey redbrick structure about 260 feet long by 65 feet wide, and was full of a wide range of cloth from across the world. It was a place to which annual operational familiarisation visits were made by all watches from our fire station, and so we had a good idea of the building's layout.

Other than the shrill ringing of an external bell, immediately apparent on dismounting, everything seemed as still as the nearby canal surface.

'Sub, you take your crew around the back, we'll check the front,' the Guvnor's voice rasped out in the still air.

91

'Send an informative, John,' said the Station Officer to John Lydus, the Pump's driver for the shift. ' *"AFA actuating, no sign of fire, search of exterior being made."*' John repeated the message in the time-honoured naval fashion, a relic of the days when many firemen were ex-sailors. It confirmed he had got the content right. He picked up the handset to transmit just as the blue beacons of the third Pump came into view from the traffic-light junction a hundred yards ahead.

We checked the front of the warehouse, our noses twitching like hunting dogs, as we tried to detect that unmistakable whiff of burning. We placed the back of our hands on window panes to check for heat, and shone our lamps through windows trying to catch in the light the reflection of smoke, and all the time the shrill bell tringed away.

The other crew did the identical exercise at the rear. But they were able to climb a metal external fire escape and check conditions at the fire exit door on the top floor, where the smoke and heat of any lower fire would be most likely to have risen, but no indications of fire were evident.

This wasn't the first time that we had received AFA actuating calls to these premises in the early hours. In fact the station's log would show that the other watches had attended as well, perhaps three or four times over the last year. These calls added to the Brigade's overall statistics, which recorded that some 30 per cent of all calls received were to AFA alarms. After about ten minutes, the Station Officer asked John Lydus to verify the origin of the 'AFA actuating', and within a few seconds Mobilising Control came back to say that it had been routed by a central alarm station company, and that a 'fire' condition was still showing on their indication equipment.

The officer in charge was now faced with something of a dilemma. The whole point of an automatic fire alarm is just that – an automatic detection and alert of a fire situation. It is the relative cost of such installations, over time, compared to the wages of night staff, which first made the systems attractive to the small to medium companies, especially as insurers would give some premium reduction if an approved system was fitted.

So a fire alert was showing, but there was no outward manifestations of fire. Increasing attendances by brigades had demonstrated that an alarm could be sounding and showing a fire even when none was present.

Were the Station Officer to base his decisions on these past negative experiences, and decide to risk sending a stop message stating that the 'alarm was caused by fire alarm system fault', he may well have got away with this most times. Eventually, however, 'sod's law' would dictate that he would come unstuck. A repeat call would be received and, on return, the premises could be alight, with all the consequences that meant for the business, not to mention the officer in charge, who could face dismissal, and the fire authority a possible civil action for loss sustained.

As a consequence, the officer in charge had two options open. The first was to force an entry into the premises on the basis that the alarm indicator was showing a fire situation. The second was to request the attendance of a key-holder via the police, and wait outside with all three appliances, until someone turned up to open the place up and allow a top to bottom search to physically check for fire. The Fire Services Act allows members of a fire brigade to lawfully enter premises where there is reason to believe that a fire has broken out, so a forced entry wouldn't be illegal. When all external checks had not discovered outward indications of fire, the usual route, option two, was taken.

A radio message had confirmed that the warehouse key-holder lived some miles to the north of London, and his estimated time of arrival was at least 25 minutes. In due course a large white Mercedes saloon drew up. The key-holder and proprietor, a short man of Middle Eastern appearance and wearing a camel-hair coat, which nearly touched his mid calf, got out. He walked up and opened the large iron-grilled front entrance door.

'I am sorry that you have had to come out like this, but why are there so many fire engines, there doesn't seem to be a fire,' he remarked to our Station Officer, who towered over the man like a Roman sentinel, his large, white, combed helmet making him appear at least another four inches taller than the six feet plus he actually was.

'Well, sir, the fact is that your automatic fire alarm is showing a fire situation. This area is what we call high fire risk and in those areas we always send three Pumps to any alarm of fire within buildings, and that includes alarms from automatic detectors. I have attended these premises at least twice in the last year, sir, and I know other officers have attended here also. Each time it's been a system fault, but we never assume this to be the case,' the Station Officer went on, in a clipped but respectful manner.

93

'Well yes, I understand that, officer. Of course I wouldn't want you having to come here if there is only a fault, but then I have paid a lot of money to have this system installed so that I can have the peace of mind that if a fire breaks out it will be quickly detected,' he responded.

'Yes, sir, and it is a wise decision, but perhaps you could have the alarm engineer attend later today to try to establish why you are experiencing these faults, and I will contact the area's fire safety officer and ask him to arrange a specific inspection with you,' retorted the Station Officer. He would have liked to go on about the fact that during the best part of an hour of being detained, someone's life could have been lost or property destroyed. However, he knew that the fault was most likely to be some defect in the apparatus, or neglect of maintenance by the proprietor, but our Guvnor was impotent as to taking any sanctions so he had to bite his tongue.

Within a quarter of an hour we had satisfied ourselves what we knew would be the case, that there was no sign of any fire, and the all too familiar 'stop' was transmitted: '*Alarm caused by AFA.*'

The warehouse proprietor's Mercedes slid away, its silky smooth purr contrasting with the harsh roar of the diesel engines of the three appliances as they pulled away in a cloud of blue diesel smoke following the long delay caused by crews having to be certain that the alarm wasn't the real thing.

* * *

King's Cross in the Early Hours

The two Pumps had only travelled a few hundred yards when the radio burst into life calling up the pump with a message prefixed with the word 'Priority'.

'*Order your Pump to fire, York Way adjacent King's Cross Railway Station,*' said the smooth female voice of the control operator.

'Received and mobile to fire, York Way, adjacent King's Cross Railway Station – acknowledged.' Station Officer Tuke simultaneously giving a blast of the siren with the switch under his right boot as we approached the traffic-lights just turning from amber to red.

Drivers of fire brigade vehicles proceeding to emergency calls are permitted to exceed the speed limit, provided all warning devices are operating, but are otherwise subject to the same requirements and regulations that apply to other drivers.

Traffic-lights are no exception, and legally, should a driver cross a red light and be involved in a collision, then that driver can be charged with a variety of offences.

However, given the amount of traffic-lights across Greater London, particularly within the inner suburbs and the West End, many minutes would be added to response times if a halt was made at every set, and those extra minutes could cost lives.

The normal procedure therefore if the lights are at red, or about to change, is for the driver to ensure that all audible devices are operating, in addition to blue beacons, and to cautiously 'peep and creep' across the junction. On the vast majority of occasions, other motorists will pull over or slow down to allow the appliances to cross. But the danger comes from not only inattentive drivers of other vehicles, but from, on the one hand, the elderly whose faculties might be impaired, and, on the other, a younger element who delight in filling their cars with high volume music. Both situations may mean that sirens are not heard, and beacons not seen until it is too late.

Given the very high number of calls responded to by London Fire Brigade each year, serious accidents en route to emergencies are rare, but fatalities have occurred across the country. In a well-publicised case in the 1960s, Lord Chief Justice Denning laid down that no fire was so urgent that risks could be taken in crossing traffic-lights at red, and that the onus lay squarely with the appliance driver.

It was doubtful if John Lydus was thinking of this distant legal ruling as he cautiously crossed the red light, but he was very aware that even with the Station Officer sitting next to him, the onus of responsibility should he be in a collision with another vehicle, cyclist or pedestrian, lay solidly at his feet.

Even in the world's busiest fire departments, most responses to fires end up as either incipient incidents or one of the categories of false alarms. Sadly, in New York and other cities in the USA, where some of the crew 'ride the back step', Firefighters have died after being thrown from the appliance en route to emergencies, which turned out to be malicious false alarms.

How many times had we thundered and blared along streets thick with all manner of vehicles, full of jaywalking pedestrians and see-mingly suicidal cyclists? Riders who often seemed to appear from nowhere into the path of the charging red engines, usually oblivious to the eight tons of steel atop them, only to return, slinking back in silent embarrassment at the cacophony of siren and bell of only a few minutes earlier.

When our rapid response enabled a successful rescue to be made or a potentially serious fire put out before it became an inferno, we were grateful for the verve and skill of our drivers. However, had we piled into cars or pedestrians killing several persons by shooting a red light, where would we be then? How would the headlines read? 'Five members of the public killed in road accident, firefighters also possibly victims in race to a false alarm'? Perhaps such reasoning was in the eminent judge's mind when making that historical judgement.

But we would still strive to get to fires as quickly as possible, certainly those in premises and locations where the risk potential for persons was high, commensurate with that legal ruling and com-mensurate with the great weight of responsibility on the driver for the safety of the public and colleagues.

The electric blue flashes of the beacons became momentarily more vivid as we hit the relative darkness and dinginess of the long parapet walls above the Copenhagen rail tunnel on York Way, just as we heard over the radio the 'booking in attendance' message to Fire Control from the local station's appliances.

King's Cross is a name possibly recognised by most people within the UK, and countless others across the globe who have either taken or left main line trains from here to the north and Scotland, or made use of its Underground facility as part of their travels across this great city. It was also the scene of one of the darkest days for both the Brigade and the London Underground network, as we will dis-cover later. For my own part, King's Cross station had often been a primary point of departure during trips to distant places when I would escape for a few days to indulge in a pleasurable break, climbing the high mountains and fells of more northern climes. Trying to replace the smoke-filled air of the fireground, not to mention the fumes caused by heavy traffic, with the pure atmosphere to be found a few thousand feet up a rugged slope.

The station was also a good place to go after a day responding to fires and other incidents. Often two or three of us could be found in the bar sampling a few pints of the more tasteful beers on sale. Our thirsts adequately slaked, and with the appetite whetted by the best beers, we would often indulge in a fish and chip supper at a large greasy spoon cafe, which existed then alongside the Pentonville Road. Or we would jump on the Underground and go up west for a few more drinks in the multitude of bars around the theatre district.

'I could kill for a juicy T-bone steak and a bottle of red,' whined Jim Peating, as the Pump braked with a squeal outside a small shop, which sold model railways. We parked opposite the two local station Pumps, the combined effects of our blue rotating beacons strobing the dingy buildings and attracting a gaggle of 'creatures of the night' from the station's frontage.

'You'll get more than a bottle of red around here, Jim,' the Guvnor chuckled, pointing to a bevy of ladies of the night, teetering in their stiletto heels and in tight leather miniskirts. The area around the precinct of the station and several of the adjoining streets was an infamous red light district, and like a number of other parts of the capital, there had been a growing presence of drug pushers and users on those seedy streets.

Only a few weeks earlier we had attended a good working job in the small hours, in a nearby squat occupied by an assorted crowd of glue sniffers, heroin addicts and prostitutes. It was a very smoky fire involving mattresses and filthy bedding, and three addicts had been dragged unconscious down a tall narrow staircase. But it was probably the drugs that had initially knocked them out, before that vile, brown, pungent smoke enveloped them.

There was no smoke here to be seen though so the officer in charge verified from Control where the 999 call had come from. All that came back was that someone had seen a fire near King's Cross station.

A blare of two-tone horn heralded the arrival of the Turntable Ladder, an automatic ordering to all calls to 'fire' in this high risk locality. The indicator plate aside the cab door showed that it had come from Euston.

Although we all suspected that this was yet another 'Mickey', our euphemism for a malicious false alarm, chances could never be taken with lives or property, so the officer in charge instructed the Leading Fireman in charge of Euston's 'ladders' to get aloft and have a good look around over the rooftops for any smoke or flame. This was a quite standard procedure, and was akin to the use of fire lookout towers in North American forests.

97

Within five minutes the ladders had been pitched, their steel pawls clanking as the telescoping extensions shot up to almost a hundred feet.

The Leading Hand, secured on his platform at the head by a safety belt, scoured the buildings around York Way, Pentonville Road, King's Cross Road, as well as the railway arched thoroughfares of St Pancras and Midland Road. The only smoke to be seen, however, was that of the blue clouds punched out of the exhaust stacks of the diesel locomotives as they inched away with their long train of northbound coaches.

'Looks like we've been effed about again,' said the Guvnor with a note of disgust and resignation in his voice. A resignation born out of having stopped trying to analyse the moronic behaviour of whoever would get a perverse thrill from a malicious call to the fire brigade.

'Do you think that some perverted and twisted bastard sees us fly past to a call, and decides it will be a wheeze to get us out again by making another "Mickey"?' asked John Lydus of the three of us in the rear of the Pump, as we headed back to the station.

'Could be, John,' replied Jim Peating. 'Psychologists have said that there is a link in the minds of some perverted individuals with everything connected with fire. It's said that they get a buzz watching fire engines racing through the streets, or from standing out of sight in a dark and dingy doorway watching firefighters rigged in their helmets and other gear.'

'Yeah, who's that watching us from the door of the model railway shop?' quipped John Lydus, and simultaneously all heads whipped round to see nothing but an empty doorway.

'Got yeh,' said John, his grinning face looking yellow in the light from the street lamp. 'In truth though, and joking apart, I do think that "Mickeys" are often down to young kids who get a buzz out of mischief,' he went on.

Whatever the motives, we were all agreed that whereas other forms of false alarms had to be accepted as genuine processes of good intent, or the malfunctions of otherwise extremely beneficial detection and fire warning devices, malicious alarms were not only sick, they were criminal acts, which could, and had, cost the lives of the public and firefighters, and there was every sign that such calls were increasing rather than declining in number.

Chapter Eleven

Whisky in the Jar

It was quite cold standing on the platform of one of those stations on the London Underground Northern Line, which are situated on the surface. My usual mode of transport to the fire station over 15 miles across the congested roads of the capital was by car.

Unfortunately, after ten years and a hundred thousand miles, the gearbox had decided to call it a day. As a consequence, here I was at four thirty in the afternoon, taking the tube, which, fortunately, was not too far a walk from the station, where the first of our two night duties would begin at six.

After waiting for a good 20 minutes in a chilling breeze, I was glad to see the red snake of the train pull in. It was good to feel the relative warmth of the carriage as I grabbed one of the few empty seats on what was a train packed with homeward bound commuters.

No matter how many times I rode on the Underground, the smell, the sounds and that tingling anticipation of new experiences that the capital provided, never left me.

To while away the many journeys I had made on the tube trains during my years in the capital, my mind would try to analyse what it was about these trains and the subterranean tunnels and stations that evoked such a strong association. Perhaps it was that unique plan of the network of lines and stations, with the different colours used to denote them. Maybe it was the names, Bakerloo, Waterloo, Picadilly, Victoria and so forth. Perhaps it was because many of the stations had names that were so familiar to so many people. Not only to the Londoner. But to those millions of visitors from around the globe who had pored over the underground plans in the information pages of countless diaries and guidebooks. Or observed the station names on the hard, folding board on which the game of Monopoly is played across the globe.

Perhaps it was the overall uniformity of the way in which the carriages and their fittings were designed and placed. The red-green patterned seats with their tough cord-like fabrics, which had supported the rumps of millions. The millions who had, and did, sit facing each other with a look that looked but didn't dwell. The millions who, in countless rush hours, had hung on those snooker ball-like spheres. Connected to those flexible coiled hangers. Or had clung to those silk-smooth steel grab-rails, fighting the clattering sway of the train, and that force caused by the gradual braking as stations were reached.

Perhaps it was the abundance of ever changing advertisements. Those long curving strips underneath the glass and acrylic cases with their stainless steel frames. So many of which evoked the London scene of commerce, leisure and endless opportunity.

Above all, perhaps that unique atmosphere, which I felt for London, arose from the packed humanity. A humanity so often crammed like matches in the tight confines of its top-curved box. But matches that differed in thickness, height and in colour, and therefore did not match.

To travel on the London Underground during the peak hours was therefore to travel amongst so much of what helps to make the capital what it is. A huge, sprawling, bustling, rushing, teeming fleshpot. A cosmopolitan container of people, which would daily disgorge its human cargo across the length and breadth of London.

On alighting, this thronging mass would make its way to countless destinations for countless reasons and countless purposes and motives, most honourable, some not. But wherever this teeming throng of people went, there would be no place within this conurbation that fell outside the embrace of the Brigade and its fire stations, the crews of which stood their safety vigil by day and during the long watches of the night.

Wherever masses of people live and work, the risk from fire and other calamity will exist. For myself, there was therefore nothing like a crammed full tube train to remind us that it is within the largest conurbations that the greatest risks to life exist.

I stepped off of the train on to the platform deep below those sometime mean streets of the inner-city suburbs, where my fire station was located. Wondering what act of human anger, weakness or mistake might occasion that urgent call of the turn out bells on the 15-hour long night duty, which we were shortly to start.

'Busy day, Mart?' I enquired of Marty Molloy as I entered the station via the open doors of the appliance room, where he stood looking on to the street. Marty was a 20-year veteran of the Brigade, and one of the most respected firefighters around.

'Nah, couple of "Mickeys" and a wash petrol off roadway after a two-car shunt outside the station. Still, if nothing else, I won't be falling asleep with fatigue tonight,' he went on. This last remark reminding me that he worked part-time on his evenings off, on the door at a local dancehall. Marty had been a useful middleweight boxer as a young bloke. Today he tipped the scales at 15 stone, and at just under six feet, with powerful shoulders, close-cropped dark hair, flattened nose and square jaw, he was a good visual deterrent to most would-be troublemakers fuelled by drink.

'Well, perhaps it is our night for some action, Marty. Just hope you don't get too much if you know what I mean – take it easy,' was my parting shot as I went up to the dormitory locker room to change into my uniform ready for the roll-call due in 20 minutes.

'Smells good, Geoff, what's in the pan tonight, buddy?' asked John Lydus of our chef.

'Sausage and mash with onion gravy followed by tinned oranges and cream, mate. How's that grab you?'

'If it tastes as good as it smells it should be handsome, Geoff. You've missed your way in life. You could have been another of those famous television chefs.'

'What, and miss working with this bunch of reprobates?' grinned our fireman chef, as he turned the browning sausages in the large, black frying pan.

The sausage and mash looked good and tasted good as I forked up another delicious slice. Before I could put it into my mouth the lights came on, followed by the sudden clamour of the call bells.

'Fire in derelict house – Euston's ground – Pump only,' the duty man called out as we sprung off the rubber pole mat on to the ridged red tiles of the appliance room floor.

Euston's appliances were out on a six-Pump fire on Soho's patch so we were called to cover part of their ground. The derelict house was not far from St Pancras railway station in those dingy back streets between there and Somers Town. A thin roll of grey smoke was coming out of a first-floor window of the derelict Victorian

101

house. We jumped down and pulled off the hose reel tubing automatically.

It was an old horsehair-filled settee burning, either ignited by kids or by dossers. Within ten minutes we had soaked it thoroughly and knew that it wouldn't be able to be reignited for a long time. Within another 15 minutes we had rewound the tubing and returned to the station.

There myself and John Lydus topped up the onboard water tank on the Pump. The hose reels and water tank were the most used pieces of equipment. Some 90 per cent of all fires were extinguished using the reinforced rubber tubing, which was tightly wound on two drums, one on either side of pumping appliances. The onboard tank contained between 250 and 300 gallons. Because the small diameter but high pressure nozzle used a relatively low amount of water, this gallonage could be used to excellent effect at all but those fires where a large body of flame was present.

The hose reel was the first line of attack on many fires. Even on the larger jobs, it could be used as a 'holding jet', whilst the large delivery hose was laid out and charged. Not for nothing then, was the equipment once known in the London Fire Brigade as the 'First Aid'.

After a quick wash of hands and face we were soon back up in the mess. The sausages had baked a bit hard in the oven's warming tray where Geoff had placed them, and the gravy had congealed, but the oranges and cream were good as was the big mug of tea poured from the huge alloy pot.

I had gone up to the dormitory at about ten thirty and lay on the hard bed reading a library book copy of George Orwell's *Down and Out in Paris and London.*

On the bed next to me John Lydus was studying for his Sub Officer's 'Ticket'. No matter how experienced a Firefighter was, or how keen to climb the promotion ladder, there were national qualifying examinations to sit and pass before permanent positions and ranks could be achieved. John had already passed the Leading Fireman's theory and practical tests. But the Sub Officer's exam, and the Station Officer's after that were much harder. Candidates had to study from a series of books published by the Home Office.

Every conceivable fire hazard and non-fire emergency likely to be encountered was within those manuals. Whole books were devoted to operational equipment alone. Other volumes covered building

102

construction, fire law, radio communications, fires in ships and in dockland warehouses. Persons shut in lifts or trapped in the lift mechanism. No wonder his brow was furrowed as he studied long into the night, even using a torch to not disturb his 'resting' colleagues around him.

Ours was a busy ship though, and more often than not sleep, rest or study would be broken by the tringing hammer on the red gong of the wall-mounted bell.

It was a Friday night. All over the capital people would be letting their hair down. Dance clubs would be filling up and the hundreds of pubs in our district alone would be pulling their last few pints as eleven o'clock approached.

It was the custom of many who patronised the dancehalls of the area to first get well tanked up in the many pubs before rounding the night off in the early hours drinking more at a dancehall, and perhaps 'pulling' a girl in the bargain, if that was a man's inclination. And there would always be those young, and not so young, bloods who were spoiling for a fight as their bravado and courage rose in proportion to the drink consumed.

Perhaps Marty Molloy might at that very moment be grabbing the collar of some guy fired up on beer and whisky for the last few hours, manhandling him out into the street. If not, giving a particularly truculent character a thumping in the dimly lit back corridor, which led to the exit door. Through which the man's coat would be thrown after him, having already been so unceremoniously slung a second earlier, black-eyed and bloody-nosed.

I must have been tired because when the lights and call bells aroused me from a deep sleep at just before a quarter to one, I was still in my day gear and the opened book was on the floor at the side of the bed.

With some of Orwell's detailed prose about dossers in London still in my head, I rubbed the sleep from my bleary eyes and grasped the polished pole, dropping swiftly down. The call bells still clamoured and the blue haze of diesel smoke followed the roar of the engines on both Pumps, which were revving loudly like growling, barking dogs, straining at their leash, ready for the charge through the early morning streets on which many revellers would still be present.

The smoke could be seen billowing out of a sixth, top-floor window from a good 300 yards away by the crews of the two appliances charging down the High Street, the electric blue sweeps of the rotating beacons bouncing off the windows and walls of the many commercial premises of this district, and the interior light of the crew cab giving a brief glimpse of helmeted, serious-faced men.

Although well after midnight, the streets of this north London inner district were still busy with cars and pedestrians on this Friday night start of the weekend break, and it was the time when the pubs, clubs and dancehalls did their best business. It was a pedestrian who first noticed the brown smoke issuing from the top floor window of the tall tenement block. As they looked around for a telephone kiosk to call us, the slow curling wraiths began to accelerate skywards. Then the welcome sight of a call box. Hope it is not vandalised with the metal reinforced cable hanging minus the handset. In luck, all was intact with that reassuring purr of a dialling tone, followed by the breathless, hurried details passed to Fire Control.

As this public spirited caller stepped from the kiosk he looked upwards. Noticed that the brown smoke cloud was now much thicker, and moving upward very fast with its underbelly reflecting the dim yellow of the tall sodium street lamps below. In the distance the caller could already hear the braying of the two-tone horns rising insistently above the deep drone of diesel engines as the two fire Pumps raced nearer by the second. The fast rising, heavy-looking smoke, which indicated a hot, rapidly developing blaze, was also beginning to bank down as the winter dampness in the air exerted its downward pressure. The sodium lamps were being masked by this smoke pall as the two Pumps squealed to a halt outside the burning tenement. On the opposite side of the street a gaggle of 'night birds' were flocking together, their necks craned sharply back and eyes drawn to the drama high above their pavement perch. Their white faces and curvaceous miniskirted thighs turning blue, then white, as the strobing light of the beacons fell on and off them.

The nearside front door of the Pump Ladder opened even before the vehicle had fully stopped. The heavy bulk of Station Officer Ben Tuke emerged, the black-booted feet on his six feet plus frame almost touching the road without him dropping down from the lofty cab, and his white-helmeted head angled sharply back as he took in the belching hot smoke 50 feet above with a critical eye born out of scores of such scenes over his fulsome operational years within inner London.

The tenement block to which we had been called had seen more than its share of fires over the years. It was divided into flats and bed-sits and a high proportion of its residents were manual-working males. In the days before fire safety legislation tightened its controlling grip, the risk from fire in such accommodation was high. Most call outs were to pans of food, which had been left on stoves and overheated whilst the tired-out resident, fatigued after a long day of heavy labour, flopped out in a chair or bed, forgetting the pan on the hot gas ring. Men had also died in fires within this building and who could be sure at this stage whether or not a similar fatal outcome might arise?

As in other parts of this locality, a fair proportion of the population were Irish and many of the residents within this tenement were of that stock. Men who had made the often rough sea passage to Holyhead, and then the train to Paddington, to seek, if not their fortune, a solid regular wage from the work to be found within the capital from the early 1950s and onwards. The Irish male, famed for his ability to carry out often back-breaking manual work with relative ease, and often in working conditions which the indigenous population could not handle, were godsends to those companies, that had recognised the money to be made from building and road construction, from civil engineering and the associated tasks of cable laying and groundwork.

Many Irishmen were single. Many remained in that non-marital state all of their lives, and for them that life was often hard and austere. Rising at some ungodly hour on a freezing winter morning from a lonely bed into a cold room, sparse of creature comforts. Cooking one's own breakfast. Making one's own sandwiches and a flask of hot drink before going to wait for the construction company's wagon. Waiting in a wind-whipped, wet Cricklewood Broadway. Sheltering from the pouring rain or from an icy blast on the Holloway or Kentish Town Roads. Then to a day of hard graft amidst a muddy, deep and treacherous trench, or high on the scaffold of some rising tower block. All the time knowing that what awaited for so many at the day's end was the four dingy walls of a seedy, dimly lit room and tiny kitchenette in such districts as Shepherd's Bush, Paddington, Kilburn, Cricklewood or Holloway.

It was little wonder, therefore, that many hard-working Irishmen found solace in alcohol, and a comfort in the company of those whose lives were following the same rugged road.

The pubs, clubs and dancehalls within the Irish exiles' community in London were the salvation of many. They provided a welcome contrast from the harsh, cold and arduous toil of their labours by the company, warmth, colour, music and drink, all of which could lift a man's mood. A mood that was so often depressed by the bleakness of their domestic surroundings within the grey confines of a seedy tenement, far removed from family, friends and the green grass and hills of Erin.

But if alcohol possessed the power to temporarily transport a man on to a happier plane, it could also hasten that same man's demise. There would, though, be very few, if any, amongst the hundreds of men and women who frequented the Irish pubs and dancehalls of the time, who would be thinking of the negative side to the demon drink, only of the lift it gave them after the unrelenting slog of working life. The districts of Cricklewood, Kilburn and Holloway contained a high proportion of public houses frequented by the exiled Irish community, and also contained three or four of the most popular Irish dance halls, the so called 'ballrooms of romance', in which they could feel at home and enjoy the crack with old friends and acquaintances. Surrounded by the thumping beat of the show-bands, the chink of glasses, the twirling patterns from the revolving ceiling globes of the dance floor lights, sometimes the 'crack' would be that of fists on flesh. A fleeting skirmish over a girl, a spilled drink, a long held grudge settled at last, and the urgent swoop of tuxedo-clad doormen, ever eager for the fray.

For all those who chose to visit these venues, it was a chance to put behind the grey grimness of their barren bed-sit, the clinging clay of the building site, and escape into a drink-fuelled haze of sound, light and pleasure. It was the custom of many to patronise the pub for a few hours and, after becoming well-lubricated with their choice beverage, head for the brighter lights and nostalgic music of their homeland. These delights were to be found in such popular venues as the Galtymore Ballroom in Cricklewood Broadway, the Forum dancehall in Kentish Town, or the Gresham Ballroom at the Archway end of the Holloway Road. Amidst the country and Irish music and songs, which sang of such places as Galway, Mayo, Sligo, Connemara and the hills of old Tyrone, hard-working folk found their temporary refuge from the weekday drudge and would be transported back across the Irish Sea.

Of course, there were other ways of gaining this release without venturing out every weekend to pub or ballroom. Some might choose to stay within their spartan rooms. Alone or with a friend, they could slip away from their confines within the heady vapour of a few bottles of Irish whiskey. Enveloped in the sharp smoke of many cigarettes, they could yarn about their youth in the old country or listen on a record player to such well-known songs as 'Galway Shawl', 'The Fields of Athenry', 'It's All For Me Grog' and 'Whisky in the Jar'.

Sub Officer Dolan Devine, himself a Mayo man, had experienced the hard and lonely domestic existence of many of his countrymen over 20 years earlier. Then he too had arrived in London as a single man, and had lived in the often down-at-heel accommodation like this to which we had responded. Many were the incidents of fire attended in such premises since he had enrolled with the Brigade almost two decades earlier.

Another such drama was now unfolding before his eyes as he dropped down from the Pump Ladder and trotted over to Ben Tuke to confirm what his guvnor's operational plan was to be. The heavy smoke issuing high above the street was no different from that encountered at hundreds of fires attended. However, at this late hour in a tenement with such a poor safety record, it was highly likely that many occupants would be asleep, oblivious to their surroundings. Indeed, it was possible that someone was already overcome by the deadly toxic gases to be found in the smoke of domestic dwelling fires. It was such knowledge that triggered the firefighter's internal pump, which caused adrenaline to course through the veins.

The men of the Blue Watch were an effective and dedicated crew, whose abilities had been sharply honed by the high number of emergency calls received to our inner London station located within one of the Brigade's highest fire risk districts. As such, actions were virtually automatic. Even before Dolan Devine had conferred with his Station Officer, men were throwing open lockers, locating, with standpipe in hand, the yellow plates that indicated a fire hydrant's whereabouts, grabbing a long line or pulling off yards of hose reel tubing with adrenaline-fuelled swiftness.

John Lydus, 23 years old and with a level of personal fitness resulting from cross-country running, had yanked the hose reel drum furiously, spinning it at speed so that a good 100 feet of the three quarter inch red rubber tubing was already on the street ready to be taken up to the blaze on the sixth floor. 'Dolan, mate, get yourself around to the rear of the block and check out the scene as quick as you like,' shouted Ben Tuke. Leading Fireman Andy Carlisle and 15-year veteran Dennis Breedon had already rigged in BA.

'Let's get a crack on, Andy, mate, I've been to a couple of nasty jobs in this effing place and this one looks as though its going to be a right bit of thickers,' shouted Dennis, using the old London Fire Brigade term to describe a fire that is generating extremely dense smoke. As mentioned earlier, it was a long-held tradition within the Brigade to 'get into fires', even at those jobs where premises were unoccupied, so as to quickly, and often without BA, crawl under the smoke to locate the actual seat of a fire and thus limit water damage as well as extinguishing the blaze as quickly as possible.

Firemen Rusty Checkland and Dick Brizer were already inside the block, their youth aiding their run up the mosaic-tiled stone staircase, anxious to get up to the fire floor when Ben Tuke's bulky form entered the ground-floor hallway, his waterproof over-trousers swishing as his huge thighs rubbed together. 'Hey, you two, bloody well slow down. Stop running and pace yourselves,' he barked at the two youngsters with less than three years service between them. 'If you keep running like that you will be breathing so hard by the time you are in the smoke you will be gasping in a lot of toxic shit and finish up being overcome. Then you'll be no use to any fucker yeah? So pace yourself, lads,' he said firmly, but tinged with an air of benevolence, remembering how green he had once been. When he had been Rusty and Dick's age, he had been schooled by a breed of officers and firemen who were almost an extinct species at the time of this account.

Those 'firedogs' of yesteryear took an almost masochistic pride in beating a fire. Holding back its fiery ferocity and asphyxiating breath in order to make a 'good stop'. When Ben Tuke was a new recruit there were few, if any, who would dare to argue about the time-honoured practice of 'getting in'. There were no shackles of health and safety law around at that time, no worries about litigation. It was the fireman's unwritten creed to save lives, protect property and carry out any other humanitarian duties without question.

When those 'firedogs' and 'smoke eaters' gained their own promotions, they came to the new rank as 'good hands' gained from hard-won firefighting experience, which was etched in the creases around the eye. Those creases were a wrinkled hallmark on skin dried by the eye-watering sting of acrid smoke, the occupational hazard of all firemen before the use of breathing apparatus became mandatory.

On this night I had been detailed to ride the Pump, and within seconds of John Lydus having pulled off that huge loop of hose reel, I had grabbed its pistol-like nozzle. Together we dragged the tubing into the entrance, pleased to note that the internal well of the stairs would facilitate a quick hauling of the hose by line up the well, rather than having to drag it around corners, which wastes a lot of time and requires a lot more length.

Even though it was now well past midnight, the staircase and landings on the lower floors still reeked of the cooked cabbage of earlier meals, but at the fifth floor this was replaced by that pungent odour of burning bedding and burning wood and cloth. It is a scent familiar to firefighters everywhere. An acrid smell, which pinches the nostrils and reminds one of the odour of burning autumn leaves mingled with that scorching smell of an ironing board on which the iron has stood on its rest too long.

The odour of smoke can be a useful indicator to what is likely to be involved before the seat of the fire is reached. In the small hours of the night it can send out a powerful signal and reminder that the situation might be one of great urgency, for at such times the average person will be asleep and oblivious to the hazard of fire. Most fire deaths occur during the sleeping hours. Within the major centres of population, especially within those places where no automatic detection of fire exists, there will be thousands unaware in all types of building of the danger that might be brewing around them. The greatest threat is that created by smoke.

The smoke at the sixth floor was now heavy, almost viscous in appearance. Its colour was a mid brown with intertwined yellow strands, which indicated the presence of sulphur, a product of incomplete combustion and giving an early warning signal of a flashover hazard. This heat within this malevolent pall had pushed the smoke up to the ceiling from where it mushroomed down, giving off its scorching radiated heat within its deadly breath, which felt like that from scores of high-powered domestic electric bar fires. Although the gaps around the windows of the burning rooms had allowed a venting release of some of the smoke and heat, we still had to locate anyone trapped and find the fire's seat and extinguish it before the whole floor burst into a fireball of flame.

Ducking very low under this baking heat cloud, and with the hose reel and its nozzle looped around my arm, I prepared to crawl towards the room in which the fire's source was suspected. John Lydus was right behind me, hauling the red tubing, which was in turn being fed by Dick Brizer and Rusty Checkland from the landing where conditions were more tenable. As we crawled along the greasy, worn linoleum towards the apartment, the heat increased, and that thin layer of breathable air an inch or so above the floor thinned and I began to cough as the acrid fumes seeped into my nose and mouth. I momentarily stopped crawling. Flattened my face to the filthy floor and felt again that life-preserving cooler vein of oxygen. I drew this in through my nose, forcing my mouth to keep shut, no easy task when the excitement and exertion causes you to gasp.

After a few seconds the coughing slowed and we pressed on, pulling ourselves along half on elbows and on hands. I could see, above, the faint light of an unshaded pendant light bulb. It must have somehow been sheltered a little from the rolling veil for me to detect it, but see it I did. Below its dim illumination I could just make out the hunched form of a man, coughing loudly. He was on his knees directly outside a door, off the corridor along which we had crawled.

'My mate Seamus, he's still in there you know, aye he's still in there,' he coughed out with an Irish accent as thick as the smoke all around us, but in the slurred, barely coherent speech of a man who sounded worse for wear from drink. 'Holy Mother of Mary, I had to leave him. The smoke was too thick, it was too hot, it's awful, can you get to him please?'

We all knew that Ben Tuke was a smoke eater from the old school, and he demonstrated this in no uncertain fashion at this point. There we were, flat on the floor, grovelling around in that barely breathable channel of air, when the footfall of his size-13 fire boots announced his presence. He was upright, his head in the thickest, hottest layers of this evil smoke, and he wasn't even coughing, as he dropped down on his knees at my side. 'You're doing fine, son, fine, but there's no time to waste. I've got a couple of BA men on their way up, but you must make a search of the far room as fast as you like if any fucker is going to come out of this job in one piece.'

'Got it, Guv,' I spluttered as he grabbed the inebriated Irishman's arm in his thick fingers and led him to the relative safety of the landing, then to the cool night air outside.

We continued, turning right, crawling over a threadbare excuse for

110

a carpet, trying as hard as we could to keep mouths closed to shut out that vile and hot toxic smoke, praying that our nostrils would filter out a lot of the poison.

Even as I crawled I was wondering how blokes like Ben Tuke could 'eat smoke' like they did. I had heard though that even he, albeit rarely, had been almost felled by the poison. Perhaps, I thought, it was a bit like drinking alcohol on an empty stomach when the drink hits you at speed. Whatever the reasons, I knew that the smoke was creasing us and behind me John was coughing uncontrollably now. It felt as if we had been inside this inferno for ages when, in fact, it had only been a few minutes since we first started our rescue and fire location efforts.

Encouraged by the sure knowledge that the two BA men would soon be with us, and spurred on by the information that there was a person trapped, we pressed on. I could now see a dancing ruddy glow about two feet above the floor some 15 feet away, the red reflecting off the browny yellow clouds.

As we got closer I could just make out what looked like the rectangular lump of a double bed. It was on the top side of this that the flames were leaping, but their curling tongues had reached up to the ceiling and spread laterally to each side, forming a moving, ruddy T-shape of smoke-masked flame. I unlooped the hose reel from my arm. The pressure built up by the water behind the pistol nozzle could be sensed like a coiled spring awaiting its release. I squeezed the trigger and the hose bucked a bit like the recoil of a high powered revolver as I gave the flames on the bed a good burst, sweeping the jet around and producing the hissing heat of steam, which momentarily darkened the glow only to light up almost at once.

'Take the reel, John, I'm gonna start a search – we ain't any time – it's too bleeding hot in here, cool the room down, mate,' I coughed out as I passed the nozzle to him. He opened up the spray and swirled it round and round in a desperate effort to lower the room temperature as I began my search in this deadly hot fog for Seamus who we suspected would be on or around the bed.

My hands felt under the bed but met no human form, only the old-fashioned 'gezunder' pot, the wet, obscene contents of which splashed on to my hands. 'He's on top of the bed – I can just make him out,' coughed John. 'He's there on your right, let's grab him and get out of this hell hole before it goes – it's too effing hot, my ears are tingling.' Once the sensitive skin on the ears starts to smart, a flashover is often seconds or so away and as I got to my feet I also sensed the blistering heat on my ears, like a hundred hot needles within this superheated woollen shawl of smoke and deadly gases.

Sub Officer Dolan Devine, here in this tawdry tenement amidst his native folk had just appeared after checking that no one was hanging out of windows at the rear of the premises. Now he was alongside us, squatting on his haunches in this furnace-like heat. Dolan was another man capable of 'eating smoke', but if it was food he was consuming the question would always be, 'Where does he put it all – there is nothing of him?' Small in stature and small in facial features he was, but his heart and spirit were as big as anyone I had ever known. There was precious little that Dolan had not experienced. His 'at the sharp end' developed nose for danger sniffed out the perilous conditions surrounding us all. He was holding a small axe and with a few deft strikes took out the upper panes of the windows overlooking the street from which that passer-by had first seen the percolating smoke pall. This life-saving piece of 'good hand' fire-manship vented the pressurised heat and smoke, releasing it to race with great heat-driven velocity up into the north London night, and lowering the potential for the deadly flashover to occur.

As Dolan was doing this my hands fell on to a stubble-covered head, the skin of which was slimy with perspiration. Moved them down over a barrel chest, bulging belly and thickset thighs which were literally cooked by the burning bedding. John gave the bed a good 'drink' from the tubing, knocking down most of the visible flame and creating a cloud of dense steam. John then took hold of Seamus's legs whilst I got my arms around his broad chest and back, thick flesh disguising the tough muscles and sinews beneath. The product of a lifetime's handling of shovel, spade, sledgehammer and pick. Seamus was, as they say back in his native land, 'a real broth of a boy'. What would he have given now, I thought briefly, to exchange the heat of this virtual funeral pyre for the cool rain and wind blowing on a Connemara shore?

BA men Andy Carlisle and Dennis Breedon were with us now, the click-clack of the valves on their sets signalling their presence. 'Take over the reel, we might as well get him out now,' coughed John to the pair as we half dragged, half carried the 15-stone form back to the relative coolness of the landing. There the hands of Rusty and Dick reached out to help us lower Seamus to the cool, tiled floor.

Dolan was squatting in the corridor, looking grey and shattered

112

from his sterling work in venting the deadly smoke and heat, whilst next to him our Station Officer was still erect but in a corridor now almost free of smoke. The weak yellow light of that unshaded bulb suspended from the old brown, twisted flex cast its jaundiced light on to the still steaming Seamus. Rising with that steam was that sickly sweet smell of burned human flesh. The whole of the Irishman's back and thighs were severely burned, so much so that the deepest fibres were visible, looking like a charred version of the human musculature printed in bright colours on an anatomical chart. 'The poor sod. Get a burns sheet up here pronto,' barked Ben Tuke to no one in particular. Within minutes, young Rusty, barely out of his probationary year, and experiencing his first nasty job, had skipped down the stairs and reappeared with a burns sheet from the Pump.

This was gently placed over the charred limbs in an effort to lessen infection within those horrific burns.

Dick Brizer, also young in service and years, was on his knees, bent over Seamus into whose tilted back head he was forcing his young, life-sustaining breath. Now stilled by that deadly smoke and shock. Ben Tuke knew that with that degree and depth of burning it was unlikely that Seamus would survive. He had once read in a medical journal that the survival prospects could be estimated by adding the percentage of the body burned to the victim's age, and if it neared a hundred per cent, chances were remote. If the victim was the 50 or 60 years he looked, then the 50 plus percentage of burns made things look very bleak and Ben Tuke just hoped that medical advancements had increased the prospects of such grievously burned victims surviving. In any event, it wasn't the fire service's job to adopt a negative approach, and miracles had occurred before. We would never give in. Those decisions were the lot of the medical profession.

If proof were ever needed of the determination of the fire service's front-line personnel, one had only to observe Dick Brizer carrying out mouth-to-mouth resuscitation on the unfortunate Seamus. While there is life, there is always hope and as I looked down at this scene, my own head now starting to clear, I observed the slow rise and fall of the victim's chest, and into my mind came the inscription that is on the awards made by the Royal Humane Society, which implores rescuers not to give up: 'Peradventure a little spark may yet lay hid.' Young Dick continued to search for that spark until relieved by the ambulance crew a few moments later.

As the fire was under control, and to get fire cover back on the local stations should other emergencies arise, the Pump Ladder was put back on the run via a radio message, after which both crews began the process of ensuring that the fire was fully out and that no extension had taken place into roof voids or adjacent rooms.

Whilst we were doing this, Ben Tuke began his investigation as to the likely cause of the blaze, including ordering on the Brigade photographer who would record the fire scene in case the victim died, which would result in an inquest and the need for a coroner's report. The previously dense smoke had now all but cleared within the affected rooms, but fire had again left its pungent calling card to show that it had yet again inflicted its damage to life as well as to cloth, timber, plastic, brick and glass. The two rooms and kitchenette, squalid and unsavoury before the fire, were certainly in a mess now. The walls and ceilings were blackened by the greasy smoke. The burning bedding and mattress had ignited an adjacent foam-filled sofa. This, in turn, had set fire to an old wooden sideboard, the varnished veneer of which added its fuel to the hot fog of fire. The double bed was now a blackened, burned, water-sodden mass. To the right of the windows, which Dolan Devine had broken to vent the great heat, there was an old oak wardrobe, superficially charred and with one door ajar revealing a scruffy old gaberdine raincoat.

'Seen this, Guv?' I said, pulling down the spalled plaster to check for still ignited embers. I pointed to the right-hand raincoat pocket where the top half of a partially consumed bottle of Irish whiskey could be seen. A few moments earlier I had noticed, amidst the wreckage of the room, two other full-sized whiskey bottles, now heavily smoke stained, but with their labels still readable. Both of these were empty and I pointed them out to Ben Tuke.

'Looks like they were having a right bleeding beano don't it?' he remarked with a wry grin.

'Sure does, Guv, I guess that the guy that you helped out will have a right tale to tell eh?' I replied. Although the man (who had been outside the affected rooms) would likely be in shock, it was vital to pinpointing the cause of the blaze for the Station Officer to speak to him while events were still fresh in his mind, or as fresh as they would be if the empty whiskey bottles were any indication of the amount of alcohol consumed.

So our big guvnor, still tall even with his large, combed white helmet under his arm, located the room where a resident had said the man would be. He knocked on the paint-peeled brown door, the steel number plate of which had fallen loose but left its imprint below. After a couple of minutes and the sound of shuffling from inside, the door was opened by a large, heavily built man with a red moonface and with a bald pate covered by some combed over hair strands. He had big, outward-turning ears and hands the size of small shovels. He was wearing a dark green woollen cardigan over a grubby white shirt. On the collar were some small specks of dried blood probably the result of a cut whilst shaving, because two pieces of tissue paper were stuck to his bull neck next to the inside of the shirt collar. His trousers were of brown corduroy, shiny with wear, and the laces on his workman's boots were unfastened and trailed on the floor.

'Good morning, sir, sorry to bother you at this hour but I need to have a word with Seamus's friend who I am told might be here. My name is Ben Tuke and I am the officer in charge of this fire and it is important that I see him soon,' he said softly.

'Oh yes, do come in, sir, that'll be Brendan you'll be wanting will it not? He's just through here. It has been a terrible night for sure, especially with Seamus getting caught an' all that,' the moon-faced man went on as he led the even larger bulk of Ben Tuke down a dingy corridor. He led the Station Officer through a tiny kitchenette. In it was a small, square table with a stained, green-checked table-cloth. On top of this there was a small, clear glass basin in which there were slices of yellow cheese and this was next to a large basin heaped with cornflakes. In the corner there was one of those tiny cookers known as a 'Baby Belling', which had two small rings, atop of which was a blackened stew pot and a small red kettle with a blackened spout. There was a small casement window overlooking a rear courtyard and below this was a brown butler sink with a draining board on which sat an old scratched Oxo tin with a thick elastic around it, no doubt a workman's sandwich container. In the air, mingling with the smell of fire smoke, was a strong rotting cabbage smell, which could either have been the residue of earlier meals, or the pungent whiff of socks not properly washed out and drying on a string placd across one end of the corridor.

Even before the room at the far end was entered, the sound of loud snoring could be heard. On entering, Ben Tuke could see in the dimly lit room a white-haired, middle-aged man sprawled unceremoniously face-up, fully clothed (save for the boots), on a large and faded old red settee. The man's mouth was half open and the snoring was that of a man who was sleeping off a skinful of strong drink. 'Brendan, Brendan, yer gotta wake up yer know, it's the officer man from the fire brigade who needs to talk wid yer,' the large Irishman shouted at the same time as grasping the man's shoulders in his huge hams of hands and shaking him until he started to stir. Staring and blinking, trying to gather his fogged and fuddled senses and trying to come around from the grogginess of an alcohol-induced sleep.

'Now, sir, do yer fancy a mug of hot tea to be supping while Brendan gathers his wits. I guess that ye will be parched after being in all that smoke and heat will yer not?' enquired the moonface.

'I could kill one, mate,' replied Ben Tuke, 'but tell me, do you know Seamus and Brendan well if I can ask that of you?'

'Oh yes. I have known the pair of 'em for well over twenty-five years. We came over here at the same time for the work on the construction sites ye know, and we've stuck together down the years for sure we have. I am a Tyrone man meself, whilst Brendan here is from Mayo and Seamus comes from a little town called Glenamaddy in Galway where the show-bands used to play back in the sixties and so on.' He rattled on in that fast delivery peculiar to men of his land, as he poured the boiling hot water on to the tea in a large chipped brown pot. 'We all met up on the ferry to Holyhead. The work back then was too good to miss as there was little chance for good money in Erin at that time for sure. None of us ever gotten wed and we used to earn very decent wages, which allowed us to send a fair bit back home each month to mam and dad down the years. Sadly they have both passed on now,' he said with a sad sigh as he pointed a thick rod of a finger at a faded card on the wall on which there was a faded photograph of an elderly couple.

It was one of those remembrance funeral cards familiar to those of the Catholic faith. Below the photo were the words: 'Pray for the souls of . . .' 'Still, when the big man above calls we all have to go at some stage,' he went on in a subdued voice as he poured the steaming tea into three large pint pot mugs, which had blue rings on their outsides and were all chipped around the edges. Then, as though the recall of his parents had reminded him of mortality, he looked straight at Ben Tuke and, in a hushed voice, asked, 'Is our dear friend Seamus going to be all right, sir, if I can ask that of you?'

Ben looked at the man's red face for a good 20 seconds before replying, 'You must remember I'm a Fireman, not a doctor, but in over twenty-five years in London I have seen people as badly burned as Seamus and survive, but they were I think a fair bit younger. So it is not easy to answer, but he will receive the best attention at the burns unit in Middlesex and we can only hope and pray for him.'

'It looks as if it is in God's hands now for sure,' responded the moonface, and as he finished that sentence, Brendan staggered into the kitchen.

'What's in God's hands, Joe?' he asked as he entered the kitchenette, his snow-white hair dishevelled and his clothing crumpled.

'Ah, there you are, Brendan, the fire brigade officer here needs to have a word wid you about the fire and we were talking about poor Seamus's burns an' all that.' Ben Tuke stood up, his tall, bulky frame dwarfing the squat Brendan, and he held out his hand: 'I am sorry about your friend and I need to try to find out how the fire started.'

'How's me old friend Seamus – is he badly hurt, sir? Where have they taken him?' he asked, his speech now barely slurred as the effects of the alcohol receded and the traumatic nature of events began its sobering process.

'Here, get this down you, Brendan, and why don't we go in the back so that you can tell the Fireman what happened,' said the moon-faced Joe.

Brendan took the mug of tea and together the three went into the bed-sitter. Over the next half an hour, with the room lit by the low-wattage bulb and by the red glow from the hissing gas honeycomb wall-heater, Brendan gave his account of what had happened that night and which had ended in such dire consequences for his friend of over two decades.

It transpired that because Seamus had been feeling very tired after a day digging a trench, a task that didn't get any easier when a man was nearer 60 than 50, they had chosen to spend the evening in the tenement rather than do their normal routine of a crawl round the pubs followed by taking a minicab to either the Galtymore dancehall at Cricklewood or the Gresham at Holloway. Instead they decided to splash out on three bottles of Irish whiskey and, with several packets of cigarettes, sit down and reminisce about their youth and the old country and play a few records on the old portable gramophone of some of their favourite tunes and songs. Brendan had said that by about nine they had seen off the first bottle of whiskey, which they were taking with water, and that they were enjoying themselves with the heat from the gas fire and the smoke from the cigarettes making things seem very pleasant.

Because of his tiredness Seamus had begun to succumb to the drink ahead of Brendan. As a result he had got on to the bed to lie back with Brendan sitting on the old settee next to him. Seamus had dozed off and was snoring. The whiskey bottle was on a small table next to the settee. Alongside it was an identical empty bottle, which was filled with water, used to dilute the whiskey – 'to make it go longer' – as Brendan had described it. He recalled having another half tumbler of whiskey and water before dozing off himself as the fug of heat from the fire and the drink took its effect. He had woken up with a sharp smell in his nostrils. Looking at the clock on the adjacent sideboard, he thought that it was showing about half past ten. Looking towards the bed, he saw a blue haze of smoke. He realised that Seamus had fallen asleep with his cigarette still burning and that the top bedding must have been set alight. Brendan had leapt up and shaken Seamus, and Brendan had used some of the water in the bottle to douse the sheet, after which Seamus got up and he recalled him going to the toilet and then flopping back on the undamaged side of the bed.

Brendan then remembered having gone to the kitchenette to refill the bottle with water and to open another bottle of whiskey. Soon they were imbibing again and enjoying the filter-tipped cigarettes. He recalled to the best of his memory that they must have got through a good half of the bottle and that this had taken them up to about a quarter to midnight, a time when normally they would be leaving the pubs to go to the dancehalls. Brendan recalled glancing at the clock just after midnight, at which time Seamus was flopped on the bed with a cigarette between his fingers, and then had felt his eyes closing as 'the old drink had really begun to speak to me for sure'.

A strong urge to relieve himself had brought him back to consciousness, if not to a clear mind, but almost at once, on starting to regain his senses, which by now were the worse for wear, his nose was once more assaulted by that pungent odour of smoke. He opened his bleary eyes but could barely see a thing. He rubbed his eyes furiously, thinking that his eyelids were stuck together. Then it dawned on him. The lack of vision was due to thick smoke in the room and he suddenly realised that the events of earlier must have been repeated. Seamus's lighted cigarette must have set fire to the bed again. Indeed, through the now thickening pall he saw red and orange flames on the bed leaping upwards with his friend still in the middle of it all. For a second or so he had frozen. Then, in a panic, he screamed to Seamus to wake up. He grabbed the whiskey bottle nearest himself from the small table, the one containing the water. He leapt up and poured its contents on the flames. There had been a vump of a noise and a blue flash and the red flames had worsened. To his horror Brendan discovered too late that in his alcohol-befuddled panic and desire to help his old pal, he had picked up the bottle half full of flammable spirit instead of the one with water in it!

In spite of his inebriated state he had the presence of mind to get to the kitchen and fill a pan with water. He had staggered back to the bed through the now dense smoke but could not locate it. Even though the top of the old sash windows were slightly open and the smoke able to partially escape, the room was full of hot, eye-smarting, lung-irritating fumes. The bed was now invisible with Seamus unconscious somewhere on its now rapidly flaming form.

Station Officer Ben Tuke listened without interrupting, taking brief notes of the salient facts and entering them with his fat stub pencil on to the numbered and ruled pages of the Brigade's official notebook. Occasionally looking up as he wrote, he saw, more than once, Brendan wiping a tear from his blue eyes with a strong stubby hand, a hand calloused and roughened by years of gripping the shafts of spades, shovels, sledgehammers, picks and drills.

What a terrible tragedy this had been, he thought. Two old pals. Once young men with all of that sweet anticipation and hope for their lives to come, the thrill and anticipation that have arisen from that great adventure across the Irish Sea like so many of their forebears. Fuelled by the excitement of moving to a city where it was once believed the streets were paved with gold. Then, realising down the years that things seldom are what they had once seemed, and, though never finding their financial fortunes, finding instead a solid friendship, which would stand the hard test of time. A friendship that had been bonded by hard physical work and by a shared acceptance of those grey and austere rooms in which they lived. A friendship strengthened in those much brighter pubs and dancehalls where alcohol would work its liquid magic and soften the hardness of a tough and sometimes lonely life.

What a terrible irony then that the alcohol, which had so often eased that rugged road of their existence, had played its part in ending the life of Seamus, who sadly succumbed to his terrible burns a few days later.

Most of those hard-working citizens of Ireland who played such a huge part over time in building this nation's prosperity would die peacefully in their beds. Few, fortunately, would die in such a tragic fashion as that which befell Seamus. Born and raised in the green of County Galway but whose demise began in the redbrick of inner London on that fateful night. Another victim of the many fatal fires, which were attended during that period, and a death that would so sadly sever a bond of friendship, first forged between three men on that passage across the Irish Sea over 20 years earlier.

Chapter Twelve

Death Underground

Over the years, the British public have become used to seeing the fire service in attendance at a variety of 'non-fire' emergencies. At road, rail and air incidents, people and animals trapped in precarious situations, major public disasters such as Aberfan and Hillsborough and a welter of other emergencies, they have come to associate these 'special service' calls as being almost as common as attendances at fire incidents.

As a matter of fact, in the period depicted in this account, there was no clear mandate placed upon the local fire authorities to attend anything other than fire emergencies (since 2004 a legal duty has been imposed on fire authorities to deal with these non-fire emergencies). The increasing involvement with what are officially categorised as special services is something that has developed in the post-war years. Increasing hazards caused by expanding transport systems, new technology and industrial processes, and a growing population, have led to an increased number of emergencies in which a guaranteed fast response is required.

Although fire stations have been sited historically in locations nearest to centres of fire risk so as to ensure that Home Office-prescribed attendance times are met, it proved to be the case that the service was as capable of attending special service incidents rapidly as it was of attending fires.

The ability of personnel to be able to work at heights, or in confined spaces, the wearing of breathing apparatus to combat toxic atmosphere, and the fact that firemen were trained and skilled with a variety of rescue tools meant it was inevitable that such a disciplined force became increasingly involved in this non-fire category of emergency work.

If a building collapses, it is the fire service who play a key role in search and rescue or retrieval of victims. If a major rail disaster happens, all emergency services would engage in their quest to save life. But it is Firefighters who, in addition to the carrying out of their legal duty of firefighting, engage in the cutting away of mangled wreckage and the extrication of casualties and bodies, as witnessed at such scenes of carnage as Lewisham, Hither Green, Moorgate, Clapham, Southall, Ladbroke Grove, Great Heck, Hatfield and Potters Bar.

Increasing numbers of cars, coaches, lorries and vans on rapidly expanding road and motorway networks have been followed by an increase in the numbers of road traffic accidents. The fire service has developed highly effective skills in relation to the extrication of casualties, and the management of chemical spillages and other hazardous substance emergency action procedures.

As a result of this additional involvement, Firefighters can be even less sure of what category of emergency will lie behind the station call-out signal.

To some people, the Firefighter's life might seem to have an element of glamour about it. In truth, there is no glamour in the work of firefighting and rescue. Whatever notions a young recruit to the service may hold in that regard are soon removed following a regular witnessing of the way that fire, heat and smoke can destroy homes, businesses and lives. Of how human tragedy can strike in a way that has to be seen to be believed.

There is certainly no glamour in dealing with a person under a London tube train. The London Underground has some 272 stations within its widely spaced boundaries. Many of these being household names. Some will be familiar with those Underground stations that form part of the sequence of properties on the popular board game of Monopoly. It was to one of those stations, through which the Northern line passes, that the call bells summoned us one early summer afternoon. The capital's Firemen had long experience of attending incidents on the Underground system.

Over the years these had included a variety of incidents. During the years of the Second World War when many of the deeper stations were allowed to be used as shelters from the air raids, a number of disasters occurred involving losses of life and serious injuries. These were the result of a station suffering a direct hit by a bomb, or, as occurred at Bethnal Green, in the East End, the result of panic.

There, the sound of the siren, along with the noise of a local anti-aircraft battery practice firing their guns, caused some to think that an air raid was imminent. and rush down the steps to the tube station. Someone tripped and this resulted in 173 people being killed in the resulting crush.

Where there are dense populations within huge cities, there are, invariably, a whole range of human dramas waiting to unfold. Most people only read about these things in newspapers. Or hear and see reports on radio and television. Such is the way of people, that matters that don't personally affect them are soon swept from the mind.

For all its eight million population, London can be a lonely place – for the elderly, the dispossessed, for those thwarted in love or ambition, and for those who are without friends and family. For these, and a variety of other reasons, some of these individuals decide that their lives are not worth living, and it is the police, ambulance or fire service personnel who invariably engage in the aftermath of events.

Person Under Train ... Northern Line

One of the most noticeable features of the London Underground stations is the strong draught. This is caused by trains moving in tight tube tunnels, and by ventilation fans. There is also the peculiar smell of burning, which is created by the arcing of electric current used to drive the trains.

Although that unique odour was present as we descended the rubber-nosed escalator to the platform, everything else appeared eerily still. No warm rush of air, and only a handful of people coming upwards on the brown, wooden-slatted escalators, which groaned and squeaked as if protesting at the daily work they had to perform in delivering and disgorging thousands of rush hour passengers.

Thankfully the evening rush hour was a good three hours away. Because it was the procedure to close stations when this type of incident occurred, the platform was deserted save for the black-uniformed station manager and a couple of other staff. The long red carriages of the train were mostly still inside the incoming tunnel. But at least two of the leading carriages behind the motive power unit were alongside the platform.

The 30 or so passengers who had been on the train had been cleared by the guard who had opened the normally secured inter-connecting carriage doors to facilitate their exit. In the small, almost claustrophobic, cubby-hole alongside the platform, which passed as the station manager's office, the driver of the train, his face almost as white as his shirt, was sitting on a chair. The old standard first aid remedy for shock, a mug of hot sweet tea, had been administered. The shock made his hands tremble, and he almost spilled that hot tea on to his shaking knees.

'I thought it was an overcoat being thrown across my path,' he was saying to the Station Manager who, before administering this help, had ensured that the line controller had been contacted to shut off the electric current, and that the short-circuiting bars (insulated handled devices to isolate the live current from the area of the train) were placed at either end.

Satisfied that this was being carried out, he had called both the ambulance and fire service, and the former had arrived just ahead of ourselves.

'John, send a priority message from me *Request traction current be shut off on southbound track, Northern line*, and then send an infor-mative: *"Person under train – ambulance in attendance"*,' said the Station Officer to the Pump's driver. In a few minutes he reappeared and confirmed that the current was off, and we moved up to the front end of the train to begin our work.

I had often been aware at such incidents, of a strange feeling of detachment. Almost as if the mind places a sheet of toughened glass between the sensitivities of the mind and the raw reality. The raw reality of the gruesome sight that may lie ahead in between the rails in that deep greasy pit under the red train.

This feeling was linked to a pride in the uniform and badge of the Brigade. A pride first sown as a small seed in the early days of recruit training. A pride which, for many Firemen, blossomed in the keen interest and satisfaction of their work. These feelings were of definite assistance to me in dealing with the sort of incident described.

I did not believe that this feeling, and the courage and conviction it gave, would have existed outside of the uniform and outside of the corporate spirit of the Brigade. Perhaps, as I later reflected, this was what the military meant by '*esprit de corps*'.

Whether it was that or not, our involvement in such situations and

124

the efficiency and effectiveness of our emergency actions were undoubtedly helped by it.

The ambulance crew of one man and one woman had already gone on to the track and had crawled under the train about 60 feet. There the casualty, a young woman, was lying, face down, in the pit, moaning gently and hanging on to life by a thread.

The yellow light of their hand-lamps reflected off the yellow fluorescent colour of their surcoats, and indicated where they were under the dark metal mass of the tube train.

If there was any hope of saving her, then it was those two who could play the key role at this stage, but the Station Officer beckoned me to follow him.

We lowered ourselves down on to the track, exercising a natural respect and fear for the electrified track, even though we knew that the current was not only off, but further protected by the short-circuiting bars already put in place at both ends of the train.

The curved advertising hoardings, such a familiar feature of the platform walls, appeared strange from this low position. If the casualty was in any way trapped by the wheels or under-train structure, then it would be the Brigade's task, assisted as necessary by the London Underground emergency team, to jack up and move the carriage to facilitate extrication.

We reached the end of the train and dropped down into the pit. Those familiar white porcelain insulators looked twice their normal size. The hard floor of the pit pressed through our leggings. Our hands fell on the greasy dust and detritus, which, in spite of a nightly cleaning and track safety monitoring service, was still in evidence. Chocolate bar and chewing-gum wrappers, discarded cigarette packets, cigarette butts, match ends, old pieces of pages from the *Evening Standard* and the other flotsam and jetsam of a mass presence of human life, crammed into the confined curves of the platform.

The light of the ambulance staff was closer now and the beam of my own hand-lamp picked up the glint of a shiny red object to my right. It was a stiletto-heeled red shoe. At first glance, in the poor light, I perceived it as having fallen from the casualty as she had gone under the train. Something made me stop and look closer. That something was the whiteness of human skin, now a creamy yellow in the light of the lamp, but with the pink and red colour of human tissue. I could now distinguish that this was in fact a human foot, still inside the red shoe. The foot must have been neatly amputated just above the ankle by the wheels of the train.

The Guvnor and I, he leading, now reached the ambulance crew. 'How's it look?' he asked in a hushed voice in case the casualty could hear him, but also as a natural respect for the obvious gravity of the situation. He had been to enough of these incidents over a long inner-city career to know that few who went under a tube train escaped with their lives. The female member of the crew was crouching over the young woman, holding her hand as she groaned almost inaudibly.

The young woman's body was twisted around with her head and upper body in the pit and her legs contorted to one side. She was not pinned by those heavy iron wheels, but it was clear that she had been under them for a time before the train stopped.

She turned her head towards the Station Officer, and, in case even at this late hour in a human life, the young woman's hearing was intact, said nothing. She simply moved her head slowly from side to side. A look of no hope on her face lit by the yellow torchlight said it all.

The unfortunate woman's extensive and multiple injuries were consistent with having fallen under the train, and, with a final moaning sigh, she expired. In that dark space. In the darkness of a dark tunnel. Illuminated only by the weak lights of our lamps.

We now had to remove this poor young soul from under the train. From this dark place of death back to the bright light of the station, which now appeared to me even brighter as we manoeuvred the special folding stretcher under the body and slowly made our way back to the platform, and to life. The amputated foot had to be retrieved. I crawled back and placed it into a plastic container pro- vided by the ambulance crew, who then placed the now covered form into a wheeled trolley. Then into the lift and from there into the ambulance, which conveyed the victim to University College Hos- pital where the ending of a life was officially confirmed

As we made our way back up the escalator to the street, I couldn't help but think of the terrible state of mind a person would have to be in to end their life in such a brutal and horrendous fashion. The fire service, especially those within the larger inner cities view their share of human tragedy, and in a lengthy career may well witness suicide in a variety of forms.

Some leap from one of the Thames bridges. Others jump from the tops of buildings. Others lock themselves in their cars after connecting a tube to the exhaust pipe, and others ease their passage into the hereafter with drugs or alcohol, or both.

Some set fire to themselves, whilst others choose strangulation by hanging. None of these situations can be anything other than sad. But to be in such a state of mind that the method of death is under the wheels of a train could only point, in my mind, to the virtual certainty of the end being quick. Mercifully, on that warm summer afternoon, and on so many other occasions when the Brigade was called to 'person under train', that was often the case.

Moorgate Underground Station, 1975

If ever there was a special service call that would test the resolve and reputation of the Brigade, and call upon a deep drawing on that well of mental steeliness in the face of human disaster, it was on 28 February 1975. It was another emergency involving those subterranean labyrinths that make up the London Underground system, and the location was Moorgate station on the edge of the City of London.

Within minutes of the arrival of the first appliances from Barbican and Shoreditch, the local Station Officer and crews had accessed the affected platform. They had been confronted with a confused and shocked crowd of commuters, who had been on their daily morning journey into the City from Drayton Park, a station not far from the Arsenal football stadium.

With a cool professionalism and skill, born out of many responses to most types of emergencies, but never one of this magnitude and complexity, the Station Officer rapidly assessed the scene. He realised that he was witnessing a nightmarish scenario in which the three leading coaches of a rush hour crammed train had crashed into a dead end tunnel into a space that was only long enough for one and a half coaches at the most.

Within minutes, the officer in charge had made the decision, never taken lightly, to transmit the priority message to activate the Brigade's Major Incident Procedure (a Brigade Control-activated alert that ensured immediate massive assistance from all emergency and medical services). With three carriages compressed into the space for not much more than one, the Brigade was faced with an awesome task. Not the least being the extremely confined space into which crews had to work, with the constant danger of collapse. A high ambient temperature, caused by the heat from hot cutting equipment, and the absence of the ventilation normally produced by moving trains, added to the overall difficulties faced.

The first impression noted by the initial crews attending was the fact that most of the disgorging passengers were covered in soot. This transpired to be the black grime encrusted on the dead end walls of the tunnel, which had built up over years and was loosened by the impact of the crash.

While the initial attendance crews and staff of the other emergency services were assisting with the evacuation of those injured and severely shocked commuters from the part of the train outside of the tunnel, the Brigade's officer in charge began to plan its own rescue efforts.

It very quickly became apparent that the tunnel into which the train had crashed would be a 'tunnel of death', and at least one national newspaper of the time used those words as a caption to the tragic story of Moorgate.

Anyone who was present on that fateful February morning will not easily forget the scene of utter devastation that confronted us, as the best way of carrying out the task of rescue, and the extrication of those dead, was worked out.

Of course, it was only after the twisted, tortured and terribly tangled wreckage was accessed that an assessment could begin of how many of the commuters packed into the first three coaches had survived. Some indications of the eventual number of fatalities occurred quite early on that first morning when the principal officer commanding the operations indicated that a temporary mortuary would need to be established to accommodate the passengers killed.

Accessing the concertinaed coaches was exceedingly difficult because of the claustrophobically cramped confines of the tube tunnel. The distorted metalwork of the pulverised coaches had spread out sideways making it almost impossible for any but the thinnest and smallest Firemen to get into the wreckage. But the London Fire Brigade had always been capable of surmounting any obstacles placed in its way. Its rescue record from all manner of incidents in times of war and peace would mean that no effort would be spared.

Throughout that first day, crews worked in relays. So determined were the men who laboured at this disaster to save those still trapped, as well as giving comfort to the dying, that some men had to be ordered away from their posts by senior officers. The atmosphere on the Underground is usually several degrees warmer than at street level. Here in these terribly confined conditions with no ventilation from moving trains, and the great heat of floodlighting and hot cutting equipment, men were soon brought to the point of collapse. Hence the firm, but necessary, orders to take a rest to permit fresh crews to take over.

On top of these physical stresses was the psychological trauma occasioned by witnessing at close quarters some of the most horrific scenes of carnage imaginable. It occurred to me at this dreadful disaster that one of the major motivations of so many of us involved in the rescue operations was the familiarity which each of us had with using the tube train ourselves. For it was surely fate, or terrible misfortune, that those who died that day were on just one of the hundreds of Underground trains running on a network that, over its long history did, and *had* carried millions of passengers so safely under the capital's streets. In short, it could have been us and our loved ones caught up, trapped in this nightmare of an environment. A setting that was so familiar to all who used the Underground.

The tough, patterned cloth of the seats, now ripped, bloodstained and tangled up with timber and twisted metal. The advertisements on the carriage walls: 'Liquafruta Cough Mixture', 'The Brook Street Bureau', the coloured route maps of the Underground network, and so on, which we would read on our rushing clatter through the tubes, now obliterated. Stained with blood and flesh amongst broken glass. The tilting seats at the end of each coach, which afforded a couple of extra places for tired legs and which we had all occupied at one time, now invisible. Hidden by a buckled, broken stanchion. Smashed by the carriage wheels, which had spun their heavy, crushing weight up through the floor of the coach, past the chassis frame to suffocate bodies, sever limbs and trap those fortunate to still be alive with their heavy, immovable form.

It was only by the tremendous spirit and professional determination of all involved that those who were alive and could be extricated had been released by the end of that first day. The story of the young, courageous policewoman, whose foot had to be amputated before she could be liberated from this horrendous predicament, is a separate story.

All major incidents, and this was one of the most notable in the Brigade's long history, will leave images in the minds of those who were close to the practical operations of rescue and retrieval.

Out of the range of images that have become lodged in my mind, there is one that would be there many years later. It had a shocking vividness, which would barely dim when recollecting my own four days at this tragic scene.

It was in that part of the carriage where those small pull-down seats were positioned. These hinged rests were positioned on either side of the central door, which could in emergencies interconnect with the next carriage. In the peak period of the rush hour, anyone fortunate enough to have got one of these seats would be surrounded by the swaying sardine-tin-packed mass of passengers.

The only way to reach those unfortunate persons trapped deep within this crushed concertina, and beyond all hope of being found alive after the first two days, was for the wreckage to be sliced into sections. Once a section had been cut through, with the vile stench of decay (exacerbated by the hot air within that death vault) ever present, it was hauled on a pulley system attached to the iron rings of the tube sections, and removed on a battery-driven truck.

I was making a check within the last carriage just after the latest slice of the wreckage had been removed. The risk from infection in the warm, fetid environment of decaying human flesh necessitated the wearing of a mask to cover the nose and mouth, but when the mask was removed away from the immediate area, that terrible stench filled the nose and assaulted the senses. The smell could be recalled even out at street level in the fresh breeze of a London morning.

In a right-hand corner of the coach, directly in front of where those hinged seats were attached, there was a bulging tangle of twisted steel. A convoluted crush of metal sheets, passenger grab rails and ripped, twisted seating. Protruding from the central and lower levels of this wreckage, in line with the position of the hands and lower legs of an average-sized woman, my eyes settled on the waxy tone of human skin, on the curving, shapely and strong-muscled calf of a woman's leg. Its foot still embraced by a high-heeled, black, patent leather shoe.

A couple of feet higher there protruded the woman's hand. Both leg and hand were unmarked of visible injury, and only the time that had elapsed, along with the hopeless crushing, removed any hope that life could have still been present.

But what has remained within the recesses of my mind, more than anything, was the glinting gold of a wedding ring. That band of gold, symbolising eternity, into which state that poor woman had been cast so violently on that fateful morning. Perhaps only a half hour after saying what would have turned out so sadly to be a final goodbye to the man who had placed that ring on her finger. I would never know if this had been the case, but the vivid image remains.

Our task was now one of retrieval, I was taking a well-earned break after involvement in the retrieval operations, and was sitting with several colleagues on the cold floor of the platform which ran parallel with the one involved in this horrendous incident.

'It's a strange old job ain't it?' said Henry Lamb, a veteran with nearly 25 years as an inner London Fireman, 'I've seen some nasty sights after all these years. Lewisham rail disaster, Staines air crash and a lot of bad fire deaths, but I always marvel at how the mind copes with some of the things we see. It's a case of getting on with it. Somebody's got to do it and I find it never pays to think too deep about things.'

'You can drive yourself mad if you keep turning sights over and over in the mind,' replied Pete Jacoby, another old sweat coming up to retirement.

'People are better educated today though. They read more and you are getting some youngsters in the job who seem too friggin' sensitive,' Henry went on. 'Look at that bloke yesterday from Clerkenwell. He's only got a couple of years in. Couldn't take it. They had to take him off of carrying out one of the bodies in a casket. He said it was too upsetting. What did he expect working in a place like London? Eight million people, road and rail systems, major airports and so on, there's bound to be an incident like this every so often. It's only three years since that airliner came down at Staines and we went on the relief. I think that they should bring in some sort of test to find out in advance if you are squeamish or not.'

I thought about what these experienced old hands had said and had to agree with them. You certainly couldn't come to work with confidence if you were always dreading what you might see during a tour of duty. If a person had over heightened sensitivities, then the Brigade life was not the job, certainly not in the large metropolitan locations where the potential for incident is much higher. Perhaps the work did case-harden you, if the first few 'bad' jobs could be coped with.

There was no doubt that most Firemen discovered that the mind can cope with far more than is first imagined. Additionally, being a member of a brigade like London, with its long and noble history and heritage, played a real part in enabling its Firefighters to face gruesome sights. A new recruit or transferee would never want to appear weak or ineffectual to their more seasoned colleagues, and it became a matter of personal pride to not do so.

This became a self-perpetuating thing. In time, in spite of retaining that necessary sense of humanity and consideration for others, an outer callus formed over the deepest senses. This provided a buffer, helping one to do what had to be done without unduly blanching.

As I sipped tea from a small plastic cup, watched as yet another victim was removed from the platform in one of the reusable coffin shells from St Bartholomew's Hospital, I reflected that my own 'callus' had begun to form.

I had over eight years of operational experience behind me at the time. The combined effect of all the sights witnessed over those years was toughening my mind to provide that protection, without which our input at this incident, one of the capital's worst ever disasters, would have been inefficient if not impossible.

In any event, in those far off days, psychological counselling and 'defusing' were unheard of. A man either steeled himself to the rawness of the work, drawing on his pride and inner resolve, or capitulated and applied for a job in a less mentally demanding arena.

King's Cross Underground Fire, 18 November 1987

The Euston Road and surrounding thoroughfares of York Way and Pancras Road appeared to be enveloped in a vile, thick smog, like that seen so often in London winters of the 1950s as fire appliances from all over the capital began to arrive on that cold November night. The strobing blue strokes of their beacons barely penetrating the dense, dark brown clouds, which were already banked down to street level as John Lydus, now a Sub Officer, arrived with his crew of four.

The many buildings to which he had responded on all manner of emergency calls over the ensuing years were barely visible as the dense pall of smoke from a raging inferno below the streets cast its shroud over so many of them. The smoke was as thick as any he had

132

seen in those earlier years in this locality, but today, unlike then, every Firefighter at least had the protection of the quickly donned compressed air sets, and the helmets were now a bright yellow, making them far more visible than the old black model.

Such was the smoke belching out of the front and sides of the main King's Cross station concourse, however, that yellow helmets or not, firefighters were rapidly enveloped in conditions of almost nil visibility.

King's Cross, York Way, Caledonian and Pentonville Roads, and a myriad other streets, alleyways and squares of this district had always held a hard to define attraction for me. Perhaps it was the 'salty' atmosphere, which had regularly seen us using the 'greasy spoon' fish and chip restaurant on the Pentonville Road after a hard day's firefighting. Perhaps the connection with King's Cross and its northwards journeys reminded me of my roots, as did the nearby Wharfdale Road, which evoked a vista of fell and bubbling streams, contrasting with the grey and grime of this atmospheric locale.

In later years, I would remember the location for many reasons. But, as is the case with so many of my colleagues, it will be remembered principally for the tragic blaze on the King's Cross Underground, which broke out on that grey early winter's evening, and which claimed 31 lives, one of whom was one of our own. A Station Officer, large in stature, and even larger in heart, who perished whilst demonstrating high courage in a Dante's Inferno beneath this world famous rail terminus.

King's Cross is one of the busiest interchanges on the Underground system, linking as it does with main line surface trains to the Home Counties, northern England and Scotland.

The main line station connects with the Underground network by a series of corridors leading to the ticket hall, and it was from those corridors that this vile, choking and superheated smoke was rushing.

Smoke had first been seen at just after half past seven issuing from one of the wooden slatted escalators, which led from the underground level to the ticket hall. The first 999 alert had been received by Fire Control some six minutes or so later, and the predetermined attendance of four Pumps and an aerial appliance were on scene at a minute or so after twenty to eight. At first there was no indication at street level of smoke or fire. The officer in charge of the first attendance deployed a crew to the ticket hall. From that position they had seen flames, about four feet in height, issuing some twenty feet down the wooden escalator, and at that stage passengers were leaving the area in an orderly fashion.

Instructions were given for Firefighters to return to the street for BA and hose, whilst the Station Officer and two others remained. These two went down the burning escalator in an attempt to stop any further use of this as an exit, and the Station Officer stayed at the ticket hall level.

At about a quarter to eight, and without warning, a huge fireball erupted, travelling up the lower level, bursting out in the ticket hall, creating severe conditions of superheated gases and dense choking smoke, which enveloped passengers and created an obvious panic as people, some with clothes alight and skin peeling, tried to escape from the nightmare surrounding them.

Station Officer Colin Townsley of Soho fire station perished in this inferno. He died trying to protect and shield a woman from the horrific fireball, which had enveloped them.

The news that a colleague has been killed or severely injured does not always arrive quickly. There is an uncertainty, jumbled messages, rumours and misinformation, but the probability of the dreadful truth emerging is often signalled by the severity of the conditions in the immediate vicinity of the fire.

Experienced, seasoned Firefighters have, over years, witnessed all too often the way that fire and superheated smoke and gas can sear the fabric of buildings and ravage the building's contents with violent heat and flame. They know that if fire can wreak such havoc on hard physical structures, the human frame can have little prospect for survival, and the minds of those who have served in the busiest units will have more than a few images to remind them how vulnerable the human form is to fire and smoke. All the signs at this blaze were that a fire of the utmost intensity and malevolence had broken out.

Such thoughts, and the loudening whisper that a colleague had been caught in such severe conditions, were evident as BA sets were donned, as crews steeled themselves for a descent into the unknown inside the tiled bowels of King's Cross Underground station on that haunting night.

Death's calling card is always a possibility to the world's Firefighters. The thought must, of necessity, be repressed, but it is hard to achieve this when a colleague has fallen, and that falling has brought home to you the vulnerability of even the most experienced

Firefighter and the physical closeness of fire's ever present and deadly threat.

If it was a haunting night for us Firefighters, professionals, rigorously trained and with many of us seasoned and case-hardened on the glowing red forge of hundreds of blazes, what must it have felt like for those passengers caught on the deep platforms below? Their exit barred by a lethal flaming monster above while trains were kept running through the station.

Perhaps some words of the late Rachel Rosser, a leading figure in giving psychological therapy to the victims of disasters, can help in our understanding:

> Imagine yourself in an Underground train that draws up in King's Cross. The doors are open but through the smoke you see people hammering on the windows screaming 'Let us in, let us in'. The horror of the fire hit people who arrived in the main station on that cold November night, who suddenly felt an intolerable wave of heat. It affected passers-by, totally unprepared for scenes of extraordinary horror. People screaming in pain ... horrific human remains ...

What is revealed in the clear light and cold of the days that follow such disasters when the inevitable post-mortems, operational debriefings and inquiries take place, cannot be easily envisaged when smoke fire, searing heat and the strong smell of death is all around.

It is one matter analysing matters under the steady microscope of a forensic investigation, when a range of information and evidence can be unearthed without physical danger. It is quite another to engage in fighting a raging inferno, deep under London's streets, when the fire's seat is unknown and when choking, deathly smoke and heat are embracing you within their deadly grip.

Sub Officer John Lydus along with Niall Pointer and Rusty Checkland, had been detailed to rig in BA and work a charged line of two and three quarter inch hose from the Euston Road side down into the ticket hall area.

Their Pump had been out on another incident, and by the time they had dealt with that and then been almost immediately ordered on, the fireball that killed Station Officer Townsley and eventually 31 others had done its damage.

The smoke coming out of the main concourse and subway stairs had been so dense on the arrival of the earlier appliances that some powerful TV lights had been brought in to try and penetrate the billowing wall of smoke but with little effect. It was still extremely thick and the heat was still great as John Lydus and his crew slowly worked their way forward. Even hotter than they really knew because the mask of the compressed air BA sets muted the warning message of great heat on the sensitive skin of the ears.

It had been even hotter a half hour earlier and the slumped and dehydrated forms of partially collapsed Firefighters, their BA sets lying untidily on the pavement beside them outside the main concourse, was evidence of the extremely punishing conditions that had existed shortly after the first attendance appliances had arrived.

When Firefighters are detailed to rig in BA and enter what is often the unknown, it would be, in the vast majority of cases, dishonest for anyone to claim that they didn't feel a shiver of apprehension. Men and women of normal sensitivities do their job by the combined forces of a rigorous, disciplined training, hard-won practical experience, pride in not wanting to let the team down and a steeling of the nerves to enter places where most would turn around and run from at a high speed.

Even the most case-hardened professional feels like surrendering to the quite natural desire to stay where it is safe when they have just lost one of their colleagues, as was the sad occasion on that black night. Instead of this retreat, Firefighters have to draw on that amalgam of discipline and courage, and push on, trusting implicitly in their BA sets and in the command abilities of the senior officers controlling operations.

All Firefighters pray that those with responsibilities for safety are 'good hands' and in possession of a wide experience of command, particularly when penetrating deep into great smoke and searing heat. And especially when the life of a colleague has tragically ended.

Flat on their bellies now, John Lydus and his crew inched forward. Slowly advancing. Seeking out the source of what had created this inferno. Opening up the nozzle and rotating it around, hoping that the water spray would lower the ghastly temperature. At least, the compressed air face-masks allowed them to communicate. Even though the voice is muted by the rubber and acrylic face-mask, tightly held to the head by three rubber straps, to ensure an airtight seal, speech is audible.

To be an unknown distance, underground, within the dragon's

136

breath of a serious, deep-seated fire, the cause of which is unknown, and whose threat is still to be controlled, shakes the poise of even the most steadfast individual. To hear, therefore, the muffled, but audible profanities, or encouraging reassurance of the officer in charge, and your crew-mates, is vital to morale and thus to the suppression of a blaze.

'Effing 'ell, talk about it being bleeding hot,' from a few feet to your right.

'Keep at it, guys, keep pushing. Now – nice and steady – give it another drink,' from the officer in charge up front.

'Eff this for a game of soldiers – I knew that I should have booked in sick tonight,' from a mate on the left, and a range of other comments, which remind one of the small boy whistling in the dark to try to dispel a fear of the unknown lurking in the unseen surroundings.

These sounds of life, along with those safety rituals, honed by regular practice in the 'smoke and heat' chambers, are the essentials that spur crews on, tightening guts and expelling that wind of natural apprehension, which always exists when the exact fire location is unknown as is the degree of hazard it might be about to deliver at any second without warning. And those same morale-boosting words were being repeated from all points of the compass, as scores of crews attempted to locate the source of this fire, which had created such a night of blackness.

Eventually, the seat of this fire was discovered, but the forensic investigation, and the ultimate conclusion as to what had happened to produce such a malevolent mix of fire and smoke, took many weeks.

That black night for the London Underground and for the London Fire Brigade was echoed by the blackened bodies on the floor of the ticket hall and in the vicinity of the escalators. Some bodies were literally cremated, and the final identifications of some did not take place for many months.

When the smoke eventually began to clear as the Brigade once more succeeded in their fire-suppressing endeavours, the full horror of this disaster became apparent. The whole of the escalator shafts looked as if they had been subjected to the incandescent heat of an erupting volcano. The escalators on which so many millions had travelled over the years on this, the network's busiest station, were scorched, blackened and buckled by the intolerable heat, and those hundreds of advertisements in their steel frames affixed to the walls, to be ignored or read by millions of eyes, had been virtually atomised.

I can, of course, only speak in truth for myself about the images burned into my mind of this disaster. But, in an almost identical way to the images retained about that other dreadful disaster at Moorgate, it is not possible to remember things without thinking of two contrasting states. First, of humanity, light and life before Damocles' sword of disaster falls. Second, the irreversible nature of death, after it has fallen, and the black shadow it casts for all of those who are personally involved in its aftermath.

Who can not visualise the noisy bustle of a massed, ethnic mix of humanity in the cosmopolitan melting pot of London's King's Cross? The varied colour of clothes, the varied pitch of a thousand talking tongues. The snap of the ticket turnstiles. The humming clatter and groan of the wooden-slatted escalators, and that ever-present draught of ozone-smelling air. An air compressed by the bullet-like thrust of the train speeding along its black barrel. The pushing draught announcing the train's imminence well before we see the bright lamp on its front, forcing that warm draught along platforms, passageways and escalator shafts. Shafts on which those sloping, stepped conveyors carried, in a seething contraflow, the anonymous faces of folk from near and far. Shafts in which that warm, pleasant breeze became, on that night, a superheated, lung-searing tempest of death and disaster.

A death that came suddenly and violently for 31 people on that night, when man's eternal enemy broke out and wreaked its havoc once more. Turning within minutes a long established scene of daily routine and normality into a deathly scene of nightmare, pain and ongoing trauma for so many. A fire that happened so quickly that most would have not realised the great danger they were in. But some were consumed by it, and like most who are caught within fire's deadly snare, never had the chance to say their goodbyes.

A scene of fire, which, as always within this huge metropolis, was responded to with an instant, unquestioning swiftness, and which drew on that deep well of high courage and steadfast resolve that is the hallmark of the fire and rescue worker's calling.

King's Cross Underground was yet another incident in a long chain of many for the London Fire Brigade, but, sadly, it was one in which a human link was lost. It called for the engraver to carry out once more the solemn task of adding a further name on the Brigade's Roll of Honour. A roll that records and honours all those who have so gallantly gone before, giving their all to protect the people and property of the capital city. Their names, like the memories of that black night, will never be forgotten.

7/7

Most who travel regularly on the Underground network will have experienced at some point that momentary concern when the train is halted for any length of time deep under the capital's streets.

This feeling of apprehension can be strong for those who, at the best of times, find that being within the tight confines of a packed train, within a narrow, barely lit tunnel creates a sense of claustrophobia. If the reason why the train has been halted is not forthcoming, such feelings can become even stronger.

At such times some of those passengers may have asked themselves how they would be able to escape in an emergency especially when the train is many hundreds of metres between stations, especially if the tunnels were filling with choking smoke and stifling heat. London's Underground is indeed a bad place for fire and other emergencies.

The only escape route in such a situation is in the barely lit tunnel, along a track from which one has a nagging fear that someone may have forgotten to shut down the 650-volt traction current to the live rail, which lies perilously close.

This escape, firstly via the interconnecting carriage doors to the end of the train, and then down on to the track and along the tunnel to the nearest station, has had to take place, albeit on rare occasions, in the past, and is frightening enough on its own.

Now try to picture the same scenario but one in which an explosive device has detonated without any warning in the midst of a tube train, cram-packed with commuters, midway between stations, with smoke and dust filling the tube tunnels deep under the capital's streets. An explosive so powerful that it has blown a crater in the very heavy steel structure of the tube train carriage, blasted the bodies and limbs of passengers a hundred metres, and demolished a tunnel wall, all without a hint of a warning. Perhaps, just perhaps this will give you some small idea of the terror that descended on the London Underground system on 7 July 2005.

It is little wonder then, now we know the dreadful truth of what took place, that the detonation of bombs on that day, the first ever

139

such incident in the 142-year history of the capital's Underground, created such mayhem and confusion.

The London Fire Brigade received the first call at just before nine o'clock and despatched a predetermined number of appliances, which roared out of their stations. Some appliances responded from the heart of the West End, others from stations in the heart of the East End, and these were rapidly reinforced by appliances and crews from across the capital as the sheer horror of the atrocity unfolded.

That morning, at King's Cross, one of the busiest stations on the underground network, and the scene of that disastrous fire a little under 18 years earlier, 47 other trains, crammed full of rush hour passengers, had already left.

It was the sad fate of those who stepped up on to the forty-eighth train to leave that they would be caught up in the largest explosion to occur on the system that morning.

At Aldgate, on the border of those parts of the East End in which some of the accounts within this book are located, and at Edgware Road near Paddington, commuters were either on trains or entering and leaving these busy stations. No doubt the conversation of many would have included the nation's triumph at being awarded, only a day earlier, the 2012 Olympic Games. Whatever the topic of conversation, or the private thoughts of those sardine-can-packed passengers, these would be stilled as three bombs exploded within 50 seconds of each other, shattering lives and chillingly confirming the predictions of those who had warned that a terrorist strike within the capital was inevitable.

Only nine minutes after receiving (at 0904) the cryptic message: 'Smoke issuing – Euston Square tube', the first fire crews arrived at King's Cross, having been rerouted from Euston Square. The crews' immediate observations were of crowds of passengers, their faces sooty and black, streaming up on to the street.

As had been the case at Moorgate 30 years earlier, the black faces resulted from fire smoke and sooty grime blown from the tunnel walls. This time though it wasn't the shocking force of colliding carriages that had dislodged the grime, but the ferocious blast of a terrorist's bomb.

Many of the bedraggled, confused, crying and shocked passengers had sustained facial injuries, some minor, others serious, as a result of flying glass, metal and whatever else a bomb macerates and projects in its explosive, atomising blast.

140

As the dreadful events unfolded it would be seen that in relative terms those walking wounded were the lucky ones, even though their minds, and in many cases, their bodies, would be for ever scarred with the horrific memories of that morning when a routine tube train journey had turned within an instant into a living nightmare.

Given that no warning had been received from any source as to a bomb threat, and given the remote, closely confined location in which the detonation had occurred, it was inevitable that it would be some time before the truth of what had actually taken place filtered up to street level.

Of course, the initial confusion and sparseness of information was such that the first response fire and rescue crews had no inkling that a bomb had gone off, and the alert minds of those racing towards the scene could only surmise what the incident might turn out to be.

I knew from long experience that they would be asking themselves a number of questions: Was this another Moorgate disaster? Was it another deadly inferno at King's Cross? Was it a fire on the heavy-duty insulation of the cables that supplied the traction current, and which some 30 years earlier had led to an evacuation of several hundred passengers along the dark and smoke-laden tunnels leading to Finsbury Park station?

Was it finally the terrorist attack with which the capital had been threatened for so long, and which some in the know had described as not being a case of 'if' but of 'when' – was this incident such an attack?

Out of these questions and uncertainty, one thing was sure and that was the presence of much smoke and dust issuing from the rail tunnels into the stations adjacent, and the earliest informative messages sent to London Fire Brigade's Control included details of the presence of this thick smoke.

It was the presence of this smoke, along with the streams of black-faced and bloodied passengers evacuating on to the street, that indicated something dreadfully serious had happened, and that this was likely to be a major incident, as potentially tragic and devastating, if not more so, than those tragedies of earlier years.

But it would be some hours later before the capital, and the world, knew how deadly and unprecedented had been the events underground, and in the street.

As the breaking news hardened, the initial relatively low numbers of fatalities and injuries began to rise, as is generally the case in human disasters as more direct lines of communication are established by all of the emergency services working together closely.

By late morning the press agencies were reporting the following dead: 21 passengers feared dead in a tube train following an explosion that had occurred as the train was in the tunnel between King's Cross and Russell Square; seven passengers feared dead following an explosion at Aldgate station; seven passengers feared dead following an explosion at Edgware Road station; thirteen persons feared dead following an explosion on a number 30 London Transport bus as it crossed Tavistock Square; hundreds of other persons reported injured and severely shocked.

The first crew to arrive at King's Cross, having been rerouted from Euston Square, confirmed that the traction current was turned off, and then began their descent into the unknown to attempt to locate the source of the smoke. A smoke and dust cloud, which was thickening and increasing in its acridity as each step was taken nearer to its source, and whose pungent, rolling clouds were illuminated by the beams from the Firefighters' hand-lamps.

Then, out of the smoke and dust-filled blackness, they saw the first carriage. This appeared to be structurally normal, save for shattered windows, which, it later transpired, had been broken with fire extinguishers by passengers, desperate to escape from the terror that had come from within without warning.

As Firefighters clambered up into the carriages, the full horror of the scene became apparent. The sickening sight of such dreadful carnage hits in the pit of the stomach like the jarring below-the-belt punch of a heavyweight boxer.

But, and as was the case at Moorgate, the sense of shock for the rescue teams was compounded by the familiarity that most people who live in the capital have with the interior of the carriages of London's tube trains.

There is no doubt that when disasters involving loss of life occur, the naturally harrowing scene appears even more shocking when such tragedies take place on our own doorsteps or within and on those places and locations which have, over time, become so warmly familiar. Death in such familiar surroundings, especially when coming out of the blue, and in close proximity to those around, can create a shock and a jolt, which has a far, far greater power to unsettle than one occurring in distant and unfamiliar environments.

Make no mistake, even to the case-hardened emergency services worker, death is never pleasant, because that irreversible state is a contradiction of the life-saving and life-preserving ethos of their occupation.

But when tragedies happen so close to home the jolt is all the greater.

This must be due to the simple truth that there must be few who live and work in London, and few tourists and visitors, who have not made use of the Underground rail network. And amongst all of these passengers, the one character who may have a deadly motive and deadly cargo in his rucksack or on his or her person.

Who could ever have known on that fateful morning that such malevolence was at large on the capital's peak period passenger systems, and that it would be the cruel case and cruel fate for so many that they were caught in the middle of this evil?

As I have remarked, when human tragedies occur within places to which most of us have set foot and become familiar, the gravity of the situation appears heightened by the fact that it has taken place amongst the familiar scene. In so doing it has turned that warm current of comfort and continuity into a chilling wind that says to the rescuers, 'There but for the grace of God go I.'

The terrible sight of those seats on which thousands have sat, reading a newspaper, doing a crossword, reading a novel or business document, or scanning those glazed advertising placards, now ripped apart or twisted into grotesque shapes by the force of the terrorists' bomb blast. The grossly distorted and smashed doors, the obliterated network maps and glassless windows. The buckled grab rails, the massive deformation of the once smoothly curved walls of the train, and the huge gash in the heavy steel floor of a bomb's blast, all these being the dreadful aftermath of a detonated terrorist's bomb.

It is because the majority of rescuers are users of the Underground that they feel that they have been so bloodily sullied and this increases the empathy felt by the rescuers with those commuters cruelly caught, catastrophically crushed or atomised by the bomb's merciless blast.

But a living rescuer cannot empathise with the dead, they can only sympathise. The Firefighters caught up in these mind-numbing scenes have to use that numbing to repress, at least until a later time, their innermost emotions and natural sympathies. Without this protective callus, it would be virtually impossible to work effectively amidst such human carnage, and, sadly, there was carnage in abundance within the wreck of these carriages.

However, no matter how harrowing it can be to work amongst the casualties of fire, the fire and rescue service's increasing involvement with those caught up in the cold chill of a non-fire disaster such as a major road, rail or air crash, can be even more distressing. It does not require much imagination to work out how the blast of a high explosive bomb, especially one within such a mass of passengers, crammed into the narrow confines of the carriages, and powerful enough to blast a hole in thick steel and brick walls, can have such a horrific effect on human skin, blood and bone.

Visible at the extremities of one carriage were literally piles of dead passengers, some with gross deformations of the human frame, and some with limbs and other body parts missing. Mingling with the acrid smoke and choking dust was the pungent odour of much spilled blood and lacerated flesh, but beneath and between these dreadful scenes lay those who were still alive, their moans and cries directing rescuers to their locations.

All of the capital's emergency and medical services had engaged in a number of combined training exercises designed to simulate major incidents, and these procedures had been strengthened post 9/11 with what was called the 'new dimension' programme.

As soon as the scale and seriousness of the incident became apparent, a message '*Initiate Major Incident Procedure*' had been transmitted, and these well-rehearsed contingency plans swung swiftly into operation.

However, even with the advancements that had taken place in radio communications technologies since the Moorgate disaster, trying to communicate via portable hand-held radios from deep within the Underground network can be fraught on account of the screening and attenuation of radio signals.

The Crew Manager in charge of the first team to enter this dreadful scene of carnage was having no success in raising by personal radio those still at street level, and sent two of the crew back up to the street to meet the supervisory officers now arriving.

As the two men descended down on to the track they could now see the massive gash in the side of the train carriage, and, in the light of their hand-lamps, could make out several severed body parts under and around the train within the tightly cramped curved confines of the tunnel.

They were also conscious of the blood-curdling screams of terror and the moaning of the many shocked and seriously injured passengers. A voice was calling for help from a point partly under the train, and the two Firefighters hesitated but they fought off their natural instinct to assist, knowing that unless they got up to the street, the vital assistance needed would be delayed.

As they hurried through the choking dust and smoke, their lamps picked out a number of corpses, some with horrendous injuries, and some 80 or more metres from the train. They could only shudder at the thought of the explosive force needed to fling an adult body such a huge distance.

Back in the grim and bloody wreckage of the carriage, the remaining Firefighters comforted as best they could those injured but still conscious and trapped. Steel grab rails and seat frames pinning limbs with a vice-like grip and imprisoning them alongside people, alive only moments before, now forever stilled.

Being present at the sharp end of such disasters as these illustrates so vividly the stark differences between what is reported by the media and what it really is like to be working amidst such human carnage deep below London's streets. The reporter has, in the main, to work from snatched reports gleaned from the press officers of the emergency services. From this information a word picture has to be produced and then the public will try to imagine the dreadful nightmare of those involved. But that is all one can do – try to imagine what it must be like, and suffice to say that there is a wide gulf between imagination and stark reality, which is so often the staple diet of the fire and rescue worker's life. A life which, sadly, but inevitably in major centres of population, does deal with death, and death in its most brutal and undignified form.

The last few decades have seen the fire and rescue services engage more and more at non-fire emergencies, and it is useful to understand the effects upon the Firefighters' emotions when confronted with death from these incidents, compared with victims of fire and smoke.

The majority of fatalities in fires result from the inhalation of smoke, toxic fumes and heat. Such victims, although perhaps blackened superficially by smoke, just appear to be sleeping, with no outward injury visible. There is no doubt that those victims consumed by severe fire do present a grisly sight, but though horrific, the impact is somehow numbed because the appearance is no longer that of a human being. It is as if the splitting and blackening of the skin and musculature disguises the fact that the life once existed, a little like seeing a fossil on a sea shore and finding it hard to think that it was once a living creature.

By contrast, witnessing the aftermath on the human frame from the severe trauma occasioned by transport accidents or from the effects of explosive devices can be devastating. Other than in the most severe injuries, the presence of a body, alive only minutes earlier, now extinct, but with normal facial features (not blackened or charred by fire's heat), is a stark reminder of the human life that has now come to such a traumatic and swift end.

These reminders of a life that was are present in a number of forms: a person's clothing, its texture, colour and style; jewellery, glinting on finger, neck or ear; a handbag's contents so rudely scattered; or a laptop computer still gripped by a cold, stiffening hand.

They are signalled by a smart briefcase of quality leather hide, the flap of which is inscribed with the owner's initials, and which is now red with his blood, and, perhaps most poignantly in the shape of a child's pink lunch box, half visible underneath the small, suddenly stilled form of its owner.

And then, in this world of mass communication, there is the plaintive call of the mobile phone or the staccato SMS signalling an incoming text. This is such an eerie and sad sound within the dreadful carnage, as loved ones, family and friends strive to seek that prayed for reassurance that the recipient is safe. Which unfortunately was not the case within London on this dark day for so many.

This then was the scene in which the men and women of the London Fire Brigade and their counterparts in the other emergency, medical and transport services, found themselves on this day of atrocity not only at King's Cross but at Edgware Road, Aldgate and Tavistock Square.

As was the case during the Moorgate and King's Cross tragedies, the professionalism of the Brigade's personnel, which has been constructed upon the massive practical experiences amassed within its boundaries during times of peace and war, shone through. But unlike these two earlier incidents, that which occurred on 7 July 2005 was murder by terrorism and the forensic imperatives of a murder scene demand that the evidence is preserved as far as it is practicable to do so.

The involvement of the Metropolitan Police and the forensic services is a story in itself, but all of those Firefighters who were involved on the front line, particularly at Moorgate, will have understood the quite horrendous conditions which those involved with the recovery of bodies and forensic evidence gathering had to endure. Working in temperatures of more than 40 degrees centigrade, with the constant irritation of the rats that can occupy these subterranean tunnels, and which would be attracted to the horrendous amount of blood and human gore on nearly every surface, crews worked on with a Trojan resolve and tenacity.

So debilitating was the heat, combined with the nervous drain of toiling amidst such carnage, and so great the risk of infection, that it was essential for teams to be relieved every two hours. At the end of each two hour session all personnel had to be decontaminated at the surface so as to minimise the health risks from working amongst the human remains. Eventually, and slowly and painstakingly, all bodies and body parts were recovered and repatriated and the logistics and recording of this grisly task cannot be described within this account.

Bodies had to be carefully sealed before being brought up to street level and the use of small motorised trolleys was invaluable in facilitating this exercise. It was only after these gruesome but delicate procedures had been completed, and all possible evidence recorded or retrieved, that the tunnels and rail network within the three affected locations could be examined for structural safety before train movements recommenced.

Those who have chosen to become operational members of the London Fire Brigade have to realise from the outset that their work is no ordinary calling, and that it can often be a most hazardous way to earn a living when the saving of life and property is called for.

The rigorous selection and training programmes, augmented by experience gained from every incident responded to, and consolidated by a comprehensive base of data and intelligence on a massive range of potential emergency hazards and scenarios, better ensures that the risk to personnel is reduced as far as is practicable.

But the reality of the Firefighter's life within any of the world's larger urban conurbations is such that sooner or later emergency incidents of unprecedented levels of hazard and challenge will occur.

Other than during wartime, the capital's Firefighters' daily workloads have traditionally arisen from responding to fires and to those non-fire special services mentioned. Such responses still comprise the largest slice of the daily bread and butter jobs of the Brigade, but the terrible events of 7 July have added a new hazard to be faced. A hazard that can come unannounced and be more deadly than a thousand fires.

So, from that date on, and like their counterparts in other parts of the world where the terrorist bomber lurks and works with such deadly intent, our Firefighters will now have to be ever mindful of this new dimension of terror. It is a threat to be added to those posed to life and property by fire or by crash, collision, collapse, chemical leakage and flooding. It is a threat in which when one bomb has exploded, the thought will remain in the Firefighter's mind that there may be others ticking away even as they work to bring succour to those caught within the first evil blast. It is a daunting prospect for sure. This then is the new dimension of hazard that the capital's fire and rescue teams must respond to unquestioningly day or night. A hazard that announced its presence with such a deadly and deafening roar, and in such a brutal and barbaric fashion, on 7 July 2005, bringing in its wake a new wave of death and destruction to the capital's streets and to those dark and confined labyrinths that lie beneath them.

Chapter Thirteen

Death on the Mile End Road

Two quick rings of the call bells by the Sub Officer signalled the end of the hour dinner break in which Mary, the daytime cook, had weighed us all down with stew and dumplings, mashed potatoes, carrots and peas, followed by a portion of bread and butter pudding almost as big as a house brick.

We were on the second of our two day duties. The previous day's nine to six shift had been uneventful, and save for the usual AFA false alarm and another infuriating 'Mickey', the only action seen had been a rubbish fire in a derelict house, which had been dealt with in 20 minutes. Yesterday had been our day for carrying out standard tests.

Virtually every item and piece of operational equipment has to be subjected to a testing regime at various periods, dependent on what it is used for. Some tests are carried out daily, some weekly, whilst others are monthly, quarterly or annually. We had been testing the rescue lines. These were subjected to the combined steady weight and pull of six members of the watch. If there was any weakness it would be revealed by this test, and far better for this to happen in the drill yard than at an incident halfway through a rescue, perhaps with a casualty suspended high above the street.

It was reassuring to know that when the chips were down, it was highly unlikely that equipment would fail.

We had been scheduled for drills after our lunch, and few were relishing running up and down ladders laden as we were with Mary's fulsome meal. It was with some relief then that the grey skies of this winter's day finally began to release the rain, which had been threatening all morning.

Safety requirements dictated that we normally didn't drill outside if the weather was inclement and so we found ourselves in the mess room to participate in 'lectures', which could cover virtually any subject relevant to our work.

'Right, listen in, you lot,' barked Sub Officer Roy, 'we can't practise our firemanship outside, so we will practise some here. Practical Firemanship will be our session for the next hour or so, and let's take a look at ventilation at fires.'

'Why do we ventilate ... Jim?'

'We all want to ventilate Jim, release some of that guff in his head that he's always spouting,' joked Niall of Fireman Peating, honours graduate in economics and one-time schoolteacher.

'Well, Niall, releasing is one part of the answer, but I'm not so sure that it is what you have just said,' retorted the Sub. 'Ignore 'em, Jim, and carry on if you will,' he went on.

'Right, Sub, well – ' In came the bells cutting off Jim Peating in mid sentence.

'You jammy sod,' quipped Niall again, 'I bet you didn't know the rest of the answer,' he laughed, as Jim gave him a victory sign as he ran to the pole drop.

John Lydus was watch room duty man for the shift and he was reading the teleprinter message as we plunged down into the appliance room, the green indicator light above the huge red station doors already lit. 'RTA (Road Traffic Accident) – persons trapped, Mile End Road – Pump only,' he shouted.

Within 20 seconds the Pump was thundering and blaring along roads made greasy by the cold drizzle, weaving in and out of the heavy traffic, which was a regular feature of this major artery into the capital from the east. A fair proportion of the vehicles were lorries transporting a wide range of goods into and out of London.

It was one of these, a refrigerated articulated truck, en route to Smithfield Meat Market in Clerkenwell, that had been in collision with a private car, at one of the many junctions controlled by traffic-lights along this major highway.

The two-tone horns echoed from the high walls of the densely packed buildings alongside, and the metallic tractor-like rattle of the diesel engine surged up and down as our driver Geoff Joynt threw the appliance in and out of the traffic, while we hung on in the rear, swaying like sailors in a force nine gale.

The radio crackled into life: *'From Sub Officer Devine at Mile End Road – one saloon car in collision with articulated lorry. Three persons trapped. Efforts being made to release, ambulance required.'*

'That don't sound so frigging healthy, fellas. Get your fluorescent jackets on,' shouted Ben Tuke above the engine's roar and the cacophony of the air horns.

As the Pump came to a halt and parked in a position ahead of the lorry and car, so as to fend off approaching traffic, it could be seen that the car had gone at least a half of its length under the semi-trailer of the lorry.

On the basis of similar incidents attended, I reasoned that the sights we might be seeing within that crumpled wreckage would not be pretty at all. I jumped down from the Pump and noticed that a young policewoman was doing her best to direct the traffic around the collided vehicles, and that the traffic-lights were not working.

Not all articulated lorries were then required to be fitted with the side crash rails. It appeared that the absence of these on this vehicle had meant that the car had gone straight under the trailer. The severe impact had caused the roof of the white saloon to split and tear back like the pull-top on a can of corned beef.

As we have seen in preceding chapters, fire and rescue crews have to become inured to the often horrific and grisly situations that their work requires them to deal with, but whereas the sight of a fire victim could never be pleasant, the sight of casualties within road traffic accidents is often especially disturbing.

As mentioned in the previous chapter, most fire victims die as a result of smoke asphyxiation. Consequently there is often little outward sign of injury. By contrast, many victims of motor accidents, and there are far more of them annually than there are casualties from fire, often sustain horrific injuries.

On top of this, it is a fact that our cars sometimes are very personal spaces. A metal and glass cocoon with the false but cosy security afforded by comfortable seats, a warm fan heater on a cold day and the pleasant background of in-car entertainment. Perhaps it is because of such reasons that the sight of that almost womb-like protection of the private car being mangled, crushed and torn apart as metal meets metal around its frail human cargo makes road traffic incidents particularly difficult and traumatic to deal with. They bring it home that it is only luck that we aren't the ones involved in our own private cars.

'What's the score, Dolan? asked Bob Tuke of Sub Officer Devine, who was on a temporary secondment, and in charge of the local

151

station ground's appliance.

'It's a nasty one, Guv. There are three trapped from what we can make out at this stage,' he replied, deliberately keeping his voice low in case any of the casualties were able to hear. 'We've laid out a hose reel in case anything lights up and disconnected the lorry's batteries. I've sent an informative plus a request for an ambulance, but for sure we are going to need the help of the ET on this one. I've got two men under the trailer trying to get into the front of the car,' he went on, his speed of delivery indicating the urgency of the situation.

'Well the ET should be here in a jiff with the heavy cutting gear and jacks. Let's see if we can get into the rear seats while we can, Dolan, eh?' said Ben Tuke.

'Niall and Geoff – get the crowbar and try to force the rear doors pronto, and see what you can do for anyone in the rear, yeah? Andy and Jim you look after the front of the car,' instructed the Station Officer.

The lorry driver, a short, wiry man with a tight crew cut, black T-shirt and trousers, and a deathly white face, was leaning on to a round-topped steel bollard on the pavement. It was one of those old-fashioned constructions placed to protect pedestrians. Its round top was burnished from a lifetime of wind, rain and the resting hands of many passing folk. It was now serving to steady his hands, which, as a result of shock, were trembling like an aspen leaf. A grizzled, snow-haired policeman was talking to him, and writing notes in his black notepad.

The roof above the rear passenger compartment was twisted back hideously. The grey-coloured cloth lining was splattered with blood, which, in its absorption by the cloth, had changed colour from claret red to a bright brown. A woman, who appeared middle aged, was on the rear seat but her left leg was twisted grotesquely around the rear of the front passenger seat, and her right leg bent sharply under her downward-facing form.

The white paint on the inside metal of the car doors was streaked with the bright red of blood, now slowly congealing and meeting up with a darker red pool running from the front half of the car embedded under the trailer. As I had thought, this was going to be a nasty job all right.

Our Guvnor bent his tall, bulky frame over the rear of the car. 'How's it look, Niall?' he asked quietly. 'It ain't good, Guv, but there's a faint pulse in the neck of the woman in the rear. We've got to get her out quick.'

The strident blare of the siren on the Emergency Tender heralded its arrival, and on its tail was the ambulance.

Under the lorry's semi-trailer the squat form of Jim Peating and the much taller and slimmer figure of Andy Carlisle were endeavouring to reach the two casualties in the concertinaed front part of the car. Andy's hand-lamp beam scanned the distorted, twisted and heavily blood-stained metal and upholstery. A former Fireman in a northern brigade, he had served on stations that attended the many RTAs on one of the country's most busy motorways. He instinctively knew that the damage to the car and the severity and position of the impact was such that it would be a miracle if anyone got out of this carnage alive.

I was crouching under the trailer next to Jim Peating, my fire boots in a small pool of what looked like engine coolant or brake fluid, which had been released on the impact of the collision.

'How's things, Jim?' I queried.

'It's bad, mate, real bad. Andy says we will need to get the trailer jacked up by the ET crew to get into the front of the car, the poor fuckers in the front must be in a right mess,' he replied, shaking his unhelmeted head (removed like ours to enable him to work under the trailer). I crawled out from under the trailer to update the Guvnor on the situation and the need to get the trailer lifted sufficiently. As I stood up, a sharp odour hit my nostrils. It was a smell that I had experienced before at other road traffic incidents and on those gory occasions when dealing with suicides on the Underground rail network.

It was a vile, nauseating whiff. It arose from not only the human blood spilled in these sort of emergencies, not only from that smell of twisted metal, which was a bit like the whiff of a burning clutch plate, but from the stomach-heaving, throat-retching stench of the involuntary opening of a casualty's bowels and bladder.

I informed the Station Officer of the need for the trailer to be jacked up. As I spoke, the large white saloon car of the duty ADO pulled up to the kerb about 20 feet behind the incident, its blue beacon spinning and then stopping as the car parked up.

Tom Monsal had been informed of the incident by Eastern Fire Control. Brigade policy dictated his supervisory attendance at 'persons trapped' incidents of this type. He walked over to our Guvnor who was detailing the leading fireman in charge of the ET as to what would be needed from them.

The eyes of 30-year veteran Tom Monsal scanned the scene. Within seconds his lengthy experience told him that this was likely to be quite a protracted job, and he was inwardly reassured that the experienced Ben Tuke, a man whom he had worked alongside for years as a Station Officer himself, was on the spot.

ADO Monsal walked up to his old colleague who then appraised him of the situation. 'OK, Ben, I've got the picture. I can see you have the job well in hand, I'm not going to formally take over, but you know what the policy is so I will be around.' (The Fire Services Act placed the ultimate accountability for events on the highest ranked officer on scene.) 'I'll get rigged in fire gear now,' he went on, and then went to the staff car and slipped into his operational uniform, which was neatly stowed in the large boot of his car.

Within a minute Tom Monsal was rigged in full gear and, firstly removing his helmet, crawled under the semi-trailer where Ben Tuke was on his knees, his huge form such that even in this position his back was almost touching the underside of the trailer's bed.

Each appliance carried a box lamp and two of these had been positioned under the trailer, their yellow-white beams illuminating the tangled wreckage of the car, and reflecting off the white paint off the bodywork, which had been smashed like an eggshell.

The ET crew, specially trained in extrication techniques were now under the trailer, assessing the situation. From vast experience derived from hundreds of incidents, they had soon formulated their plan. 'We'll need to jack and block the trailer, Guv,' the Leading Fireman remarked, his advice directed to both the ADO and Station Officer. 'First though, the articulated tractor unit will need to be uncoupled from the fifth wheel and service cables,' he went on.

'Of course, LF, but let's get it done like yesterday, we have three trapped, and if there is to be any chance for any of them we gotta be sharp so go to it,' replied Tom Monsal.

Before the jacking up began, one of the ET crew dealt with the uncoupling of the tractor from the trailer. The police had already done their photographs, marked the surface of the Mile End Road for evidential purposes, and taken the 'spy in the cab' tachograph from the lorry's cab, so the tractor could be uncoupled and moved enough to permit the trailer to be raised. Within no more than 15 minutes, the trailer was being lifted inch by inch, the groans and

154

squeals of impacted metal sounding as the weight of the trailer was taken slowly off the car. Whilst this was taking place, the ambulance crew plus two doctors and a sister from the casualty department of the nearby Royal London Hospital in Whitechapel were attending to the grotesquely contorted rear seat passenger.

Displaying his customary presence of mind, born out of long experience, Ben Tuke had sent a priority radio message requesting a medical team. If the passenger could be saved, they were the ones to do it. As the weight finally came off the car, the rear passenger who had now been extricated, was rapidly conveyed to the nearby hospital.

Now that the trailer had been raised clear of the car, it could be slowly pulled back the eight or so feet it had travelled under the trailer. Over an hour had gone by since we had first arrived. It was getting dark now, and the tall lamp standards alongside this major East End highway were flashing into their sodium yellow light, which cast long shadows around the concertina-like crush and severely smashed structure of the car. The front roof of which was almost flattened to steering wheel level by the pulverising pressure of the heavy refrigerated rigid box van of the trailer, under which the car had gone.

It took another forty-five minutes or so of careful cutting before the tortured, twisted, tangled metalwork could be removed. Throughout this time the second ambulance waited to the rear of the scene. Its bonnet already pointing towards the hospital's direction. Its rear doors wide open and its white, bright interior lights revealing the familiar red blankets of the London Ambulance Service.

Unfortunately, and sadly, there was no longer any need for an urgent blue beacon and braying siren dash to Whitechapel's famous infirmary, and this became all too horrifically apparent as we cut through the confused convolutions of steel, walnut fascia, rubber, glass and velour cloth, to uncover a ghastly scene of carnage, in which death would have been instantaneous.

Instead, the ambulance, so often a speeding chariot of hope and salvation, would become a respectfully slow conveyor of death. Only an hour or so earlier the driver and front-seat passenger had been talking, feeling, thinking human beings. Now they were as lifeless as the cargo of beef inside the trailer under which the unfortunate car had impacted with such a shocking severity.

There had been little that all of us in attendance at that dreadful job could have done to assist save for the releasing of the rear-seat passenger, who, in spite of severe injuries, did survive. Had there been the slightest prospect of salvation, then that well practised, daily drilled and instant response of all present would have ensured that this was achieved.

There is a natural sense of loss and dismay at the waste of human life, caused, it was later revealed, by the car shooting the traffic-lights.

The fire service exists to save life whenever it is humanly possible to do so, and these non-fire special services had become an increasing part of operational work. But our sense of the futility of needless fatalities was never lessened, no matter how many fatal incidents we attended.

However, the deaths of those two men that afternoon were not totally in vain. Across the nation, a large number of fatal collisions exacerbated by trailers not having rear and side crash rails, led, in due course, to amendments to the law relative to the safe construction of heavy goods vehicles.

In future years we attended increasing numbers of road traffic accidents. More than a few would result in fatalities, but the fitting of crash rails did increase the safety of those unfortunate enough to become involved in collisions with heavy goods vehicles, and that had to be a good thing for all involved.

Chapter Fourteen

Ally Pally

'Smoke issuing, Alexandra Palace, London N10', were the words tapped out by the teleprinter on that early afternoon in 1980, ordering the Pump to this famous north London landmark adjacent to the capital's Muswell Hill and Wood Green districts.

'It's a bleedin' wind up ain't it?'asked our Station Officer as he read the message slip. There were a couple of spirited souls on the watch who weren't averse to the odd prank. It was a simple matter to use the teleprinter like a typewriter and tap out a 'spoof' message, especially during slack periods of operational activity, as had been the case up until then on the watch.

But the call bells had rung, and even our two pranksters knew that it was more than their lives were worth to actuate those call out bells as a joke.

Within seconds we were away, the two-tones parting the heavy north London traffic like Moses parting the Red Sea. We were heading in the direction of the leafy suburb of Muswell Hill, on top of which sat the 'Ally Pally' as the giant edifice to Victoriana is affectionately known.

My own first sight of the Alexandra Palace, with its towering radio and television mast, had been from the King's Cross to Edinburgh railway line some years earlier. It had been through the window of a southbound train that I had first set eyes on this broad domed structure set on its green terraced hill, dominating the scene and overlooking the far distance, above the roads and rooftops of such places as Finsbury Park, Holloway, Islington and Shoreditch, wherein I was to witness so much drama over the years.

In later years, more familiar with this part of the capital, I learned that the steel-latticed mast was the same one that for years had

157

provided the black and white backcloth to the BBC television news broadcasts.

Then 'radio waves' had rippled around the mast's structure, accompanied by a stirring tune before the announcers' BBC accents informed the nation of the latest information from around the globe.

The Alexandra Palace first opened in 1873, but within a little over two weeks, it had been destroyed by a fire in the huge dome, before being rebuilt two years later. Now, over a century later, we were charging towards a report of 'smoke issuing'.

'Well, if it isn't a "Mickey", there can't be too much going on,' shouted our Guvnor, above the roar of the diesel engine as we started to descend the steep road down to the pleasant residential district of Cranley Gardens, where the future mass murderer and body dismemberer Dennis Nilsen was to carry out some of his grisly deeds.

'We would have heard a "make up" by now if it was a job ... Christ, take a peep at that,' he faltered. His eyes, and then ours, took in the 'Ally Pally' atop its hill as we rounded the curve of the steeply sloping road.

'Stack me, Guv!' exclaimed Jack Towleen, the Pump's driver, 'look at the bloody smoke – it looks like a right goer.'

Sure enough, from out of the Ally Pally's huge dome, a thick brown smoke pall was rising a good 50 feet into the blue sky. This was no wind-up, no 'Mickey'. The Ally Pally was on the patch of the Hornsey fire station, only a few minutes low-gear-straining lug of eight tons of appliance up the winding and steep public road, which led to this now burning Victorian pile.

Buildings of the profile and size of the Alexandra Palace were categorised as 'Special Risks'. As such, every call to fire received resulted in a predetermined number of Pumps, aerial ladders and other specialist appliances. In later years, as fire prevention, fire safety and building regulations began to prove their effectiveness, fewer appliances and personnel would be initially despatched. Back in 1980 though, tradition still held a large sway. Better to be pre-pared for the worst on every fire call and send the full circus just in case. On this occasion, the 'worst' was about to happen, if that ominous, now hundred-feet high smoke pall was anything to go by.

Jack Towleen dropped the gearbox into second as we toiled up the steep road, the blare of the two-tone horns seeming incongruous to our slow, lumbering speed. What wasn't going slow was the thrumming beat of our hearts as we crested the steep slope and turned left into the access road, not knowing what the next minutes would bring as we looked up to the obvious indications that here was a major blaze.

I caught a glimpse of the delivery hose being slung out along the tarmac and of a crew connecting up the suction hose, preparing to lift water from the boating lake some 160 feet to our right. Yes, there was a 'job' on here all right!

Although there were fire hydrants sited on the complex, a huge conflagration requires a massive capacity of water to bring it under control. Depending on the diameter of the mains, and the flow of water available, there is a limit to the number of Pumps that can draw on such a supply, especially where the fire is on top of a hill.

The boating lake would give a reasonable number of firefighting jets before being exhausted, but it wasn't very deep, and thousands of gallons being pumped out would mean that the supply from here was limited. To compound the problem, any hilltop location can create its own difficulties as the pumps of reinforcing appliances drawing water from the larger diameter mains at the bottom have then to overcome the frictional resistance encountered when pumping it uphill.

Pete Revell, our Station Officer, jumped down from the Pump, instructing us to remain whilst he trotted over to the white helmet of the ADO, who was frantically waving his arms, beckoning him to report to him.

'What do you need, Guv?' he asked, at the same time as noting the red and yellow tongues of flame now becoming very evident from the dome many feet above.

'It's going like stink inside, mate,' the ADO exclaimed. 'I need you to get your crew to get a large jet to work via that big entrance door yonder,' he went on, pointing to a massive steel structure, which led into the main hall. 'Set into the boating lake pronto. You'll need to take care, it's a bloody big area, long, wide and high. Whatever has caused this bastard seems to be burning at the upper level. There's a massive volume of air in there, which is being drawn like a giant chimney – so watch out, right? Got me?' He swivelled around and jogged up to another Pump, which had just arrived, about the same time as one of the division's top brass.

'Yeah, I got you, boss,' replied Pete Revell, turning himself to run back to our Pump where the four of us were waiting. Anxious like all keen Firefighters to get into the fray of this fire, which even a raw recruit could see was no run of the mill job.

'Right, listen up, men. Jack, take the Pump over to the boating lake. We are going to set in the hard suction and get a large jet to work in the main hall, which is going like billy-o. Whatever you do, don't position the Pump anywhere but over at the opposite side from the entrance to the lake. If you set in near the entrance, you are gonna prevent other appliances setting in, yeah?'

'OK, Guv – will do,' replied Jack Towleen. Before he had clambered back into his cab, the rest of us had grabbed the rolled lengths of two and three-quarter inch delivery hose from the side lockers. Each length was 75 feet. It was about ten lengths from the lake, over the car park to the huge steel doors where we would get our jet to work. Lengths were spaced equidistant from the lake to the door, and after this we trotted behind the Pump as Jack drove it smartly over to the far side of the lake, where dumbfounded members of the public, out at the Ally Pally for the afternoon, stared transfixed by the huge fire that was growing by the second.

'Effing 'ell, Guv, it's not often that we find ourselves setting into open water is it?' said John Lydus, as we connected up the reinforced suction hose, before dropping it into the water.

John wasn't wrong. The vast majority of fires fought in London utilise the water drawn from the street mains, via the hundreds of hydrants situated across the capital. I had spent some time on a station not too far from the docks and wharves alongside the Thames. Even there, it was rare to have to set into the river to draw water. On those occasions when it had been necessary, it had been on some of the biggest fires ever experienced, like the major fire in 1972 in a disused warehouse in Tooley Street, where it took more than 50 appliances and over 200 men to bring it under control.

There was every indication that almost as many appliances might be required here, high above north London, and the constant blare of sirens and roar of Pumps straining their eight tons up the slope signalled that a huge 'make up' fire was in progress, and our work was only just starting.

The competent 'good hand' Firefighter never tries to make an entry into a burning building without the protection of a charged hose line. To do so would be like the SAS soldier bursting into a room with suspected armed terrorists inside without a weapon. A deadly fate could await them both, and whether a hail of bullets, or the lung-searing heat and flame of a flashover, you end up just as dead.

The boating lake water soon surged along the delivery hose, engorging its flatness as it raced along to the hand-controlled nozzle, which I was holding firmly just outside the 15-feet high, 9-feet wide door to the great hall.

I was crouched very low, a safer position than standing should the inrush of air ignite a fireball of smouldering hot gases, enabling it to go over my head once the door was opened a fraction. My heart thumped as I gripped the nozzle-opening lever like a vice.

Ricky Tewin, our 15-stone, rugby playing Leading Fireman, cautiously gripped the handle of the huge, outward-opening door, preparing to pull it open enough for me to get the jet to work into the inferno inside. As hefty and strong as he was, the terrific suction draught being produced by the fire consuming the thousands of cubic feet of oxygen inside the cavernous Great Hall was such that it was like trying to shift a 40-ton truck. In spite of this, he managed to open it just enough for us to feel the heat emanating from the shimmering maw, before the massive suction off the draught slammed it shut.

Eventually, this huge door was opened and wedged and a ground-mounted water monitor used to direct a powerful stream into the roaring hell of the Great Hall, from which huge heat waves surged on to us, like those hot blasts from the open doors of a turbo fan oven, which take the breath and parch the facial skin in a second. The fire had developed at a rapid pace. The round window frames at the front encircled angry looking flames, which rolled and roared as all of what would burn was consumed by this inferno, which was forcing its destructive heat and flame laterally.

An officer ran up to our position. He had a lined face, and the twin black bars encircling his white helmet denoted the rank of Divisional Officer. 'Listen up,' he shouted out. 'Shut off your branch and reposition it in the hall on the eastern side inside the complex. We've got no chance of saving the central portion, we gotta concentrate on preventing lateral spread,' he went on in a calm, unhurried voice, which spoke of long experience of dealing with pressure situations. Such a situation certainly existed here. One of north London's most famous buildings was well alight. An historic venue where some of the earliest television transmissions had been made from, and a leisure, exhibition, entertainment and drinking location that attracted folk from near and far.

This was no dingy back street blaze to which the television and press reporters would have difficulty locating. Standing in its commanding position, visible from afar, and overlooking the very busy east coast main line railway route, this huge blaze was like a hilltop beacon, advertising the effectiveness of the Brigade in its firefighting endeavours

The relative paucity of water supplies in the immediate vicinity had necessitated the area Hose-Laying Lorry being deployed. This vehicle carries a huge bed of flaked, preconnected large diameter hose. It moves along disgorging this hose, whose huge diameter permits a less hindered flow and delivers far more gallonage than the standard two and three-quarter inch variety.

Given the massive size of the Alexandra Palace, and the rate at which the flames were spreading, every last drop of water would be needed, and the on-scene presence of the local water authority turn cocks would play their own role in diverting all available mains supplies to the huge extinguishing task confronting us all.

All things considered, the measured calmness of the Divisional Officer was impressive, a sure sign of the 'good hand' officer. Assured, confident and able to cool the surge of hot adrenaline that can overexcite the young and inexperienced hands.

Within ten minutes we had dragged the charged hose across the building's frontage, an energy sapping task given that a gallon of water weighs ten pounds, and that the total hose line from the boating lake to our position was some 750 feet. Sweating profusely now, we made an entry to the east of the Great Hall, where flames were breaking through the large windows in a separating brick wall. These darting, scouring flames were threatening to destroy the place from which the BBC produced some of its Open University programmes.

At first the location in which we were standing, sweeping the powerful jet into and across the rolling flames, was virtually free of heat and smoke, the result of that huge draught inside the Great Hall forcing the fire and smoke up and out through the 'chimney' created by the burned through dome. But the combined effect of the thousands of gallons being delivered began to supress the blaze and lessen that draught causing the hot smoke to bank down, enveloping us intermittently with its acrid, pungent, cough-inducing, eye-watering blanket.

Four separate crews were at work from this position. The

discomfort of smoke, although not as pungent and dense as that I had encountered in the rag warehouses, dockside wharves and garment factories of the East End, was nonetheless wearing. But it felt good and satisfying to feel that we were making what the fire service terms a 'good stop'. Beating back the all-consuming flames. Preventing the searing heat from radiating its surging waves across the hall in which we were working to save the masses of books, films and other educational material of the Open University. Struggling to stop the 'University of the air', as it was first known, from going up in the air!

We worked for two hours beating back this inferno, but no structure could withstand indefinitely the terrific heat being generated in this massive blaze. Roof timbers, exposed to heavy fire, char at first. Indeed, on the thickest beams, this charring does act as a form of insulation, protecting the unburned wood underneath, but eventually the heat and flame will burn their way through all but the thickest beams and lead to a structural collapse of the roof.

Once a roof has burned through, the heat and flame and smoke do have a path by which they can ventilate, and this lessens the risk of lateral spread. However, such spread of fire was a real danger here because the body of fire was massive and generated huge heat. A heat that was not much less than that experienced during 1940 and 1941 when the blitz raids turned the London docks and the City into a seething cauldron of fire.

It was this rarely experienced sort of conflagration that had made our own efforts so draining during that long afternoon, but breaking through the roof of fire did improve our position and relative comfort.

The downside is that without the roof, walls can lose their brace and become liable to collapse. Structural collapse has killed as many Firefighters as those who have perished in flashovers, and lessons have been learned from each tragic episode.

One of the most important was the requirement to have safety officers positioned at strategic points in and around the perimeters of buildings involved in heavy fire. It was one such officer detailed to monitor the northern flank who first noticed a crack developing in the upper wall, which supported the dome, and all personnel were withdrawn from the vicinity in case a collapse occurred.

Safety from collapsing walls doesn't simply mean standing 20 or so feet back. When a wall topples over, it will often cover at least the number of vertical storeys, or the vertical height of the external wall. In addition, huge swathes of the roof trusses may be pulled down with the falling wall, and end up, in an average four-storey structure, some 40 feet at least away from its base.

Those charged with the safety officer's role, as I would be so often on future occasions across the capital, will often find it a nerve-stretching duty if death and serious injury to Firefighters are to be avoided.

At least four safety officers were detailed on this memorable afternoon, and were positioned at all compass points where the main body of fire was rapidly weakening the structure. Identifiable by yellow tabards, each held a loud hailer in their hands.

Walls, roofs and floors have to be scanned for tell-tale signs of collapse. A dropped window arch. A crack in a tall unsupported wall. A wall out of plumb. A sagging timber floor overloaded with water or goods. And the bulge in an end wall caused when steel joists expand from the great heat of a severe fire.

Safety officers have to have a diligence and gimlet-eyed focus which would not be shamed by those Secret Service agents who scan the crowds whenever the President of the USA is about in a public cavalcade, looking, all the time looking for signs that could lead to death and disaster.

The potential dangers to fire crews from collapsing buildings, such as those which took the life of a young fireman in Paddington's Maida Vale in 1975, and that of another on the boundaries of Kentish Town and Euston in 1978, are never forgotten.

But whenever crews are withdrawn, and fires fought 'from the street', the safety officers' task, rather than diminishing, can actually increase. The size and pressure of firefighting jets often have to be increased in order to ensure that the water reaches the flames. Aerial appliances such as Turntable Ladders and Hydraulic Platforms have to be carefully sited, and the huge water monitors atop these used discriminately if sudden structural collapse is to be avoided. When a monitor is delivering say 200 gallons a minute, then each and every minute of uninterrupted flow will mean that a weight of going on for a ton will be deluging into a building. This great weight and scouring pressure can soon overload floors and walls, and wash out mortar from walls, perhaps already weakened by time and lack of main-tenance, and no more so than from the monitors atop the Turntable Ladder.

164

Dennis Breedon had been detached on 'out duties' to cover for a sickness at a local station and was riding the Turntable Ladder. He was one of the most experienced and enthusiastic men on our watch, and still kicked himself after over 15 years of service if he missed a good working job.

When a major incident occurs, the whole Brigade, or large parts of it, soon becomes aware either by teleprinter printouts ordering standby appliances in towards the incident from outlying districts, or from overhearing the radio transmissions from the scene.

'There's a big "make up" fire on at the Ally Pally,' shouted out Nick Pyrland, the duty watch room attendant to the crews just assembling in the yard for drills.

'Just my effing luck to be out on detached duties,' moaned Dennis to Leading Fireman 'Dicky' Bird.

'Come on, Dennis, mate. Ain't you had enough of wanting to go to every make up fire that's on?' the Leading Fireman asked sarcastically.

'Seemingly not. But I bet my own station's pair, or at least the Pump, will have gone on, or will do, if another make up message comes in,' he responded.

Dennis Breedon was still inwardly cursing when the shrill teleprinter bell was followed by the harsh clamour of the call bells. 'Turntable ladders to fire – Alexandra Palace – J26 Hornsey's ground,' the duty man shouted out.

'Bleedin' 'ell, Dennis, you're the kiss of death,' shouted out 'Dicky' Bird as he watched Dennis dart, like a startled silver fish into the appliance room, punching the air in his delight as he climbed into the rear cab of the huge red and chrome Turntable Ladder.

'Right, position your ladders on the east side of the central hall and get a monitor to work,' the Divisional Commander instructed. Within a few minutes the hundred foot steel ladder was being elevated, and before it began its clicking extension, Dennis Breedon mounted the ladder from the rear of the appliance, the huge safety belt with its big karabiner, like dog clip glinting in the light. He slammed the footplate down at the head of the ladder and hooked on the safety clip to a metal ring. He stuck out his left arm horizontally, the standard signal to show the operator that he was secured and his toes away from the ladder's rounds, before it was extended.

Before climbing on to the ladder, Dennis had, with the assistance

165

of another crew, connected the permanently connected monitor hose pipe to an incoming supply, which would feed the huge monitor nozzle at the ladder's head. Only 20 or so minutes back, Dennis had been cursing his luck at missing out on what would be one of the biggest and most memorable north London fires of the twentieth century. Now he was on it, and would soon have one of the best vantage points going!

Dennis checked that the sharp safety knife was present in its space just before his slow ride high above the ground started. Turntable Ladders are self-supporting, held stable by the weight of the appliance, the correct and secure positioning of outrigger jacks on solid ground and the use of safety tables and cut-outs designed to prevent a capsize.

However, should the weight and pressure of water, or the recoiling reaction of the outgoing jet, create any instability that could lead to the tall ladder rocking, risking a capsize, the safety knife is there in readiness. It was used to slice into the hose and release the water pressure that could create unstable conditions.

The smoke from the burning Ally Pally had by now formed a column of at least 200 hundred feet, and was visible for miles around. The huge fire that was generating it had forced its heat laterally, before venting as the roof of the dome above the Great Hall was breached. This superheated smoke, and the rolling, roaring flames enveloped within it, had raised all that was combustible to a temperature in which ignition occurred. Internal fire spread had penetrated the ceiling structures aside the Great Hall, and had begun to consume the roof trusses and other timbers within the void, and the fire had breached the roof covering here as Dennis Breedon, secure on his platform, rose slowly above the roof line.

From his high vantage point, Dennis looked down at the toy soldier size of the scores of Firefighters battling this massive outbreak. 'Extend another fifteen or so feet, and train the ladder to the right, Mick,' Dennis voiced into the intercom to the operator some 70 feet below.

'Got you, mate, extend fifteen to twenty feet and train to the right,' echoed the operator's voice, which confirmed that the instructions were understood.

'Water on, Mick,' squawked the voice from up on high. Within the next minute the water surged its upward way to the huge monitor positioned in front of Dennis Breedon and which was moved by a long steel lever, which linked with a joint permitting vertical and horizontal movement of the jet. A whistling rush of air being forced ahead of the rapidly rising surge announced the imminence of the jet from the monitor, which Dennis had already aimed into the centre of the huge fire below. A fire which appeared from his position like an erupting volcano, spewing out thick, rolling brown smoke, and red and orange timber brands, some a couple of feet long, thick, heavy spars, but forced up by the fast rising heat as though light as feathers.

Like Japan's silver-liveried bullet train, exiting from a long dark tunnel into the bright light of day, the thick tube of water shot from the monitor's nozzle, boring its way through the dark tunnel of smoke to reach the molten heart of the blaze many feet below, and causing the tall ladder to gently sway.

In spite of the massive gallonage and weight of water pouring down, in spite of the great cooling effect of the Firefighter's principal weapon, the heat was so terrific that a high proportion of the water would be converted to steam before the knock down force that such a large deluging stream contains could take effect.

Dennis Breedon moved the monitor slowly up and down, then slowly side to side, always trying to cover the greatest area with the stream, but cautious not to cause too great an oscillation of the gently rocking, self-supporting ladder.

Turntable Ladder accidents were rare, but they had happened, and some with fatal results, hence the rigour of the Brigade's specialist training course, one of the biggest chunks of which concerned stability in operation. Because of the weight of water being delivered, and because of the powerful force of the stream on a building's weakened structure, crews inside burning buildings are normally withdrawn when aerial appliances are at work above them as water towers.

Because the body of fire was so huge in the Great Hall, there were no personnel in there, but the safety officers had to keep a constant watch on structural stability, especially below and around where aerial equipment was in operation. As a result of the decision to withdraw for safety reasons, we engaged with a firefight from the street, and slowly, the raging beast, high in its north London lair, began to be tamed.

Atop his ladder, Dennis Breedon was pleased to note that the brown smoke was becoming grey, a sure sign that the water was having its knock down and cooling effect. It was also pleasing to note that the monitor's jet had helped prevent the potential spread over the top of the east side of the Great Hall, where his station colleagues had worked so valiantly for the last few hours.

About three hours after we had first arrived, the combined effect of many large jets and monitors, supplied by the boating lake, the internal hydrants, and by a relay of water pumped from the large mains at the bottom of the hill, had brought the main fire under control, but final extinguishment would take several days.

So, 107 years after the first blaze to destroy the Alexandra Palace, disaster had struck again. How sad to see that in spite of the efforts of over 150 Firefighters, so much damage had resulted to a building for which so many north Londoners held a special place in their hearts.

Our efforts on that afternoon played their part in saving those parts that it was possible to save, but, as pleasing as this was, no firefighter worth their salt could ever be pleased at seeing the devastation that this conflagration had caused. Going off duty much later that evening, I stopped on a high road from which the still burning Ally Pally could be seen by the many north Londoners crowded at this vantage point. The red and yellow flames were only intermittent now in the windows, and the huge edifice seemed to my eyes like a huge warship, struggling to remain afloat after taking a pasting from enemy shells.

Back in 1900 an Act of Parliament had been created, which required trustees to maintain the Palace and park and to 'make it available for the free use and recreation of the public forever'. The public of north London and further afield had made good use of this availability over the years up to that memorable but sad 1980 afternoon, when this place of leisure and pleasure for so many was all but sunk.

But there must have been the spirit of the Phoenix present in the north London air, because eventually the affected parts were demolished and the old place rose from the ashes of its former self, enabling all those who returned to once more make use of the new leisure, catering and exhibition facilities provided.

In my years in London, many enjoyable visits were made to the Ally Pally, and I remember all of them. Over the years, I have taken trains from and to King's Cross many times. On every occasion my eyes have automatically strayed to the sight of this huge monument, and I am always reminded of that afternoon in 1980 when a call, which our Station Officer at first thought to be a prank, turned out to be one of the London Fire Brigade's largest and most notable fires, and one that added another chapter to its long and eventful history.

Chapter Fifteen

Down and Out

Most large towns and cities have their vagrants, homeless people, and those who choose to squat in either derelict or unoccupied houses, factories and even inside old cars and vans. London is no exception to this general rule, and the East End and parts of the inner suburbs have always had their quota of such dispossessed people.

Within such areas, there's usually a fair proportion of buildings in various stages of dereliction. These either await the steel ball and sledgehammers of a demolition crew, or the purchase of the structure by some developer hoping to carry out a minimal cost refurbishment, prior to making a healthy profit on a future sale. Over a long period working in and around most of the inner London boroughs, calls to derelict premises were a regular occurrence. Although it was easy to treat such fires with complacency, one could never be certain that within the depths of what appeared to be a totally uninhabited property there were not vagrants or squatters sheltering from the elements, and often anaesthetising themselves with a variety of alcoholic beverages.

Our evening meal of boiled beef and carrots had been interrupted at just after eight fifteen on an icy December evening by a call to 'Rubbish Alight' in the rear of Christ Church, Spitalfields. This was directly opposite the vegetable market, and in the heart of the East End. Such calls within the inner city usually involved a pile of commercial waste such as empty cardboard boxes, wrappers and refuse sacks stacked at the rear of commercial premises, and ignited by children playing with matches, or by a discarded cigarette end. Or they involved the hand-and-body-warming small bonfires set up by some of the area's down and outs.

171

The location was a regular one. The rear of the church was known as 'Itchy Park'. Its title derived from the bodily scratchings that accompany the lives of those who have worn the same garments for a long time, and who have not bathed or showered in many cases for months.

The ruddy orange and yellow flames in a corner of the area illuminated the weathered faces of about six men and women. Faces that were blackened by the greasy smoke of their fire. Faces whose deep-etched lines illustrated the highs and lows of their lives, in the same way that the contour lines on a map indicate the existence of high and low terrain.

Someone passing by had noticed the flames. Perhaps unfamiliar with the area, and with the vagrants' haunt of 'Itchy Park', they might easily have thought that a more serious blaze was afoot than a bonfire, and considered it prudent, in this high-fire-risk locality to dial 999.

A virtually toothless woman, her head half bound in a ragged tartan scarf against the cold, grasping a wine bottle, of which all but the neck was inside a brown paper bag, was sitting leaning against a wall. Her croaky voice giving a faltering rendition of the old nursery rhyme ' ... Oranges and lemons said the bells of St Clements ... When will that be said the bells of Stepney ... When I grow rich said the bells at Shoreditch ...' She broke off to bellow out; 'Look, it's the fucking firemen here to piss on our lovely fire.'

Her equally squalid looking comrades chortled out a drunken cry of 'Piss off. Effing leave us alone,' waving their cans of strong lager and bottles of 'Red Biddy', a lethal throat-tearing concoction of cheap wine and methylated spirits. Experience had shown us how lethal such a liquid could be if the consumer of it rolled too near the flames of a fire, setting themselves ablaze. We had been to a number of fatalities caused by this hazard.

In any event, the fire was too big and was sending up a load of sparks and embers, which only needed to find their way through an open window of one of the commercial premises adjacent to start an inferno. But we also appreciated that it was a freezing cold night, and for these people, their fire was the only warmth they had. If we doused it completely they would light another one a few yards away, so we had found that the most prudent compromise was to reduce its size.

As our Station Officer, a burly ex-Royal Navy sailor, approached

172

the group and the fire, one of the men, his senses befuddled by the potent drink he had consumed, grabbed a flaming brand and waved it at him shouting in a broad Irish brogue, 'I'll effing brand you if you touch this fire.'

'Now, now, let's not do anything we might regret,' boomed out the Guvnor, striding purposefully up to the drunken Irishman. 'We are not going to put the fire out, just reduce its size, Paddy. OK, understood,' he said, his six feet one inches and seventeen stones towering over the fire-wielding man, who had threatened him so aggressively.

'Well, make sure that's all yer do,' he snarled back, a spray of alcohol-tainted saliva accompanying his words.

With a few bursts from the hose reel, and by breaking up the bonfire with a ceiling hook, we soon had reduced the fire to a level we could live with, and within minutes we had wound the hose reel on to its drum. Fifteen minutes later we were able to finish off our boiled beef and carrots, which was by now, after almost half an hour in the oven, more boiled than we would have liked.

There were six of us sitting at the formica-topped table in the mess room just after midnight. It was a narrow room, about eighteen by nine feet, and the peeling cream paint on the walls of this Victorian era fire station was crying out for refurbishment. There was an old radiogram in one corner, and next to it a battered wooden bookcase with a sliding glass door, which contained a range of reading material. Some fire brigade oriented, plus various paperback novels and a pile of old *Playboy* magazines, the latter's pages dog-eared from the thumbs of three shifts of firemen who had scanned the coloured photographs with a voracity or nonchalance depending on their age and attitude.

On this inner-city station, in the heart of the East End, where at any second those shrill bells could despatch us to a wide range of fires and emergencies, it had become a habit for men to congregate here. Sipping mug after mug of tea or coffee. Preferring to be alert and conscious should the bells come in, rather than take that fitful rest, which we were all permitted, on our army style iron-framed beds in the shabby dormitory.

'I reckon it's better for you to stay up at night, rather than jumping up from a sleep when we get a shout,' said Jim Laine, a thickset veteran of 22 years. 'I read somewhere that the average Fireman only lives about five years after retiring at 55, and I wouldn't mind betting that it's all that sudden action from rest to firefighting that starts the rot,' he went on.

'For God's sake, Jim, leave it out, you morbid bastard. That means I've only got six years left if I retire next year,' responded Bert Braxton, at 54, one of the oldest men in the division.

'Yeah, but you've probably spent half your career sitting in here after midnight, and the old ticker won't have had the strain put on it like what happens when you are suddenly woken by the bells. Christ, take a look see next time we turn out at night at those blokes who always like to kip, they look like death warmed up,' Jim went on.

Most of this club of nocturnal tea and coffee guzzlers were still around the mess room nearly three hours later. The air was now a fug of dry heat from the radiators, fuelled by the coke-fired 'appy', the affectionate name given to the heating furnace apparatus ensconced in the basement, and from the blue haze of cigarette and pipe tobacco smoke.

Few would have envisaged in those days how, in the future, most organisations, including the fire service, would be so reformed in their culture of health and safety that smokers would be in the minority. Bert Braxton and Jim Laine had, in the raw days before the advent of breathing apparatus for every crew member, probably inhaled far more lung-damaging fumes and smoke during hundreds of fires than a whole room full of smokers could ever match. As a consequence they gave not even a thought to a colleague exhaling cigarette or pipe smoke in their presence. Indeed, at the time, cigarette and pipe smoke was considered a natural part of that cosy, warm fug of the fire station rest area, by smokers and non-smokers alike.

Three of the six men remaining had whiled away the last couple of hours playing cards. Another had stretched out in the battered old armchair with a novel, whilst the two veterans of the station had indulged in their nightly reminiscences of fires and characters, looking back over a long period spent within the 'London in the East'.

Only about a half mile away from where these six night owls were sitting dry and warm, and where the remainder of the watch were dozing fitfully on their iron beds, in what had been an unusually quiet tour of duty, another six people, four men and two women, were huddled and slumped in the rat-infested remnants of a once proud house.

174

Brick Lane, London E1 is a slightly curving thoroughfare of about half a mile in length. At its northern boundary it makes a junction with Bethnal Green Road. Travelling in an easterly direction are such streets as Cheshire, Buxton and Old Montague, which themselves run into Vallance Road, the one time home of three men, two of whose names, Ronnie and Reggie Kray, have become synonymous with the East End of the sixties and seventies.

At its southern end it becomes Osborn Street for a short stretch before meeting the major highway of the Whitechapel Road. Within a little over half a mile on the left is the Blind Beggar public house, reminding us again of the infamous Krays, for it was in this drinking place that Ronnie Kray killed an old enemy, George Cornell, by means of a close range bullet to the head. Some 80 or so years earlier another period of infamy had helped create the folklore and history of this district when a certain slaughterer of prostitutes became known as Jack the Ripper.

During the 1980s and 1990s, there were, and indeed still are, many streets and alleyways, which, save for the replacement of gaslights with electric ones, could still pass for the grey stone and soot-blackened redbrick buildings and cobbled streets of that period.

Brick Lane, and many of the surrounding streets, had witnessed much of the work of the London Fire Brigade over its long history during which a succession of immigrants including Huguenot, Irish, Jewish, and latterly Asian races had occupied the houses, tenements and factories in successive waves. Most striving to make a living, and in some cases their fortunes, from involvement with a variety of trades, but especially that centred on the garment and furniture industries.

If there is such a thing as spirits from the past, then, in fire brigade terms, the atmosphere will be dense with them. There will be the clatter of the hooves of horses, which once hauled the steamer fire pumps. The cries of the Firemen drivers who urged their horses on to a blaze. Then, in later years, the haunting clamour of bells and sirens. The orange and later blue flashing beacons. The drone of powerful diesel engines pumping water on to fires in a multitude of factories, workshops, villas, houses and tenements. Fires whose thick smoke will have drifted across and over the rooftops of this cosmopolitan inner-city district. In its drifting it will have added its distinctive sharp odour, and will have draped its hot, twirling cloak over the homes of the hundreds lying asleep.

Asleep and unaware of the drama taking place in the darkness and shadows of the East End night, and of how that darkness was now being rapidly illuminated by the lurid glow of leaping, searing flames. The bone-chilling coldness of the night, exacerbated by a biting wind from the north-east, had forced the inebriated inhabitants of 'Itchy Park', whose fire we had been forced to dampen, to seek out some shelter from the elements. They headed for one of the derelict buildings that stood in such streets as Fournier, Heneage and Chicksand, minor grey backwaters branching off Brick Lane.

They had to stagger no more than a quarter of a mile to Brick Lane from the site of their earlier bonfire, the embers of which were now turning slowly black as the fire cooled from its abandonment. Just off Brick Lane, they arrived at a partly boarded up house, whose crumbling walls and holed floors had provided sanctuary on several occasions in the past.

Before going inside via a hole they had previously made in a rear fence, the small, grizzled Irishman who had threatened to 'brand' our Station Officer some four hours earlier, had shouted out that he was going back to the soup wagon outside Christ Church opposite Spitalfields Market. With a snarl and cursing of the cold the whole group of six, their old dirt-stained coats flapping in the rising strong wind, and their worn out shoes dragging over the hard London pavements, reeled off, clutching their bottles and paper bags of wine and spirits. They eventually reached the mobile 'kitchen' adjacent Christ Church, and they huddled around the stark white light of its illuminated serving hatch like moths around a flame, the bright light standing out like a beacon amidst the dark alleyways and courtyards of the Spitalfields Market opposite.

By half past one, the thin, hot onion soup and ragged slices of bread doing their best to soak up some of the alcohol inside their stomachs, the six had made it safely back to the derelict house. A box of matches was pulled out of the greasy inner pocket of an old and ragged gaberdine raincoat. A small pile of paper and cardboard was pushed under a pile of old broken picture rail and lit. It was only a small fire, but because the fireplaces were all boarded over, it had to be positioned against a wall of a rear room. The rear room best disguised their presence from any patrolling police officers, who might have noticed the shadows cast by the dancing yellow flames, but the smoke, which found its own way out of the few upstairs

176

window openings could still be smelled if the now gusting wind was blowing in the right direction.

As the warming and soporific waves of heat enveloped them, their fingers, numbed by the low temperature, began to thaw. Soon bottles were at lips, and over the next few hours the six would gradually drift into a slumber, their bodies slowly sinking on to the broken timber floor, which was covered in crumbling plaster, broken laths and skirting boards.

Before finally succumbing to the mind-numbing effects of half a litre of Red Biddy, the small Irishman had broken some of the old skirting by placing it on the lower edge of the old timber staircase and stamping on it.

Armed with about half a dozen pieces, he had placed these in criss-cross fashion over the hungry flames, whose appetite, whetted by the melting layers of old paint, caused them to stretch their hot tongues up to the timber. With each passing second as the six down and outs snored and grunted, from their chosen positions around the ground and top floors of the three-storey house, the flames became length-ened and grew hotter as they consumed their fuel.

London's streets are, of course, the workplace of the police officer. It was one of them who had first caught the sharp tang of burning in his nostrils just after half past three through the slightly opened window of the car. He knew the direction in which the biting wind was blowing from and had soon begun to walk towards the smell of smoke. He walked slowly at first. Then faster as the smell became stronger. As he approached the street's junction with Brick Lane, his heart leapt as he made out fast swirling wreaths of smoke, racing past the pale yellow of the street lamps, and inhaled that peculiar odour of smoke from a burning building. A smell now so strong that he could almost bite on it.

Jim Laine and Bert Braxton had almost covered the combined 51 years of their service in their nostalgic reminiscing when the bells came in. If they had been the sort of individuals who kept diaries, then there would have been many days and far more nights recorded during which they had made the same urgent but cool response to the trilling red call bells.

On all of those occasions, their pulses had quickened with the anticipation and uncertainty of what might confront them. That anticipation had never really lessened with time. It mattered little that one part of their minds was telling them that out of all the thousands of emergencies responded to over the years, relatively few turned out to be dramas. Nor that within minutes the thundering, clanging engines charging to an address could be slinking back to the station at half the speed of their earlier charge because of yet another false alarm. Nor did it matter that most fires attended were dealt with by a deft and swift application of water from the hose reel rather than through the huge snaking tube of cotton and canvas.

Such incidents, the daily fodder of all city fire crews, registered in the mind, but only in a blurring of a thousand minor images. It was the working jobs, those fires and special service calls, that drew from them that energy-giving boost of adrenaline, that became etched in the mind and that could be recalled even years later with such clarity. It was that mental gallery of images that fuelled the anticipation and uncertainty to come when the Pump Escapes, Pumps and Turntable Ladders finally screeched to a halt.

No greater was such anticipation and apprehension than when the ordering message contained the words 'Fire','Smoke issuing' or 'Premises alight'. Those words were the mental triggers that placed those past images on display. At no times were those memories triggered faster than when they accompanied a call in the dead of the night when fire so often strikes.

It was dead of night now, and the teleprinter had punched out 'Fire in derelict house Brick Lane E1 – time of call 0355.' No more than three minutes had elapsed when the officers in charge of each of the appliances 'booked in attendance' by radio. The thick grey smoke of a fire illuminated in their headlamps and reflected back like a dense fog, in spite of the strong gusts of wind blowing spasmodically.

A sudden gust cleared the smoke momentarily and in front, on our left, a heavy body of fire was showing in the second and third storeys of a typical early Victorian house. The red and yellow glow at the ridge of the house indicated that the fire was through the roof. A not unusual occurrence in houses fallen into dereliction, where rotten timbers, plus the breaking up of rafters and purlins by down and outs to build fires, had opened part of the roof to the elements. This was also a good thing in the sense that the fire and smoke could vent itself. This helps improve conditions of visibility and breathability for crews working inside without BA, and provides vital air to anyone trapped within the building.

Unlike an occupied dwelling, where, in the earliest hours persons are likely to be asleep, fires in derelict premises, however severe, did not give off that sense of urgency. This was an area of commercial premises intermingled with tenements and houses, with a fair proportion being in various stages of dereliction and disrepair. Although we knew from experience that in such parts of the capital down and outs could be sleeping inside, our automatic search routines, which we would deploy immediately at any conventional residential fire during the sleeping hours, could be easily pushed into second place at fires in derelict buildings.

Within this high risk tinderbox of an area, suppressing fires in 'derelicts' was crucial if spread to the densely packed commercial premises all around was not to occur. The body of fire was such that the two and three-quarter inch diameter hose was the preferred choice for a quick knock down. The gallonage of water delivered per minute via a suitable sized nozzle was such that the maximum absorption of heat, combined with the weight of water striking the flames was very effective. I flung open a side locker, grabbed a length of the large hose and threw it along the road where it unrolled with a crack. Just as I was connecting the coupling to the delivery on the pump at the rear, a terrible scream cut through the air from above.

I looked up. There, at the very centre of the window frame on the top floor, the form of a man, his clothes alight from head to toe, was silhouetted by the fire in the room behind.

'Send a priority – *make Pumps – four persons reported*,' the Guvnor shouted out. 'Slip and pitch plus a covering jet'. At 54 years, and with only a year left before he had to take compulsory retirement, Bert Braxton could have used all of his 'ringcraft' to ensure that at most fires the heart-pounding stresses and lung and leg bursting efforts of rescue were left to the younger element. But he was a Fireman's Fireman. An individual who was just as motivated here, at this ungodly hour, confronted by the sight of a burning man, 40 feet atop a virtual funeral pyre in the heart of London's East End, as he had been all those years before.

Back then he had first felt that surge of adrenaline, that hard to describe buzz, after bringing three small Jewish children down from the upper floors of a burning tenement no more than a few streets from where we were now. In that rescue, Bert Braxton had ascended and descended the wheeled escape three times to rescue those screaming, sobbing children.

The ladder was almost enveloped in the rolling, rising flames issuing from the lower floors, and although a young man then, the effort and energy drain of those rescues in the darkest, deepest hours of the night had all but laid him low. The Bert Braxtons of the Brigade never sought glory or reward. Fire and rescue was their noble calling. Human life was precious. A sentiment that, in later years, and amongst an increasing number of the general public, would be derided in the selfish, materialistic world, which so many seemed to inhabit, caring only for themselves. It was good, therefore, that the Honours and Awards Board of those far off days had seen fit to commend his heroic actions as above and beyond the call of duty. The framed certificate on the watch room wall spelled out his bravery that night, a fitting reminder in later years of the spirit and courage displayed.

Although time is always of the essence in firefighting in general, and in rescues in particular, Bert knew that a man could move too fast when smoke and fire were about. He knew this from experience gained at hundreds of emergency attendances over nearly 30 years, all of it spent on inner-city stations. Such experience had taught him and his colleagues how to conserve that energy and strength so vital to the saving of life.

His ascent of the pitched ladder was a lesson in how to move briskly but not recklessly. Conserving his breath, and reducing his need to pull in huge amounts of air and smoke, as would have been the case if he had run too hard up the huge 50 foot rescue ladder.

Jim Laine, another veteran, was providing the covering jet and his first task was to shout up to the screaming and burning man at the window, 'Stay put, mate – we'll have you in a second,' after which he allowed the powerful jet to crash into the brickwork just above the head of the unfortunate man, the icy water deluging the burning clothes. Bert, calm, controlled, but with his 54-year-old heart thumping like a pile driver against his breast bone, was now at the head of the escape. Moving with an agility that would have shamed men 20 years his junior, he clambered into the burning top-floor room.

The water from the jet had virtually extinguished the burning garments, but the man, still in a drunken haze, and traumatised by his ordeal, was reeling from side to side. Bert could see that there was no way out of the room. The flames, heat and smoke were too much, so without hesitation, he bent his near six foot frame over. In a flash

180

the small Irishman, the very same one that had threatened to 'brand' our Guvnor the previous evening, was slung across his shoulders like an uncomfortable, filthy stole. With burning skin from the man's hands and legs filling his nostrils with a sickly hot odour, he remounted the ladder and executed the classic fireman's lift carry down to where willing hands relieved him of his badly burned human burden.

'If there's one in there, then there's probably others, get a jet in via the front and get the BA men rigged,' shouted our Guvnor to Sub Officer 'Ziggy' Apted.

After connecting the large hose to the Pump delivery I had taken a standpipe and a hydrant key and bar and located the nearest hydrant. From that we laid out another line of hose to provide an unlimited supply to the Pump. By this time the ladder had been pitched to rescue the blazing man, and we were ready when the Station Officer ordered the large jet into the house via the front door. Although locked, this soon succumbed to the weight and blows of the 14-pound sledgehammer being wielded by former heavyweight boxer Jim McBreen.

As Ted Smart and I humped the now charged hose line up the small flight of stone steps, which led to the front door, I could see the BA men rushing to rig. To save time, always of life-saving essence when persons are reported, two men had entered without the protection of BA, and these two were quickly inside, crawling around the smoke-filled house, searching for any other persons.

Because the fire had vented through the roof, the smoke and heat were a little more bearable than was usually the case. As we hauled the heavy hose into the ground floor it became clear that the fire had apparently started on the ground level but had bypassed it to create fire on the top two storeys. We soon had the charged line up to the second floor where there was a heavy body of fire in two rooms and hallway to the front of the house. As the powerful stream of water hit the ceiling and walls, in its ever moving sweeps, we were drenched with a deluge that was already warm because of the fierce heat absorbed in its cooling and knocking down effect. In later years, when looking back at the so many working fires like this one which we responded to in those times, I never failed to be surprised at the minutiae of detail I was able to recall.

I recalled the broken wall and ceiling plaster with the broken laths. The patterns on linoleum, stained and worn with rain from leaking windows and roof, but which once had been shiny and new in the past home of a family from distant shores. The remnants of furniture from another era, which stood, sad and abandoned in a far corner of a smoke-laden room. Above all, I recalled the past spirit of lives moved on. The bedrooms of love, life and death. The dining-rooms or kitchens, the food which fed the children before they danced off to local schools, and parents to their work, many to the clothing and furniture trades, which then made up such a large part of this cosmopolitan inner city. Spirits of the past. Memories, which not even this fierce fire could ever fully erase.

Our two colleagues, Jonnhy Depthard and Mitch Rolinger, who had responded to the Station Officer's urgent request, had done a search of the ground floor, made hazardous by its missing floorboards and general state of dereliction. Their bare hands had recoiled from the hot embers and ashes of the fire set by the squatters some four hours earlier, and which had grown out of control after the broken timber was piled on to it. The heat and smoke had risen to the ceiling. From there it had raced up the hallway and up the stairs, its superheated gases raising the temperature of the dry timbers, old paint and wallpaper of the upper floors, to the stage where they burst into searing flames.

'I've got somebody here,' coughed Johnny Depthard as his hands fell on to the unconscious shape of a body. 'Grab the legs, Mitch, and drag it out back to the street quick.'

Retracing their route in, they manhandled the dead weight across the broken and litter-strewn floors to the front door and down the unforgiving stone steps to the pavement, just as the BA crews were going in to take over the search and rescue effort.

It was a man. He was dressed, if that was the right word, in a greasy old, once sand-coloured gabardine raincoat. A coat that was now almost brown with the polished shine of too much wear. Too many days and long nights in which that raincoat, fastened round the waist with a section of brown cord, had acted as the only piece of material between his malnourished frame and the cold, rough floor of a derelict building. His trousers were corduroy. Once green. Now almost black, with frayed bottoms and shiny with wear like the coat. He must have taken off his shoes before lying down to sleep, and on his feet were the black remnants of socks through whose sweat-matted, blue-veined-cheese-stinking smell, poked his big toes, the nails of which were black, long and curled back into the skin.

A quick check of the carotid pulse in the neck detected a still beating heart, and the welcome attention of the London Ambulance Service took over the next stage in the rescue and revival process.

We had soon knocked down the fire on the second floor, and in spite of the noise made by the powerful water jet and crashing plaster and hissing steam, we could hear the welcome sound of braying air horns, which heralded the imminent arrival of the reinforcing appliance.

Within minutes we had negotiated the staircase. In a short time our 60-gallons-a-minute of water had put paid to the inferno in the room from which veteran Bert Braxton had carried out his carry-down rescue with such aplomb only a few minutes back.

The BA men located four other occupants on the ground floor. But because the fire had bypassed them, because its fury had been diluted by the open roof, allowing heat and smoke to ventilate, their unconsciousness was more a result of the alcohol consumed earlier than from the malevolent smoke surrounding them. It was most likely though that had the policeman not detected the pungent smell of burning and called us, they would have ended up on a mortuary slab, rather than the pavement of Brick Lane. To which good fortune and the well-drilled search and rescue efforts of the London Fire Brigade had mercifully delivered them on that bleak winter morning. 'Down and outs' brought 'out and down', as so many had been during those busy years when fires surrounded the beating heart of the East End.

Chapter Sixteen

Fire Law

The East End districts of Shoreditch, Whitechapel, Shadwell and Bethnal Green, in which I had seen so much of life and death, were characterised by more than vagrants and dispossessed persons. They were also prime centres of a wide range of manufacturing industries.

Historically, these had included such sweated trades as brush-making, matchbox production and garment manufacturing, to name but a few. Sweating meant the production would be broken down into its simplest components, permitting the deployment of the cheapest unskilled labour.

Within the congested streets, alleys, turnings and courtyards of this colourful cosmopolitan quarter, hundreds of people earned their meagre wages in helping to produce goods to be sold at profit far and wide. In the middle part of the nineteenth century, Henry Mayhew had chronicled the often appalling working and living conditions in his *London Labour and the London Poor*.

It was within some of those workplaces and dwellings featured that many fires and other alarms would be responded to in the ensuing years by London fire crews.

On that hot summer Saturday, on the second of our night duties, I was lying flat on the iron-framed bed provided to permit an official rest between the hours of eleven to seven. It was just before eleven o'clock, and since coming on duty at six, we had turned out four times, twice to false alarms, once to 'person shut in lift' and once to a fire in an abandoned old Jaguar car. I reflected on the vast potential that existed for a fire in the thousands of different buildings and premises located across the capital. Within this huge city were 32 London boroughs. Within those were some of the most extensive fire and life risks to be found anywhere in the world, and, even as I lay there, some deadly fire might just be being ignited as a result of electrical fault, a carelessly discarded cigarette or by the malicious actions of an arsonist.

A red-faced infant of a flame might be growing slowly to maturity, filling its surroundings with its thickening smoke and toxic fumes. Rising fast via open doors, lift shafts or stairways to ignite, with its rising heat, other fires many floors above or below its origins, until hours later, perhaps, it announces its presence by the shattering of glass or by its menacing, dancing flames breaking through a roof high above.

Such potential for fire within the East End's wide-ranging types of industry and its Thames-side warehouses stuffed with a powder keg of combustibles, was augmented by the multitudes of high-fire-risk premises of the West End.

Within that district were the major department stores, nightclubs, theatres, hospitals and dwellings in street, courtyard, estate and square. There were the massive and impressive embassies and royal buildings. Overarching all of these in the business of human life risk from fire were the hundreds of hotels, guest houses, boarding houses and bed and breakfast establishments. These sleeping risk premises ran into thousands. As one of the world's most visited cities, London sees thousands of tourists and others laying their heads upon pillows every night, and placing their trust in the fire safety of this accommodation.

I must have drifted off into sleep because when the sudden illumination of the lights and harsh clamour of bells startled me into consciousness I could see through heavy-lidded eyes that it was just before three in the morning on the large electric wall clock. I reached out to encircle the coldness of the sliding pole, and dropped 15 feet to the large, round mat below, wondering if my earlier musings were to be realised.

The order was for the Pump only to a call to a fire in a furniture makers on an adjoining station's ground. It had been sticky in the dormitory and the open windows of the Pump's cab provided a welcome cooling draught as we roared out into the night. Even after all the years in the capital, I had never ceased to be interested at the sight of someone out on the streets no matter how late or early the hour was.

This early Sunday morning was no exception as a group of six or seven men and women, probably having just left a nearby late-night dancing venue, made their way home as we charged past. The beacons of blue revolving light caused them to turn, gesticulate and cry out, their peals of drunken laughter just audible through the opened crew cab window.

The radio squawked into life with the '*in attendance*' messages of the first two appliances to arrive. A minute later, our Station Officer booked us in also, and we halted just 30 or so feet behind them opposite a two-storey redbrick building from which a thin sheet of brown smoke, illuminated by a nearby lamp standard, was slowly percolating from around the top-floor windows.

How long had this fire been building up? This was the universal thought of all present. If it had been developing slowly it might just be at the point of 'lighting up' as soon as crews started to gain entry. The consequences of that could be fatal to fire crews and disastrous to the property and the furniture maker's business.

'Pitch the Dewhurst and carefully take out a top part of the pane,' shouted out the Station Officer to his own men, 'then lay out a charged line ready to go in,' he went on as our own Station Officer walked over. 'Morning, Tom, what do you want from my boys?' he asked.

'Morning, mate, can you take a shufty around the rear?' he replied. Two of our crew were detailed to make their way to the back of the building to check if fire was showing at that point. The rest of us, the remaining two plus the Station Officer, stood back ready to engage once the entry was made. The 30-foot extending wooden ladder, known as the Dewhurst, was up in a flash. With a deft strike of his axe, the man at the head, keeping below the pane, released the built up pressure of smoke.

This was not unlike the lancing of a boil, and, as the pane shattered, the hot yellow pus of pressurised smoke rapidly shot out and raced up into the warm night sky.

The ground-floor door had been forced. The charged hose was taken up the small flight of stone stairs, ready to drive any fire out of the window, rather than forcing it back into the factory, which could create an immediate spread of fire throughout the floor, if directed from the outside.

Fortunately it soon transpired that heavy smoke was the only hazard. There was no flame, and in a few minutes all of the front windows had been opened and the pent-up brown fumes rushed up into the warm summer morning air, rapidly improving conditions.

187

'See that?' our Station Officer said to me, as he pointed to a still burning gas ring on the workbench, which ran adjacent to the external wall. 'They are always doing it, leaving a glue pot on and forgetting the burner is lit.' Evidently, some worker had been in the workshop on the Saturday and had forgotten to remove the glue pot from the ignited gas ring. The glue had eventually boiled away and the pot had overheated and filled the factory with smoke. That factory had a lucky escape, but it was increasingly being realised that the reliance on good fortune to preserve human life and property was something that an increasingly safety conscious society would not tolerate.

During the 1950s and 1960s, a number of serious fires had occurred in places of work and in hotels and boarding houses, and these had resulted in multiple losses of life. Many of these hotel and boarding house fires occurred in London, and some of the more infamous locations were referred to earlier.

The public clamour that resulted from these incidents, which had involved amongst others a Yorkshire textile mill, a Liverpool department store and a Bolton drinking club, had resulted in the enactment of a progressive programme of statutory fire safety legislation.

Following a particularly tragic fire at a guest house and inn in Saffron Walden, Essex, on Boxing Day, 1969, in which eleven people perished, and following those many fatal fires in London hotels and boarding houses during the 1960s, the Fire Precautions Act was introduced in 1971. This legislation was designed to protect people from fire. Its aim was to ensure that the fire safety provisions of a premises were of such a level that occupants would be alerted to an outbreak and be capable of making their own, unaided escape to safety. With only a few exceptions, this legislation, thanks to the diligence of fire brigades in carrying out a sound inspection and enforcement programme, would prove to be instrumental in significantly reducing the previous unacceptably high numbers of fire deaths and casualties sustained within commercial premises and other places where the public resort.

In those years before these new fire safety laws began to bite, London's fire crews within the inner suburbs had their own involvement in monitoring the compliance with another significant piece of law. A law that was unique to the capital. That law was the London Building Act, and within its embrace were many of those huge warehouses alongside the Thames.

Chapter Seventeen

A Night to Remember

The heavy steel sliding fire door rolled along the sloping rail on which it was hung and slammed shut with a metallic, crashing thud.

'This door will hold back fire and smoke for as long as the thick wall in which it is set,' boomed the strong voice of Station Officer Jim Cronine to the four assembled members of the Pumps crew, who were taking part in an outside duty known as a 'One One D'. These were visits to familiarise crews with selected premises. They were sanctioned by Section 1(i) (d) of the 1947 Fire Services Act, hence their name. It would clearly have been a practical impossibility to visit every premises on a station's ground, and we therefore concentrated on those that held the greatest potential for a serious fire, or were buildings of a large or unusual construction, or had a high life risk. Falling into these categories were the major hospitals, factories, department stores, prominent buildings such as St Paul's Cathedral, the Bank of England, Tower of London and the massively constructed warehouses besides the Thames, in the interior of which the five of us were gathered on that morning.

The 'One One D' enabled fire crews to gain information on such areas as the water supplies, the presence of sprinkler and fire alarm installations, the materials stored or industrial processes carried out, the numbers of employees and their locations, and such internal provisions as fire-resisting walls, floors and steel fire-stopping doors.

These familiarisation visits were often combined within the inner London suburbs with inspections carried out under the London Building Acts (LBAs), which were regulations unique to the capital and which could historically be linked back to the Great Fire of London of 1666, from which the dangers of small fires spreading from their source to neighbouring premises and then adjacent streets and thoroughfares had been so vividly and catastrophically demonstrated.

A progressive series of fire-protective structural developments over the next 300 years, honed to greater effectiveness by conflagrations experienced within the capital, culminated in the introduction of the London Building Acts. The 1939 amendments to these Acts embraced any commercial premises whose cubic capacity exceeded preordained limits. It required the provision of automatic sprinklers, fire-resisting walls, floors, doors and shutters. The purpose of which was to contain the spread of fire and smoke long enough for the Brigade to gain access and extinguish any fire occurring. The proliferation of many massive warehouses alongside the Thames, along with other huge structures, which were often united into constructions covering a very large number of floors, made these regulations vital to the process of fire protection in these high-fire-risk localities.

The steel fire door, which had slammed shut so loudly, was one of four positioned on each of the six floors of this massive warehouse. It was adjacent to the Thames. Only a river's width from the majestic structure of the much loved and much visited Tower of London and next to the Pool of London as it used to be known. Then, cargo from across the globe found its way to the heavily fortified dockside complexes. These were massively built to protect such goods as ivory, silks, spices, timber and precious metals from the pilfering and wholesale theft, so rife before their construction.

The LBA requirements were such that any fire starting would be held in check by the actuation of the sprinklers, and by non-perforate walls. These, along with the steel fire doors and shutters, would prevent any fire and smoke spread outside of the compartment of origin. Each door ran along a slightly sloping rail. It was held in the open position by a counterweighted cable. At the centre of the cable there was a fusible link. A soft piece of metal designed to part on exposure to the heat of a fire, causing the door to be freed from the counterweight and slide down its rail to close the opening in the thick fire-resisting wall.

'Of course, arsonists have been known to wedge these fire doors in advance of their horrible deeds so as to prevent them from doing their job, in addition to them shutting down the water supply to the sprinkler system,' Jim Cronine went on.

'So they then torch the place and the fire spreads throughout the warehouse?' asked Sevvy Malt, a former policeman who had resigned for personal reasons. Now, in only his first few months out of probation, he was proving himself to be a keen and capable addition to the watch.

'You have got it, young man, and don't forget that if the doors to the stairs are wedged open as well, the fire can spread from floor to floor, a real nightmare scenario, yeah?' replied the Station Officer. Jim Cronine had been to many nightmare scenarios in his almost 30 years of service, the vast majority of it being around the East End and its environs. Like Ben Tuke and Tom Monsal, he had seen it all and nothing seemed to faze him. Although he was not a man to cross, or question when out on the fireground, he was a considerate individual who cared about his men. But he knew that caring for men meant being uncompromising and ultra-disciplined when danger was afoot, and in blazing warehouses there was danger afoot in abundance.

So it was a nightmare scenario, given the nature of the warehouse, and the high fire risk of the surrounding areas. There had been a spate of fires in some of the warehouses in this locality over the last few years. The area was a prime spot on which the developers of the highly sought after Thames-side properties would be anxious to lay their hands. There had been rumours circulating that most of these fires had been of 'suspicious' origin, which was police and fire brigade speak for deliberately ignited.

Only a few months back we had attended a ten-Pump blaze nearby. It had been a rapidly spreading fire, which often meant that accelerants had been used to hasten the spread. It had occurred on a Saturday evening when the chances of detection would be less than in the week. I had been a designated BA wearer on that occasion. I remembered the incident clearly because as we waited to receive the order to start up our sets and make our way via an escape ladder to the second floor, a flashover had occurred inside, catching a crew who were working a jet there. Not the sort of thing to build up confidence just before we had to enter ourselves.

Within seconds a ladder was repitched to the affected level and in minutes the Sub Officer in charge of the crew was being carried down, but fortunately his burns turned out to be only superficial. After that flashover, the officer in charge had made the decision to withdraw all crews and we spent the next few hours fighting the blaze from the street.

The London docklands had suffered some of the heaviest damage of any British city during the bombing raids of the Second World War. The firemen of that period had, to quote former Chief Officer Cyril Demarne of the West Ham Brigade, 'packed a lifetime's experience into a matter of months'. Then, whole rows of warehouses and riverside properties were alight. Surrounding streets were rendered impassable by melting paint and tar, and even the most powerful jets of water were largely ineffectual against the massive conflagrations that developed. None of us present on that outside duty that morning would have envisaged that we would one day be returning to this selfsame structure, to a blaze that the television newscaster would describe as 'one of the largest fires to be experienced in London since the blitz'.

It had been a long-standing custom of the London Fire Brigade, especially on the 15-hour stretch of night duty, to have a mug of tea. This followed the six o'clock roll-call and the routine check of lockers and breathing apparatus. Unless we were called out, the evening meal was always scheduled for eight o'clock. The tea was a little hot liquid nourishment prior to commencing drills, technical lectures or going on outside duties such as hydrant inspections or topography.

Before running up the stairs to the mess room I had carefully checked the breathing apparatus set to which I had been assigned along with Sevvy Malt and John Lunsett. Along with Jim Breen the driver and Station Officer Jim Cronine, we made up the Pumps crew.

The 'Proto' oxygen breathing sets in use in London on all front-line pumping appliances up to the late 1970s were a world-renowned piece of equipment. Like the black melton fire tunics, shiny black boots, leggings and distinctive combed helmet, the set was synonymous with the press images of London's firemen, and had been so for many years.

'Proto' had been a loyal servant at countless numbers of fires and other emergencies. Although the set would eventually be phased out and replaced in total by compressed air equipment, the London fireman had a great confidence in it.

Even though the preceding shift may not have involved the use of BA, it was still the individual wearer's responsibility to carry out his routine checks. These included the amount of oxygen remaining in its cylinder, the satisfactory operation of a warning whistle (automatically sounded to remind the wearer that the oxygen supply was nearing exhaustion), and a general check.

Each of the three sets on the Pump and Pump Escape had their own plastic tally. On these, the wearer's rank, name and the cylinder pressure were appended in chinagraph pencil. Before entering an incident this tally was handed to the BA Control Officer who was located outside in fresh air.

These complex but vital procedures had arisen from a number of historic fires in which firemen had lost their lives. In 1949 at the then Covent Garden fruit, flower and vegetable market, a Station Officer had perished when he ran out of oxygen in a smoke-filled basement. Nine years later, at one of the most arduous and demanding subterranean fires ever handled by the Capital's fire-fighting force, two men, one of whom was a Station Officer, died when their supplies ran out whilst searching in extreme conditions of smoke and heat for the seat of a fire at Smithfield Meat Market in Clerkenwell.

These innovations, when coupled with a specially designed guide line, had greatly improved firefighter safety. As reassuring as all of these safety features were, the sense of apprehension and tension that existed at serious fires into which BA wearers were committed, could often be palpable. Little did we know as we informed the nominated watch room attendant of our BA numbers, which he annotated in the station logbook, that within this tour of duty such apprehension would arise.

That first gulp of the hot, tannin-brown, sugar-sweet 'Rosie Lee' had been barely swallowed when the urgent ring of the call bells reverberated across the mess room. Within 30 seconds both appliances were thundering, and blaring through the tall canyons of the city of London's near deserted streets. The cacophony of noise echoing back, and the slipstream of the two engines throwing up a discarded copy of the *Evening Standard* into the air. As we neared Tower Hill the unmistakable pungency of fire smoke stung our nostrils.

'Probably some bonfire set alight before tomorrow,' shouted Jim Breen as he tugged at the gear lever. It was the night before 5 November, and maybe, out in the residential suburbs Jim's surmise might have been correct.

'Bonfire around these parts, Jim? Don't be a plank,' retorted Sevvy Malt.

'Christ, if it is a bonfire, it's a bloody biggun, mate,' chipped in John Lunsett, 'look at the effing smoke!'

A heavy swirling fog was banking down to pavement level. In the 1950s and 1960s London was notorious for its pea soup fogs, which blanketed buildings, people and vehicles in their suffocating veil. This wasn't 1950 or 1960, and this wasn't a London fog in that sense. It was a fog though. A hot, pungent, rolling brown blanket whose texture was so closely woven that both Pumps were forced to brake, so reduced was the visibility.

And then, a breeze of night air, funnelled into a gust by its passage through a narrow alley, drew back the smoke curtain to reveal centre stage, with the majestic Tower of London in the wings, the selfsame warehouse we had visited only months before. But now, ominously, and with Jim Cronine's words about arsonists returning to our minds, huge inverted cones of thick dark smoke were racing out of windows on all visible sides and shooting rapidly towards the dark November sky.

The two appliances hadn't yet come to a halt when the radio's metallic voice sang out, '*Priority from Station Officer Sands – make Pumps ten, Turntable Ladders two*'.

'Fuck me, a straight ten – we've got a real goer here, boys,' shouted out Sevvy Malt, whose enthusiasm for 'make up' fires was a facet of the ex-policeman's keenness. This enthusiasm was not born out of any wish for anyone to suffer, but was instead the same sort of enthusiasm displayed by the military when they are being despatched to a trouble spot. There they will be able to at long last display all of the skills learned via hours of simulated exercises and drill evolutions, and feel the real adrenaline rush that springs from the raw reality of life, rather than the oft stale and repetitive routine of practice.

At many fires, the initial officer in charge, conscious of the numbers of appliances on the first attendance, will be conservative in their requests for extra appliances. Often the real extent of a fire is not evident on arrival, and a quick reconnaissance has to be made unless embarrassing situations are to arise by premature requests for additional appliances.

A straight 'make up' request, which at once calls for seven more Pumps plus an additional Turntable Ladder, is a sure indication that a potential conflagration is afoot. Especially when a man as seasoned as Biff Sands, a Station Officer of the old, grizzled, fire-forged and case-hardened steel of the London Fire Brigade of yore, is the one who initiated it.

He had spent the whole of his long service in and around the East End, progressing slowly from Fireman to Leading Fireman to Sub Officer and then to his present rank of Station Officer, which he had held for a decade. He had tackled and commanded hundreds of emergencies amongst the closely packed buildings and warehouses of East London. Like so many of his era, he would not initiate any 'make up' message lightly. He was of that breed that had such a pride and confidence in the competence of his men that every effort would be made to 'stop' fires without needing to call for reinforcements. It was an almost jealous guarding of his patch. 'Make up' fires always resulted in a supervisory officer coming on from divisional headquarters, a few of whom did not measure up to Biff Sands' strict criteria of being a 'good hand'. As a consequence 'make up' assistance messages were only sent after his developed instincts had left him in no doubts that without additional Pumps and men, the fire would 'get away'.

It was almost a form of management psychology. One in which, by convincing his men that they were the most efficient firefighters around, they would believe this and live up to it. Because these 'hard' officers were invariably natural leaders, every 'man jack' on the watch would invariably hold their Guvnor in the highest regard and respect him, being far more ready to please and support than to undermine by dissent and backchat.

When Biff Sands had enrolled, following his conscripted service in the army, there was none of the often pretentious management theories, jargon and philosophies of later years. There, in too many cases, style would take priority over substance. In later years style would all too often be perceived as more important than hard-won experience and its corollary of full competence and capability on the fireground. Burgeoning regulations on health and safety, and an altogether more gentle style of management, influenced by the politics of a rapidly changing society, would virtually outlaw the raw 'in your face' style of firemanship that was so often the fully accepted norm in Biff Sands' era.

Given this background, if Biff Sands had requested a further seven Pumps plus a second set of ladders within a half minute of arriving, there was every prospect that this blaze could become a conflagration. Such a prospect was becoming evident with each passing

195

minute. A glance at all of the warehouse windows over the whole frontage of the five-storey warehouse told its own story as the squawk of the radio confirmed Station Officer Sands' informative message

'From Station Officer Sands at ... General warehouse, five floors, approximately two hundred feet by two hundred feet, seventy-five per cent of all floors alight.'

From each of the square, prison-like windows, inverted cones of browny yellow smoke were funnelling upwards at a speed that suggested only one thing, arson! Just as our own Guvnor, Jim Cronine, had talked about back in February during our familiarisation visit. No matter how combustible the contents, fire would never be able to develop so rapidly, especially in a building like this, which was subject to the massive fire protection provisions of the London Building Acts already described. In fact it now seemed extremely likely that someone must have entered the warehouse over the weekend and carried out exactly what Jim Cronine had said could happen.

Station Officer Sands' men had already got two large-diameter jets to work, their silver streams playing into the windows in some effort to quell this fiery monster. Our own Station Officer was liaising with him, and as we awaited instructions, we looked up at the belching smoke and saw a ruddy glow moving in a veiled dance behind the dark curtain of smoke.

Barely visible, and initially only at first floor, the red glow, like that of a ring on an electric stove on its lowest setting, gradually began to appear at all floor levels. The redness then started to further increase, looking like the stove ring now turned up to its maximum temperature. Then, as if liberated from its smoky shackles, the vicious fire burst forth, turning the darkness of the November night into almost the light of day, and casting a vivid, shimmering reflection on the adjacent cold, black water of the river basin to the east.

'There goes the eggs, beans and chip supper,' quipped Sevvy Malt, secretly bubbling inside at having 'picked up' a blaze of this magnitude.

'You are not kidding, mate, and you can probably say cheerio to breakfast as well, looking at this bastard,' retorted John Lunsett, who had himself attended some of London's largest infernos in his 17-year service.

The duty ADO from Shoreditch Divisional Headquarters arrived, his white car screeching to a stop. He alighted hurriedly, flinging open the cavernous boot from where he lifted out his fire kit, into which he rigged, balancing precariously on one leg as he moved from shoe to boot.

He was a tall, youngish man, probably a decade younger than Biff Sands, towards whom he purposefully strode to get an appraisal. Not that it wasn't plainly visible to all as to the scale of the fire. It was the scale and size of the fire, measured in terms of the numbers of Pumps requested, which triggered a number of predetermined procedures at Control level.

As soon as an assistance message was received for eight or more Pumps, the Brigade Control at Lambeth on the Albert Embankment, mobilised the Brigade Control Unit and alerted the London Ambulance Service, in addition to notifying a number of senior officers attached to Brigade Headquarters.

The duty ADO knew that a 'make up' of ten Pumps plus the additional TL would see the duty DO from Shoreditch on scene, and, in view of the rapidly deteriorating conditions, knew that a further 'make up' message calling for a further five Pumps wouldn't be too many.

The ADO's 'make Pumps fifteen' was received just as the grizzled form of the duty DO arrived in his chauffeur-driven car. He finished off the cigarette, which was seldom out of his lips, quickly stubbing it out in the car's ashtray. He clambered out and temporarily placed both of his huge hands across the small of his back in which a bout of lumbago was giving him hell and shortening his already quick temper.

We had been instructed to lay out four large jets. With these we were to mount a 'from the street' attack into the burning warehouse windows in an attempt to lessen the searing waves of heat radiating from it. These were quite capable of igniting the office block adjacent even though this was a good 30 yards away. The terrific heat being generated by the rapid burning of such a huge fire was sending clouds of smoke and huge chunks of white-hot firebrands and embers hundreds of feet into the night sky. This was creating real concerns that some of these embers might set fire to one of the capital's most prized and historic monuments, the Tower of London only a few hundred feet away.

'Effing hell, if the Tower lights up, the Chief Officer will end up in there,' joked John Lunsett.

'Where will that put us then? We'll be bloody burnt at the stake,' chuckled Sevvy Malt, as, with me, leaning on to the hard canvas of the hose, he struggled to control the jet. This was working at over 75 pounds to the square inch pressure, in order to throw the solid white lance of water into the shimmering maw.

The fears for the Tower, and the many other commercial premises in the vicinity, was such that two of the reinforcing crews were detailed to slowly tour the surrounding streets. This was to look out for fires started by the showers of embers, whilst the security staff and guards within the Tower were alerted to carry out a similar task.

The DO, ADO and Station Officer Sands had by now done a 'reccy' of all accessible sides of the warehouse. It had become clear that the fire was involving a good half of the building at all levels, but that the fire doors might be still in the closed position in the rear portion. This suggested that there was the potential to make a bridgehead against the blaze at the landing levels at the head of each staircase. There BA crews would get large jets to work at these positions as soon as possible. Given the rapidly developing conflagration, and the manpower that would be needed to provide the water, and emergency standby BA teams, the DO sent a further message making the Pumps up to 25.

At all fires requiring 15 Pumps or more, the policy at that time was for a Principal Officer to be ordered on from Brigade Headquarters. The Assistant Chief Fire Officer (ACFO) was telephoned in his penthouse flat, which overlooked the Thames at Lambeth Bridge on the Albert Embankment. He looked out towards the illuminated face of Big Ben. He saw that it was ten minutes past seven, before taking the lift down to the appliance room where his staff driver was already revving the engine, anxious like all firemen to get to a major blaze.

The Assistant Chief took a long pull on his pipe as his driver sped across Westminster Bridge, and then turned right on to the Victoria Embankment. Over the city, he saw the huge, red, shimmering light illuminating the eastern sky. It looked for all the world like the scenes he had witnessed over 33 years ago as a young Fireman involved in fighting the tremendous fires caused by the blitz. It signalled another inferno that he was once more racing towards.

There were over twelve large jets playing into the windows now

198

from the ground plus the water from the monitors atop the two Turntable Ladders. These were sending a crashing deluge into the upper floors. Those monitors deliver hundreds of gallons a minute and their capacity for absorbing heat is tremendous. But there is a downside. The disadvantage is that not only does the Firefighter's main ammunition weigh over ten pounds for every gallon, but in these old warehouses the floors are supported by cast-iron columns. As Firefighters know, cast iron has tremendous strength in compression but it has a fatal weakness in that its tensile strength is low. The sudden cooling of a cast iron column by the water deluging in from jets and monitors can cause it to crack and collapse, leaving floors laden with heavy stocks of goods to be partially unsupported.

It then only needs the additional weight of thousands of litres of water to cause a sudden and massive structural collapse. It is for this reason that whenever fire crews have to enter a burning building for firefighting or rescue purposes, some jets, especially those on aerial appliances, are shut down.

Jim Cronine strode over after visiting the BCU (Brigade Control Unit). 'Right, listen in. BA men are to get rigged. Five teams are going in via the south west corner entrance. One team is going to each floor, but only in sequence. That is no one goes to a floor above, until the team below have got their jet on to the fire. At the bridgehead, any closed fire doors are to be carefully opened just enough to get a jet to work. If the fire is too fierce close the fire door and retreat – any questions?'

An identical briefing had been given by the Station Officers of the other four teams, and after others had taken over our jets, we went over to the Pump Escape and Pump to begin the tedious process of donning and starting up our old friend 'Proto'.

As I went through the start up procedure, taking the small personal head harness from under the inner shell of the helmet, which secured the mouthpiece to the face and head, I looked up at the massive inferno confronting us. I then glanced across at Sevvy Malt and John Lunsett. The brown rubber goggles pushed up on to their foreheads revealed a sense of apprehension in their eyes, an apprehension that I could feel in the pit of my stomach.

No matter how well trained a Firefighter is, no matter how experienced, one could never get away from the fact that we were heading into the unknown. Especially at the once-in-a-decade conflagrations like this into which we would soon be entering. And

199

placing our trust in the 30-pounds of breathing apparatus to safely see us through the heavy rolls of superheated smoke. Now almost viscous in its appearance, and with the searing heat of fire all around us.

On later reflection, I would wonder how many of my colleagues of those days had felt the nervousness born out of our knowledge of those earlier incidents at which Firemen and officers had perished, some of which have been mentioned earlier on in this account.

This apprehension could easily enter the thought process. We were only human, no matter how well drilled and experienced. But the thoughts had to be repressed. There was usually an ominous, sub-conscious, stomach churning, not dissimilar to the butterflies felt by the boxer before a fight. But, like the boxer, whose tension dissipates on the clang of the bell and changes from inertia into hard physical action, so too did the apprehension lessen as we commenced the tasks for which we were employed.

The BA entry point was set up and we handed in our tallies, and prepared to begin the hard graft of working the heavy charged hose lines up to each floor as instructed by Jim Cronine. No sooner had we taken the first steps towards the south west entry when a ripping, tearing crash rent the smoky atmosphere aside. A huge portion of the top three floors of the warehouse cracked open creating a huge split about twelve inches wide, narrowing to a few inches, thirty feet below. Angry tongues of white-hot flame blasted out as if from a gigantic blow lamp. Hearts leaped into mouths of all those positioned with their jets at the northern face of the warehouse where the huge fissure had occurred. We all froze, fearing the whole facade would collapse on to us.

'My God,' I thought, 'not another Cheapside.' (See Chapter 9)

'All crews withdraw, all crews withdraw,' came the urgent voice of the duty ADO through a loud hailer.

The ACFO from Lambeth had only just finished being appraised of the situation by the DO, and had just assumed command when the huge crack appeared.

Although the Fireman's primary duties are to save life and property, there was a time, even in those 'raw' years before health and safety law shackled decisions, when the safety of personnel became paramount. Especially when no occupants were reported to be inside a building. The Assistant Chief didn't have to think twice about giving the decision for all crews to be withdrawn. He had in his 30-plus years attended some of the largest fires ever seen in London. His instant command decision arose not only from his expertise, developed over those years, but also out of a genuine concern for the safety of crews now under his command. He had been present at too many harrowing visits to inform relatives of firemen killed at incidents. He had attended too many Brigade funerals that followed to be prepared to risk his men when no persons were inside. Above all, he knew that this was a conflagration. No different in size to those massive dockland fires of the 1940s, when the only recourse was to attack from the outside. The urgent order for withdrawal obviously meant that our own task of gaining entry to attempt to cut off the spread of fire was immediately aborted.

'Saved by the bleedin' bell there all right,' said Sevvy Malt, his speech no longer impeded by the mouthpiece as we closed down our BA sets and unrigged.

'Not half, mate, another few minutes and we'd have been inside. It don't bear thinking about, although it ain't collapsed yet,' said John Lunsett.

'No, but I bet it won't be long before it does,' Sevvy went on, as we carried our sets back to the Pump now surrounded by at least 15 others, and amidst a web of snaking hose lines.

Such was the concern of the officer in charge that the front portion of the warehouse would suddenly collapse that he had detailed officers to begin a retreat of those appliances parked closest to the weakened structure. This was no simple matter. The first couple of Pumps to arrive had set into the street hydrants straight away in their urgent need to get jets on to the blaze. The whole area of road and pavement behind them was a mass of charged hoses supplying the jets to quell this conflagration. But there was no option unless we wanted to see several front-line appliances crushed under tons of debris. The hydrants feeding these had to be shut down, along with the firefighting jets, and the disconnected hose dragged away to allow the Pumps to be reversed out of the path of the collapse, which was looking more imminent each minute as huge chunks of masonry crashed to the ground. Of course, the premature shutting down of these jets gave this massive blaze the chance to grow even bigger.

It took about ten minutes of heavy frantic effort before the Pumps could be reversed, and this wasn't a moment too soon. Very shortly afterwards, a massive section of wall and floors from the top down to the first floor broke off from the gaping canyon of a crack and hit the ground with a massive crump, throwing up a massive dust cloud to mingle with the smoke.

Virtually everything that Jim Cronine had talked about on that earlier visit to this warehouse appeared to have happened. The sprinklers must have been shut off, and all of the fire doors wedged for a fire to have spread to this size so quickly. Petrol had probably been liberally used and the speed with which those inverted cones of smoke had been shooting out of most windows, along with the ruddy glow on all floors on our arrival, pointed clearly to the use of such an accelerant. The intense heat produced by the use of petrol would have quickly ignited the tons of combustibles on each floor. With the absence of sprinklers and the wedging of fire doors in the open position, the superheated gases and smoke would have soon raised the internal temperatures to a level where everything combustible burst into flame.

Such terrific heat expands steel floor joists or burns through timber floors and the combined effects of this leads to structural collapse as walls are pushed out by the forces created from weakened floors loaded with heavy amounts of goods.

Because of the risks to surrounding buildings from flying burning embers and white-hot sparks, especially the Tower of London, and to those even closer premises from the scorching waves of radiated heat, massive amounts of heat-absorbing water had to be applied.

Now that any hopes of cutting off the internal fire spread had gone, all that could be done was to apply the greatest amount of water to protect these surrounding structures. Accordingly, the assistant chief requested a further ten Pumps, making this blaze one of the biggest attended since those long nights of the 1940s when 'all of London seemed to be alight'.

All our efforts now had to be concentrated on to getting the fire surrounded, and applying such a force and amount of water that the aforementioned risk to surrounding properties was reduced as soon as possible. Opposite the northern collapsed wall of the warehouse was an office block, and its flat-railed edge roof provided an ideal position from which firefighting jets could be positioned and directed.

The one hundred feet long general purpose lines were taken up on to the flat roof via the internal staircase, the keyholders having been alerted much earlier. They were anxiously praying that we would save their office block from the radiated heat, flying firebrands and embers falling from the sky. The GP lines were lowered down to the road and the uncharged large diameter hose and branch pipes were hauled up to the roof. Before the 'Water On' instruction was given to the Pump operators far below, each of the half-dozen or so jets were lashed to the stout steel tubes of the railing, which guarded the edge of the roof.

Such a lashing made the job of directing the powerful jets far less strenuous as the very heavy weight of charged two and three quarter inch diameter hose makes for heavy work. Especially when water is being pumped at the high pressures necessary to overcome the frictional resistance encountered by the water in ascending from the street. Plus throwing the jet the 60 or so feet on to the blazing warehouse opposite.

'That's a bloody good jet, fellas,' said Jim Cronine. He stood behind me as I directed it in a sweeping arc by moving the large branch pipe in its lashing. It was of little use to keep the jet stationary. The idea was to keep it slowly moving, thus knocking down flames and cooling down the heat over as wide an area as the lashing would allow. The fire was still of terrific proportions a good two hours after we had first arrived. But it only felt as if we had been there half an hour or so, such is the effect of the adrenaline, which pumps into the system at incidents of this magnitude.

Once the adrenaline begins to subside, and it seemed to do this in direct proportion to the stage which an emergency was at, a sudden lethargy could occur. It was at such times that Firemen had to dig into their physical and mental reserves, especially during fires being fought from the street, and particularly when it was becoming colder as the pre-bonfire night rolled slowly onwards. Details that go unnoticed during the frenetic activity of the first hours, become more and more evident and annoying as the initial excitement subsides and the night hours drag by. The barely noticed leak of water from a defective coupling washer on to the hands, wrists and arms can seem like a Chinese torture as the temperature falls over time.

The same water and spray-filled air that soaked the rear of our blue overalled legs, and which was not even felt during the first adrenaline-filled hour, slowly became evident. Soaking through with a cold that seemed to penetrate through to the bones.

The full-length yellow over-trousers were still some time ahead at that period in the Brigade, and our soaking was occasioned by the smart-looking black polished leggings. Smart-looking but extremely ineffective at keeping the back of the legs dry.

If there was one antidote to this somewhat miserable and wet state of affairs, it was the arrival of the canteen vans from Brigade Headquarters and from the Salvation Army respectively.

Suitably refreshed, we returned to our rooftop post. Some 25 plus jets and monitors were now attacking the blaze from all sides and from aerial appliances sited at strategic positions, and in due course the officer in charge sent the standard message '*Fire surrounded*'. I glanced at my luminous wrist watch and saw that it was just before eleven o'clock. We had been here from just after six thirty. As part of the initial attendance, we were due a relief soon.

Those Pump Escapes which could be relieved had already gone, including our own. They were still the principal life-saving appliance then, on account of the wheeled escape, and it was Brigade policy to always get those back to their stations ready for any other emergencies.

It was the officer in charge who made the orders for relief crews and appliances, and the wait to be relieved would depend on a number of factors. If there were other serious incidents going on across the capital in which large numbers of Pumps were attending, then being relieved could be a long wait because fire cover could not be denuded over large tracts of London.

At a fire of this magnitude, it would be many hours before the 'Stop' message could be transmitted. The potential dangers to adjacent high-risk properties, and to fire crews present from further structural collapses, meant that a proportion of the relief Pumps would need to have a Station Officer in charge for reasons of command, control and personnel safety.

Pumps satisfying this rank requirement might have to travel across London from as far afield as Feltham or Heston in the far west near Heathrow, and this could mean a long wait for some before finally returning to home stations.

Crews would need to be kept at this fire for some days. Their numbers gradually being reduced as the operations would change from quelling the still huge body of fire, right through to the damping down and cutting away stages, and with the district building surveyor on hand to advise what parts of the structure were unsafe. Our relief arrived at just after midnight, and so, some five and a half hours after we had driven into that hot, brown fog of smoke, we were able to leave the fireground.

The cold night air was still heavy with that unique odour of burning, but the massive volumes of water delivered from all vantage points had finally begun to tame this conflagration, and that dense smoke of earlier was no more. The ten o'clock TV news had reported the blaze as one of the biggest to have been seen in London since the blitz. As I looked over to the scene as the Pump headed back along Tower Hill, the comparison with that era, in which the London docklands took such punishment, was not entirely inappropriate.

The massive warehouse, which we had known at its best, now appeared like so many of those dockside buildings captured by wartime photographers. A once proud structure reduced to a shadow of what it had been earlier. But tonight, unlike then, no matter how hard we had worked to suppress the inferno, no matter how palpable had been our apprehension as we had prepared to take our BA-festooned forms inside the blazing building, we could not have begun to imagine the feelings and fears of our forebears of those nights. Nights where the dangers of firefighting were magnified so much by the terror that rained from the sky above. A terror created by a deadly screaming load, which could, and often did, obliterate so many, without regard for rank, age or gender.

Midnight had passed and it was now 5 November. 'Remember, remember, the fifth of November, with gunpowder, treason and plot.' The old familiar nursery rhyme came into my mind as the Pump slowly wended its way through the city streets, the strong smell of smoke still heavy over almost a mile from the blaze.

In another eighteen or so hours, the Brigade would begin its annual ritual of responding to those bonfires which had grown too large for neighbour comfort. We had seen enough flame tonight to ignite a million bonfires. The damage caused was immense, but the surrounding properties, especially the historic jewel of the Tower of London, had remained unscathed through the combined efforts of over 200 personnel and 40 appliances. It certainly was a night to remember.

Chapter Eighteen

Hook Ladders

History teaches us that what was the norm in one era can rapidly appear to be anachronistic, even an oddity, less than a generation later. The oxygen BA sets, so synonymous with the London Fire Brigade for many decades, had been replaced completely by compressed air apparatus by the mid 1980s. At about the same time the solid-wheeled escape ladder, in use in London for over a hundred years, was withdrawn as was the unique hook ladder. Both these ladders had become synonymous with the images of firefighting and rescue in the capital, and of the courage so often displayed in their use.

The public services had been subjected to a range of increasing financial stringencies. These fuelled the need to find the most cost-effective ways of meeting their statutory obligations, at the same time as ensuring that employees had adequate levels of personal protection mandated by health and safety law.

But as welcome as increased levels of personal protection were, the Firefighter's job, especially where human life is at stake, will always call for a level of courage and commitment and a willingness to face personal exposure, which few other occupations require. In any process of change, especially in a brigade with such a tradition of using time-tested methods of firefighting and rescue, it followed that those at the sharp end needed to be confident that any new equipment had to be as good, if not better, at doing its job than that which had preceded it. For it was, after all, the personnel on fire stations who would be called upon by day and night to use this equipment and place their faith in its capabilities.

Many of these changes took place around the early and mid 1980s. However, these changes were never clearly envisaged by the average

Fireman as depicted during the period of this account. The wheeled escape and the hook ladder had helped provide succour to the capital's citizens for many decades. Fire crews on the front line of the busiest inner-city stations had no reason, during the 1970s, to believe that their use would not have continued indefinitely.

Accordingly, any policy decisions to remove from front-line operational usage previously revered and time-tested equipment was often viewed by a fair proportion of the 'traditional' school with a professional concern, and in many cases no small amount of anger.

Nowhere was this more clearly illustrated for some than in the decision to withdraw the hook ladder from front-line operational use.

For many Firemen, the potential for the hook ladder to become unstable caused a good deal of nervous apprehension before drill training or fireground use. The fact that, in spite of these quite natural fears, men would still view with a real professional concern any proposal to withdraw the ladder, demonstrated the natural inclination of all those 'good hand' Firemen to place the fire safety of the public before their own necks.

The hook ladder had already been a part of the essential equipment of the Paris Fire Brigade for some time when a serious daytime fire broke out in 1902 at Queen Victoria Street in the city of London. Paris Firemen had found the lightweight hook ladder to be vital during rescues when fighting fires within the narrow congested streets, alleys and passages of the inner city. A city where, like London, there were many tall buildings where persons might be trapped on upper floors, and where conventional ladders could not access and reach.

It was because of the inability to position a wheeled escape, and reach upper floors, that nine young women perished high above the streets of London on that fateful afternoon. As would turn out to be the case in a number of multiple-life-loss fires in succeeding years of the century, the public and parliamentary clamour resulted in the introduction of measures designed to prevent or severely lessen the repetition of such disasters in the future.

In the same way that the fire safety legislation outlined in Chapter 16 grew out of the soil of earlier multiple-fire fatalities, the terrible events of 1902 led to the Brigade adopting the hook ladder, already in use across the English Channel, but adapted and modified to meet its own stringent requirements for effectiveness and efficiency.

HOOK LADDERS

The hook ladder was carried on all front-line pumping appliances as well as on the Turntable Ladders from its introduction in 1902 to its disbandment in the mid 1980s.

The ladder was a little over 13 feet in length (or height) and some 28 pounds in weight. It was constructed of ash with piano wire and steel rod strengthenings, and attached to a steel stanchion at the centre of the upper end was a serrated, toothed hook of some 30 inches, this culminating in a curved bill. When not in use the hook folded into the central stanchion to facilitate stowage and manoeuvrability.

All recruits to the London Fire Brigade had to become proficient in the use of the hook ladder by the end of their basic training. If they could not achieve this proficiency they could never become a Fireman within the capital. Although other fire brigades across the country had carried the hook ladder, and although there had been successful rescues carried out using them over the years in the provinces, the ladder was essentially something associated with the London Fire Brigade. Other than a basic confidence builder on recruit training courses, most brigades in the country had withdrawn the hook ladders from front-line use some 20 years before London finally withdrew it.

The ladder could be used on its own or in pairs. In the former, the ladder was hooked over the thick wooden sill of the drill tower's unglazed windows (something that differed totally from an actual building of course, where glass had to be broken and cleared before use in most cases).

The teeth on the underside of the hook bit into the timber and the weight of the user was transmitted back to the ladder by the user leaning back on outstretched arms along with a synchronisation of hands and feet, and this kept the ladder stable.

The points of most danger were during the entry and exit from a floor of the drill tower, when the ladder could capsize, and during the time when the ladder was unhooked from the sill and pushed up to the next floor, or lowered through the hands when descending.

To carry out a two-man drill with two ladders, the first man would wear a hook belt, a thick, stitched leather construction fitted with a large snap hook, similar to a rock climber's karabiner.

This was attached to a polished steel ring at the hook ladder's head, and by placing total trust in this belt, the wearer would take a half turn with the inner leg braced to help stabilise the ladder and the outer leg rigid in space.

The man below would push up the second ladder to the first man's outstretched arms, who would take it and from his precarious stance push the second ladder to the floor above. The first man would then pivot back to face the tower, unhook the belt and ascend to the next floor and continue in this way with the man below following until the required floor was reached.

Although the hook ladder drill was a potentially dangerous exercise, with some fatalities and serious injuries occurring during training, the time-tested method of instruction was of such a high level that compared with the thousands of drills completed, injuries were extremely low.

With the massive benefit of hindsight, it becomes increasingly clear that as well as being trained to competently use a piece of equipment, which might be the only means of gaining access to upper floors to save life, the ability to conquer the quite natural 'white knuckle' apprehension that arose for the majority during training was a source of inner pride and confidence.

The discipline over one's nerves and senses, which was necessary to apply when ascending the drill tower to its highest level, was a developer of courage *par excellence*. If one could master the hook ladder, and trust to its sway, every other ladder felt like a solid staircase.

'Sub, get the escape into the drill yard will you,' the loud voice of Ben Tuke boomed out on that early autumn evening, as the mess manager cleared up the now empty mugs of tea from the long formica-topped table.

Our watch comprised a mix of men whose ages ranged from as young as 19 to the mid-fifties. Such age discrepancies displayed themselves in the naturally differing attitudes and beliefs to be found amongst those of differing generations. But on the whole, it was good to have this diversity. The older element, schooled in the more stringent discipline of earlier times, acted as a ballast and counter-weight to the often impulsive and hot-headed behaviour of some of the younger men.

It was no easy task for Ben Tuke to balance the efficient running of his watch, in which he applied his philosophy of running a tight ship, with the oft repeated moans of some of the younger element that some of the neighbouring stations were run in a much more relaxed manner by their officers. Ben knew that a few of his Station Officer and Sub Officer counterparts on some of the surrounding stations were doing him no favours with their laid-back attitudes and lack of tightness. It was his confirmed view, however boring it might have seemed to an increasing number within the Brigade over the last few years, that as a public servant in one of the potentially most hazardous of occupations, the safety of the public and their property, along with the safety of the men under his command, was paramount.

Unfortunately, it only took one rotten apple in the barrel to taint the rest. Among most of Ben's peers, the consensus of opinion was with him, in that some pretty weak man managers had been placed in charge of some stations and watches.

When their 'weaknesses' were combined with a watch of 13 men, who gained a collective strength from their numbers, it wasn't too long before the tail was wagging the dog.

Ben was convinced that it was the exposure of some of the more impressionable younger elements of his shift to the sloppy standards witnessed in respect of a few of the adjacent stations, when they were on 'out duty' there, that was creating the undercurrent of unrest.

This unrest was manifesting itself in more than the usual moans and whines. All of which were a normal part of station banter, especially during a quiet period with few emergency calls. A grizzled old Divisional Officer had told Ben only a few months back that the busiest stations were usually the happiest in terms of morale and that most of the personnel problems in the Brigade occurred on the station, seldom, if ever on the fireground.

It had been an unusually quiet few months over the summer. Most serious fires, especially in the dwelling houses of the time, occurred in the winter months. Although the other watches had been quite active, his watch had been in the doldrums operationally. But Station Officer Tuke had been around too long and had been schooled too well in the thinking of the London Fireman to buckle to their dissension, to not know how to neatly 'draw things back into line'.

The fire service like the military and the police service had strong codes of discipline. After all, it would do little for the public's confidence if on being instructed, say, to carry a victim down a ladder at a burning building, the Fireman could refuse and there be no sanction available.

However, to men of the character of Ben Tuke, and there were far more like him in the Brigade than otherwise, the day he had to resort to the disciplinary regulations to handle his watch would be the day he would retire and take up his hobby of deep-sea fishing full-time! There was more than one story about the Ben Tukes and Jim Cronines of the Brigade (both huge men and handy with their fists should the need arise), having 'tamed' the more unruly, by a walk to the back of the drill tower!

He had already briefed Jim Roy, his burly second in command, of what he wanted out on drills, and to emphasise that this drill would be more frequent. The last session he had seen had given him cause for concern as to the efficiency and safety of his crews on this particular evolution. Safety of Firemen was not, of course, solely connected with the practical competence that results from regular drilling. There were other factors, and one of the most important was having a mind that was not overburdened with problems, especially those of a personal and emotional nature.

In the same way that a soldier when training with live ammunition has to be totally focused on the job in hand, so has the Firefighter. When external worries impinge on the normally clear thought processes, the risk to the safety of the individual and others increases. To not be constantly thinking what one was doing when engaged on hook ladder drills could end in death.

Sevvy Malt, the young man who had resigned from the Metropolitan Police to enrol with the Brigade, was in the middle of a personal crisis, which seemed to affect no small percentage of those who served or had served as police officers. During his seven years police service he had seen the personal relationships of several of his colleagues run into difficulties. At least five of those he had served with had gone through divorce or separation, and it seemed that those who served in the CID were particularly prone.

Sevvy had always wanted to be a detective, and at the first opportunity had applied to join the CID. Like the vast majority of those he worked with, he put in very long hours. He found that the business of detecting crime was a process that could become addictive, especially if one was of that fastidious temperament, allied to great tenacity, determination and high sense of right and wrong, which appeared to be the hallmark of the most successful crime busters.

There is usually a price to pay for anything that gives satisfaction, and Sevvy gained a sense of public service and job satisfaction from being a detective greater than he ever thought possible. Unfortunately the price he paid was that which those colleagues of his had paid, a breakdown in his marriage. Only married a couple of years, his young wife was unable to cope with the loneliness experienced as Sevvy worked sometimes more than 14 hours a day. On top of that he brought his work home with him, and the many frustrations felt when case leads collapsed or seemingly watertight cases failed in court were more often than not exorcised by his irritability and impatience.

By the time he had decided to try to salvage his marriage by resigning from the police and enrolling with the Brigade, his wife had started to see someone else and divorce was in the offing, even though this was the last thing Sevvy wanted.

Sevvy Malt had only confided his problems to me. He thought, seeing he was just out of his probation with the Brigade, that it would be best not to tell his officers in charge.

'Crews – crews fall, in' barked out Jim Roy to the ten men making up the combined crews of the Pump Escape and Pump that evening. 'Hook ladders, it's about time we did some as we are well down on our drill book quota. Who knows, in the wee small hours we might pick up another Hills Hotel.' This was a reference to a very serious West End hotel fire of a few years back, when the hook ladder had been used to great effect in the rescue of some trapped residents.

'Oh shit, not effing hook ladders, I hate the bleedin' things,' piped the thin tones of one of the main whingers of the watch.

'That's precisely why we need more drills with them,' retorted Jim Roy. 'The more you use them, the more your confidence returns, yeah? Anyway, we will be doing the two-man drill with the hook belt so let's get the standard tests done, fellas, on the ladders and belt, please – all right?'

Such was the importance of efficiency during incidents, and of crew safety, that some equipment had to be tested before drills, and the hook ladders and hook belt were two such items. In a few minutes we would be entrusting our lives to the strength of a leather and steel belt, and to the ash wood and steel parts of the hook ladder. All the while suspended precariously, many feet above the concrete of the drill ground. Very conscious that there was no safety line or net to protect you if a slip occurred.

Like the military system of drill, the fire service in basic recruit training uses the system in which members of a crew are 'numbered off' relative to the type of drill being carried out. Once on an operational station, it was down to the watch officers as to retaining the numbering off system. For men like our Guvnor, the Ben Tukes and Jim Cronines of that time, and there were plenty still around in the 1970s and 1980s, such semi-military training techniques satisfied that sense of regimentation and order, which was as natural to them as breathing. They knew that numbers on drills, not names, could be vital to safety. Not only did numbers remove personal sentiment, not only could an officer unfamiliar with men's names still call out instructions, but of greater importance was that there was no confusion in the response from men to safety commands. Life-saving instructions which might have to be shouted out in a split second to prevent a tragic accident from occurring.

'From the right in twos number,' barked out Sub Officer Roy. I was second in from Sevvy Malt who was on my right. I was therefore number two in the hook ladder drill to follow. 'Right first two – two-man, two-ladder drill with hook belt, scale the tower to the fifth floor – get to work!' barked out Sub Officer Roy. We marched to the drill tower on which the ladders hung.

As number one, Sevvy was wearing the hook belt; he had previously fitted it around his waist ensuring that the huge double prongs of the shiny steel buckle were fully engaged in their holes, and that the huge 'dog clip' was working freely and correctly.

No matter how talkative a squad of men had been, the effect on them of hook ladder drills was such that a hushed silence descended. No more was this so than when awaiting one's own effort and where we had to totally trust the belt, the ladders and the competence and nerves of oneself and one's opposite number to prevent a plunge into almost certain eternity. It was not the best sort of drill for men with their head full of pressing emotional problems. But then, at such times, one always hoped that your opposite number had the character to put such matters to one side, at least until the manoeuvre was safely completed.

With heart going like a trip hammer no doubt and with palms moist with the sweat of nervous apprehension, even fear, Sevvy ascended the thin ladder. The thump of his leather fireboot soles echoing through the rounds and down to the small toe plates at the ladder's foot, which held it away from the drill tower wall. Because it was only a relatively short time since Sevvy Malt had passed out of recruit training, the automatic sequence of coordinated movement of feet, hands and outstretched arms still had the polished gloss of a newly minted coin.

At the head of the ladder, and keeping one hand connected with it at all times, Sevvy's opposite arm encircled the ladder's horns. With the other hand the large snap hook on the waist belt was snapped on to the polished steel ring affixed to the central metal stanchion of the ladder. He now had to place all of his faith in the belt, steel clip and ladder ring, and do a half pivot, firstly calling out 'hooked' to signal to me below that he was hooked on and ready with outstretched arms to grasp the second ladder, which I would push up to him.

'Hooked', cried Sevvy, and made the 90 degree pivot. His inside leg braced on the ladder round and the other leg out in space, tensed and his arms outstretched horizontally in front. His whole future health now relied on a number of things. The barbed teeth on the billed hook, which bit into the wooden baulk of the sill. The steel 'dog clip'. The ladder's central steel-polished ring into which the clip was secured. The soundness of the wooden ladder itself. And his own physical and mental control and coordination in order to keep the hook ladder stable and vertical as it and he hung on the precarious perch.

Although the ladder weighed only some 28 pounds, it could and did feel much heavier. If not positively handled, the second ladder could 'take charge' and its weight lever you over and capsize the whole set up and cause a fatal plunge to the hard drill yard below.

How good that initial instruction had been, and how many recruits had steeled their nerves and muscles to master the hook ladder drills, which, if not achieved, meant that one's career in the London Fire Brigade would be over before it had hardly begun.

These thoughts briefly flashed across my mind as I looked up and watched the one-time copper and detective punch the ladder up, hand over hand, looking up to the next window-sill some ten feet above, before turning the ladder and hook at just the right time to engage its sharp teeth into the thick timber sill of the first floor. Before I could follow Sevvy, he had to transfer from the first ladder to the other, releasing the 'dog clip' of course before making the critical move.

Now for the critical bit, the transfer from the first ladder to the second. One of the points where past mishaps had occurred. He moved his right hand across to the waiting round of the second ladder. 'REST, NUMBER ONE!' shrieked Jim Roy, who was watching our every move as closely as an army sniper sights and locks on to his prey. Sevvy instinctively halted, awaiting his next instruction.

'Foot-hand, you clown, not hand-foot just yet – now carry on!' In spite of the excellence of basic instruction, his nerves had got the better of him, or his thoughts were not totally on the vital job in hand. Placing the right foot, which was nearest to the second ladder, across first helped stabilise the second ladder before transferring the full weight. Then, only then, could the hand on the same side move over. Then the left hand and foot followed in that order. Once in position the shout 'Climb when you are ready' was given.

I then climbed the first ladder to the first window and entered the opening after firstly leaning back on outstretched arms. Then, with one leg tight into the rounds to keep the ladder from capsizing, the other leg was cocked, up and over the timber sill. By jamming that inner thigh close up to the internal wall of the sill, I was secure and ready to repeat the sequence until the fifth floor was reached.

It was as Sevvy was making his 90-degree pivot, the hook ladder hung over the fourth floor sill, that disaster struck. He had shouted out 'hooked'. I looked up from my precarious perch, leg locked into the third-floor sill, high enough to smash my brains out, preparing to grasp my ladder and punch it up when something must have caused his normally tensed inside leg, braced on to the round, to slacken. Perhaps his thoughts had strayed into marital problem territory. Perhaps he didn't care what happened now that his personal life was in such a state. Perhaps he was merely tired, unfit, weakened by the hair-raising ascent. Whatever the cause, there was the sound of metal scraping on brick, as the toe plates that held the ladder from the wall moved across towards me slowly but surely. The stentorian shout of 'STILL!' followed by 'Number two, steady number one's ladder,' cracked out like a sniper's rifle shot, the same time time as Sevvy let out a 'Fucking hell, I'm coming off.'

I instinctively tightened my inner leg and grabbed the base of the moving ladder. That terrifying slide stopped. Sevvy was securely held by the clip and ring, but his ladder had moved from the vertical by a good foot. Only the barbed teeth gripping the wooden sill, the hooked bill and my hands were preventing a capsize and most likely fatal plunge to the drill yard where the other eight stared up, their faces as white as flour. Their subdued talk now silenced completely.

'Number one, do not move an inch. Number two, very slowly straighten number one's ladder,' barked out the Sub 50 feet below.

'Keep bloody still, Sevvy – I'll push the ladder straight now.' Slowly, very slowly the metal toe plates and the ladder were shoved back to the vertical.

Once straight, Jim Roy waited a second. As vital as it was to train on the hook ladder and carry out the drill evolution set, he sensed that it would be prudent to call it a day. Perhaps he sensed that Sevvy Malt had other things on his mind. He therefore gave the instruction: 'Don't proceed to the top floor. Descend when you are ready.'

'Eff this for a game of soldiers,' gasped Sevvy as we began the descent back to terra firma, where the rest of the watch, their turn still to come, looked from here like a row of toy soldiers. As we finally reached the ground and marched back to the lined-up watch, I noticed, as all who had participated regularly in hook ladder drills will have noticed, the extent to which even the most garrulous were quietened when required to scale the drill tower to its highest floors.

On this day, when, as I later discovered, Sevvy had indeed lost his concentration because of the emotional problems in his head, that collective silence was all the more deafening.

Sevvy was new to the Brigade, but his police background had honed his understanding of the old-fashioned tricks of man management psychology. 'Have you noticed how the older, experienced guvnors always concentrate on hook ladders when a few silly pillocks start getting bolshie?' he remarked. His face white and hands still trembling.

'Yeah, I sure have. But have you noticed how quiet they are now? And they will all be even quieter by the time they've been up and down. Talk about the death sentence focusing the mind. Next time keep your mind on the drill. You are lucky that Jim Roy is the "good hand" he is, and an ex-recruit instructor at Southwark, or you might not have been here now,' I remarked, inwardly relieved that this good man, with all his personal problems, had not come to grief.

On reflection, there was no doubt that as vital as the requirement to maintain safety and proficiency was when using the precarious, swaying hook ladder, the particular drill evolutions with this piece of equipment served also as a useful management tool. It was a calming dose of medicine, which relied upon the potion of fear to help retain watch harmony and order. With the massive benefit of hindsight, the Brigade hook ladders engendered a special sense of pride.

This was not a pride born out of the nostalgic sentiment of hindsight. Indeed many secretly feared the ladder. The studied silence when men scaled the higher reaches of the drill tower regularly confirmed that. It was, instead, a pride born out the sense of achievement. A special, unique satisfaction gained by entrusting one's life to this flimsy piece of equipment, and to having faith in the competence of one's opposite number on the drill. A drill that could be converted into reality at any time, when it would be brought into swift operation to save the lives of those trapped by fire and smoke, when all else had failed. As had been the sad case at that tragic city fire of 1902 following which the hook ladder was introduced and maintained in service for the greater part of the century saving many lives through those years.

Chapter Nineteen

Fire in the East

The capital had been a magnet to many from foreign shores for hundreds of years, and it was in the 'London in the East' that the majority of immigrants had found themselves. The East End, with its cheap accommodation and mean streets became, therefore, the new world for a large proportion of these immigrants. From as far back as 1690 when the first Huguenot settlers arrived, the area had witnessed huge influxes of displaced people from mainland Europe, Ireland and the Orient.

Between 1870 and 1914 some 120,000 Jews who had taken flight from the Russian pogroms came to London. As well as these, there were Chinese, Lascars, some Scandinavians and many hundreds of Irish, who left their potato-blighted land to seek new lives in North America and England. The buildings of the district often acted as witnesses to the transient nature of these incomers.

One particular building, situated at the corner of Fournier Street and Brick Lane, mirrored the successive periods of immigrant communities. This structure, first erected in 1743, had been a French Protestant church, a Methodist chapel, a synagogue and, following the arrival of the Bangladeshi community, one of a number of mosques built or converted in the area.

Within and around the same streets were the homes and workplaces of these people. The London Firemen who responded to so many fires and other emergencies over the long and noble history of the capital's Brigade were first-hand witnesses to those often raw and brutal dwelling and factory environments as they carried out their daily work of firefighting and rescue.

With immigrants come differing religions, cultures, associated rituals and festivals, which commemorate and strengthen belief systems and values. It was the variety and diversity of these that added a wider range of colours to the often grey and bleak streets of the East End. For the personnel crewing the local fire engines, the local population provided a rich vein of human interest, and, all too often, human drama. Dramas created by the eternal hazard of fire in both dwelling and workplace, in which this rich brew of humanity lived and toiled.

How many times had we crawled along the floor of long corridors? Our noses almost touching the greasy linoleum as we tried to inhale the little air remaining below the smoke that enveloped us, as we moved towards the orange glow of fire in a distant room of a tenement flat or workshop?

How many times had we to witness the ravages of fire and smoke on the human form before the processes of fire prevention and fire safety became so effective that such scenes would be substantially reduced?

In an ideal world, all buildings and their contents would be incapable of burning, and the hazards to persons from fire and smoke would disappear, along with the grief and pain that inevitably accompany the loss sustained. But absolute safety is an unrealistic goal in a world occupied by humans with all of our vagaries, weaknesses and personal ambitions. A world in which the majority tend to believe that fires only happen to others.

But fires, in essence, are caused by people. The more people that occupy an area, the greater the hazard from fire is likely to be. When the hazards posed by fire exist within communities in which the process of communication and education about those intrinsic hazards is made more difficult because of language and perception differences, then the task of those charged with attempting to maintain and enhance public safety from fire are magnified accordingly.

It has always been the case, whether we are talking about New York, San Francisco, Paris, London or any other great cosmopolitan city, that many immigrants will have little option but to be accommodated in areas of deprivation and inferior dwelling stock. These twin factors of poor communication and sub-standard accommodation can create a real breeding ground for serious, life-threatening fires. As experienced in those types of socially deprived districts such as New York's South Bronx in the 1970s and within some districts of inner and suburban London.

220

* * *

The traffic coming out of central London was even heavier than usual as I drove the 15 or so miles to start the night duty at six o'clock on that sharply cold early winter's evening. At least I was driving 'against the outgoing stream' of cars, vans, buses, the ever present London black cab and the motorbike despatch couriers who weaved in and out of the lanes with a thousand-cc-powered nonchalance between their leathery limbs.

Against the stream or not, the inward bound traffic still comprised nose to tail queues. When reduced to this snail's pace, I couldn't help thinking about a recent article in the *Evening Standard*, which said that London's average traffic speed in the rush hour was now less than that of a horse-drawn hansom cab at the turn of the century, about eight miles an hour.

The stop-start journey, exacerbated by the sets of traffic-lights, allowed me to look over to the fire-blackened building to my right abutting the Farringdon Road to the City. About 60 of us, riding on some 15 Pumps, had fought a rapidly developing blaze in an unoccupied six-storey building a few months back. More and more fires were being attended in buildings that were either up for sale or awaiting refurbishment, and an increasing number of incidents were being treated as arson. We were, in fact, beginning to experience something of what our New York City colleagues had been living with for a long time. This was the deliberately ignited blaze, started either for reasons of insurance fraud or to hasten the demolition of buildings that were obstructing the insatiable appetites of some involved with the development processes, which are such a huge aspect of inner-city life.

The street and building lights around me highlighted the inky, star-spangled sky, whose clarity heralded a sharp frost, following the bright sunshine and blue, clear sky of the day. The cold, thin air appeared to magnify the globe-headed lamps stretching out along the street as I made a series of 'back double' short cuts, which allowed me to make better progress towards the East End.

The huge sprawling bulk of the Smithfield Meat Market lay on my right, the internal illumination reflecting off of the blood-stained white smocks of the porters. Once again my mental library of epic London Fire Brigade incidents clicked in. I took in the iron-plated covers on the pavement, which led to the subterranean labyrinths under the market.

A Station Officer and one other Fireman perished under there back in 1958 in one of the most difficult fires the Brigade had been called to deal with in peacetime. They were victims of a choking, disorienting smoke. A smoke so thick that they lost their way, never to retrieve it before their life-sustaining oxygen expired. And before they could be located by colleagues, who, roped together to avoid further casualties, had given their all in attempting to save them.

Much progress had been made in terms of BA wearer safety procedures over the many years since that tragic fire in Clerkenwell. But a moment's reflection on such tragic events was bound to make one think of the potential for danger within one's daily work. It was not something that could be dwelled on for long. However, it was our Guvnor's belief that such a recall, stimulated by the sites of earlier incidents such as that at Smithfield, did have a part to play in preventing complacency.

Experience over time had clearly demonstrated to him that, in all spheres of hazard and human disaster, complacency, created by the lengthy periods devoid of incident, led to the erroneous and potentially fatal conclusion that safety was assured when, in fact, the exact opposite applied.

'What's on the menu tonight, Geoff?' I asked our inscrutable mess manager and chef. Like me, he was in the gear room cleaning off his gear, still grubby from the rubbish skip fire we had picked up just before the last of our day shifts ended some 24 hours earlier. 'Well,' he replied, 'provided that we get some peace tonight, you will all be feasting on a load of spiced chicken I got at an unrefusable price at the wholesale cash and carry place at the back of Rodley Road.'

'I hope that it's bleedin' safe, Geoff,' piped in Niall Pointer. 'Someone told me that place is known as "Salmonella Sid's"!'

'Don't worry, Niall, old son,' Geoff responded. 'When I've finished dousing it with my extra strong curry spice, there's no bug out that will live through that,' he half smiled.

Our watch had been unusually busy over the last few weeks. Fires and emergencies often come in phases, with one shift picking up most of the working incidents while the others remain relatively quiet. It was that busyness that had prompted Geoff's reply about our enjoyment of his supper depending on us having some peace

222

from what had seemed like a never ending series of turn out bells on both day and night shifts.

As it transpired, we were blessed on that evening with no more than a call for the Pump to a false alarm on the edge of Whitechapel. Geoff's spiced chicken plus lashings of mashed creamed potatoes had gone down a treat. Either the chicken was good and fresh or his pungent curry powder had sanitised the low cost poultry, because by midnight as men began to rest on their bunks or sit around the TV or mess table, no one had complained of any upset stomachs.

The pungent aroma of spices, curries and other exotic, often mouth-watering cooking smells had become an increasing feature of life in those parts of the inner East End. There, as we have already seen, a growing number of immigrants from the Indian subcontinent had begun to take up residence. A sure case of East meets East. As the earlier immigrants had prospered and moved into better districts, their places had been taken by others who followed them. Such streets as Brick Lane, previously the enclave and ghetto of earlier immigrant communities, were seeing the businesses and residential accommodation occupied by another culture. All of which added to the rich tapestry of cosmopolitan colour and bustle.

I had been a London Fireman a good number of years now. Like most who had served the largest parts of their service on the busiest inner-city stations, I had developed an ability to feel what was almost a premonition about the next serious fire. Perhaps it was no more than the subconscious mind working out that by the law of averages a station bang in the centre of some of the highest fire hazard locations in the country would be bound to pick up the out of the ordinary incident sooner or later. On top of any such perceptions was the fact that on this night, the temperature was a good few degrees below freezing. With that, the risk of fire in many residential properties would be likely to increase, especially where portable heaters were brought out to counter the bone-chilling harshness of the cold.

Medical experts testify that the normal human adult enters into their deepest sleep around four in the morning, and that at that period the body's natural rhythm is at its lowest ebb. It is, they say, the time at which the old and the very sick are more likely to die.

Fire experts will tell you also that it is when the body is so deep in sleep that the chances of never waking should a fire break out are at their highest as the suffocating smoke and poisonous gases fill a home with their hot, malevolent wreaths.

223

In later years, technological advances and mass publicity campaigns would see many homes fitted with low cost smoke alarms, whose piercing blasts, if not quite loud enough to wake the dead, would save many from entering that realm before their time.

Although automatic fire-alerting systems were commonplace in many commercial premises at the period in question, few, if any, domestic dwellings could boast of them. As a consequence calls to fires in houses, flats, tenements and hostels, especially in the deepest hours of the night, would be often received with a strange sense of foreboding, which somehow intensified the urgency of the response.

Although ADO Tom Monsal, in his small office-cum-rest-area at Shoreditch Divisional Headquarters, was provided with a bunk, identical to those in the dormitories of all London stations, he seldom slept. He preferred to catch up on his paperwork, or read a book, propped up on the iron-framed bed, his shoes on the floor being the only concession towards relaxing. He had put the novel he was reading down for a while to enjoy a cigarette and was lying back with the long filter tip between his fingers, slowly exhaling the strong smoke. Suddenly the black telephone on the small cabinet at his side startled him with its loud ring.

'Hello, Guvnor,' said the soft voice of the duty officer in the Mobilising Control room at Stratford. 'Just to give you early notification that we are receiving multiple calls to smoke issuing from a house somewhere near Whitechapel or Shoreditch, it was a garbled, frantic message, Guv.'

'Thanks for that, I'll switch on my listening post,' Tom Monsal replied quietly.

He glanced at the luminous watch hands and saw that it was just after 0420. He was feeling a little peckish and had been contemplating driving his staff car to one of his favourite all-night refreshment facilities, the 24-hour bagel shop at the top end of Brick Lane. He would often park the powerful two-litre white car near to the take-away cafe and treat himself to a couple of freshly baked bagels, stuffed with cream cheese, and, if he was feeling particularly deserving, some smoked salmon too. He would wash it down with a large polystyrene beaker of steaming sweet coffee while sitting in the car.

Even after over 30 years with the Brigade, the vast majority spent in the East End and its near environs, he had never tired of the endless sense of variety and anticipation that his work in this huge city provided. Often, he would sit sipping the coffee, never failing to be intrigued by the 'creatures of the night' who would still be about on the streets at the most ungodly hours.

He appreciated, of course, that, like himself, there were others whose employment required working through the early hours. The constant stream of black cab and minicab drivers, and the occasional policeman and woman, in and out of this particular all-night watering hole, testified to that. But it was the motivations and reasons why so many other folks were about that fascinated him. Not all of the women would be prostitutes, though perhaps many were. Some of the men around would be seeking the services of these 'women of the night'. But what about those who were not? What were they doing out in the grey streets at such an early hour? Perhaps some were returning from nightclubs and gambling dens, or were on their way to work? Perhaps an early start as a cleaner in the many offices within a mile or so of this area? Perhaps they were men and women with a mental illness? Possessed of a troubled mind to which rest and above all the healing balm of deep sleep would not come.

With the steam from the hot coffee condensing on the car's windscreen, he would wind down the window and catch the sweet, hot smells drifting out of the bagel bakery. He would peer out at the down-at-heel buildings all around him here in the heart of the East End.

He had likened his feelings for the place to that of a child for its favourite rag doll. A battered, pulled about, raggy object, but with an undefinable attraction and sense of affection, which was at once comforting and, at the same time, slightly perverse.

Such thoughts were mingled with a great sense of anticipation. Not quite a churning of the stomach, but, certainly a gentle tingling, which came from the very real awareness that you can never know what the next second might bring in terms of fire, calamity and human drama, even the loss of one's own life.

He only had to close his eyes to bring back the countless fires and emergencies he had been involved with in his long years on and around the busiest inner-city stations. With eyes shut, he could recall so many memories and images. He could see that pall of dark smoke rising above the East End buildings as the shiny red Pumps charged towards it, a blur of headlamps, spinning blue beacons and throaty roar of engine.

He could see the angry, billowing fire as a corner was turned. He could see the black on faded white street name plates – Commercial Street, Aldgate, Leman Street, Curtain Street, Rivington Street, Cannon Street Row, Bethnal Green Road, Shoreditch High Street . . .

He could recall the billowing clouds of heavy yellow smoke, banking down to the street, obliterating the yellow light of street lamps like an orange filter on a camera lens. He could hear the sounds of a burning building. The shattering of glass, the thumping crash of racks of goods collapsing in the inferno inside. The heavy crash as the slates and roof tiles plunged through burned away timbers to release the pent-up heat, smoke and pressure. He could recall the sight of how that pressure, in its newly found freedom, rose at a rapid pace to form swirling, roaring, crackling, spitting columns of flame and embers, like a million fireflies shooting towards the night sky.

He could smell that evocative tang of fire smoke. Still see the urgent movements of the men as they slung rolls of delivery hose along the highway. Lifted the lids of hydrants. Screwed in the standpipe with a rapid twisting of the hands and wrists. Racing to tap that life- and property-preserving water surging through a 24-inch main below the street.

He could see the snaking, thick, spaghetti-like coils of charged hose. Hear the lurching heave and crash as the 50-foot wheeled escape was slipped and pitched. Could see the black-helmeted Fireman, silhouetted in the lurid glow of flames, uncharged flat hose over the shoulder, briskly climbing a ladder to get a jet to work via a window three floors aloft the smoke-filled East End street. Could see the 'Proto' BA men standing with legs braced. Barrel-chested with the canvas breathing bags around their chests engorged with oxygen awaiting use. Rubber mouthpieces stuffed in. Pinching nose clips. Goggles pushed on to the forehead in that stomach-churning wait for instructions that would send them into an unknown deep basement filled with fire, great heat and deadly thick smoke, with no guarantee that they would return unscathed.

He could see an unconscious form, draped like a stole across the shoulders of a Fireman bringing them 40 feet down a ladder from a smoking top-floor window. The carrier's hands and feet moving in unison. Head looking down to ensure surefooted steps on ladder rounds made slippery with jet spray. Then the outstretched strong hands to relieve the weighty burden and place the victim gently to the ground.

All of those experiences, sights, sound and smells had amassed over time. First at Shoreditch as a Fireman, then a short move down the road when promoted to Leading Fireman. Sub Officer had taken a few years more, but in his day, becoming the 'good hand' needed time, patience and the gradual learning curve of experience. An experience constructed from the hot metal of those working fires poured into the mould of his mind and shaped gradually on the hot anvil of hundreds of fires. Fires in tenements. Fires in clothing factory sweatshops, fires in reproduction furniture factories. Dockside warehouses filled with rags, cardboard, paper, cloth and timber, and those so clearly recalled blazes where, in spite of all human effort, lives had been lost. Lives of men and women, young, middle-aged and old. Above all, the tragic deaths of young children, plucked from life and parents without the chance to say goodbye.

By the time he had attained the white helmet and single black rank mark of Station Officer, he could enter the sharpest of sharp end fire stations with the confidence that his reputation as a 'good hand' had preceded his arrival. All of those experiences were augmented by his five full years commanding a watch within the very district in which he now sat, but now his shoulders carried the rank markings of ADO, and the heavier command responsibilities that came with the post. He had held this rank for ten years now, throughout one of the Brigade's most busy periods for fires. In spite of his extensive experiences, or, perhaps because of them, he was just as charged by that silent tension of the unexpected now as he had been all those years ago.

This anticipation was heightened by the quiet squawk of the Brigade-wide radio system. A Priority Assistance '*Make Pumps four*' in Brixton across the river in south London. A '*Smell of burning, search of area being made*' in Belsize Park. A '*Sprinkler gong actuating, no sign of fire, search of premises being made*' from appliances in Oxford Street. All of these and more echoed across the airwaves from these diverse locations within this mighty metropolis.

The black bedside telephone began its urgent ring. A shrill tone, which sent a shiver up Tom Monsal's spine like some portent of foreboding, only a second or so after he had intercepted the breathless voice from appliances requesting assistance via the '*Make Pumps four – persons reported*' message, not too far from those mean streets where his crews had rescued those down and outs in the past.

The Pump Escape and Pump had arrived on scene within a few minutes of the call out bells starting their urgent clamour. Just in time to witness the horrific sight of a person, their clothing alight from head to foot, plummeting from a third-floor window to lie impaled on the spear-like iron railings below. Their still burning form hanging like a rag doll over the entrance to the basement flat.

The blazing house was almost identical in size and construction to that in which Andy Carlisle and Jim Pile had rescued the two women and young boy, on a similar freezing night in the past.

'We have got a right fucking goer here, boys,' shouted Bert Braxton, and he ought to have known, with his solid and lengthy East End pedigree.

The Station Officer had detailed me and Sevvy Malt to check out the situation at the rear. The sight that met our eyes almost froze us to the ground. High up on the steeply pitched, slated roof, we could make out at least three people clinging to the ridge plate. They were clad in the long gown so familiar now in this Asian-occupied ghetto. Seemingly, they had somehow climbed out of the burning house up on to the roof to escape the billowing flames and smoke issuing from all the windows on the upper two floors.

'We will need to get up there to calm them down else there's going to be others ending up impaled on those street railings,' I blurted out to Sevvy.

'Yes, mate, but how do you propose we get up there with all of that fire issuing from the rear, and probably the street side as well by now?' he replied.

'Hook ladder, mate, and the Dewhurst pitched to that second-floor window on the gable end wall,' I responded, my eyes having at that moment spotted the six-feet-wide window on the end wall, which was at right angles to the frightening flames and gushing brown smoke emanating from the front and rear of this Victorian structure. I knew that the 50-foot wheeled escape ladder would reach up to the roof from the gable end. But this had already been pitched and a covering jet got to work on the front of the house, and there would likely be a delay before a second escape ladder arrived.

From high above the street, the wails and cries from those trapped mingled with the drone of the diesel engines pumping water into the couple of jets already at work. In the distance the staccato burst of bell and urgent rise and fall of two-tone horn heralded the rapidly nearing reinforcing Pumps.

As I shot back to the front of the house to appraise our Guvnor of the situation, and of what we were going to do to try to reach those stranded high above this deadly fire, the radio echoed a message:

'Received from Station Officer Tuke ... house of four floors and basement, twenty-five feet by fifty feet. Fifty per cent of basement, fifty per cent of ground floor, seventy-five per cent of first floor and whole of second floor alight. Unknown number of persons involved, building being searched by BA crews. Escape in use. One person jumped from upper level before arrival of Brigade, injured, awaiting removal.'

I breathlessly informed Ben Tuke of the situation involving the three persons up on the roof and of the action to be taken. 'Right, do that, and take one other to assist you and Sevvy pitch the Dewhurst. Try to get 'em all secure as possible until we can knock this bastard down, and for God's sake mind how you go.'

Tom Monsal was in his car in a flash. Long experience in these parts had given him an uncanny sixth sense about incidents and he felt a strange sense of unease that this fire was somehow going to be a bad one. His feelings were confirmed as the informative message from Ben Tuke crackled over the car radio. He subconsciously pressed the accelerator a little harder as he hurried through the mostly empty streets to the fire scene, the single blue beacon on the roof of the white staff car striking the surrounding walls and windows with its lightning flashes of electric blue.

He manoeuvred the large saloon behind the control van from Shoreditch Divisional Headquarters. He opened the boot, quickly got into his fire kit, pressing his battered helmet on to his balding crown. He pressed the stud on the strap under his chin with a click and sought out Station Officer Tuke. On his way he paused to enquire after the unfortunate man whose badly burned body was impaled on the railings, and who was being supported by two firemen anxiously awaiting the ambulance's arrival.

The Dewhurst ladder could easily be slipped and pitched by three men and we soon had it at not too steep an angle up to the window from where Sevvy was going to get on to the roof using a hook ladder.

With a rescue line over his back, rucksack-like in its container, he ascended to a position close enough to smash out the sash window.

'Stand from under,' this being the fire service's standard warning to those below that something is on its way down, as with his axe he broke the lower window glazing and then the wooden frame. With sweat running hard from his contorted exertions, he managed to get from the Dewhurst astride the window-sill, at which point I brought up the hook ladder. We reasoned that the ladder should hang from the small flat top of a parapet wall, which rose above the ridge plates. Sevvy, casting all thoughts of plummeting to the ground to one side, slowly pushed the ladder upwards before turning it to hang on the small wall. 'Thank God that we trained hard on hook ladders,' I thought, looking up to Sevvy.

Very gingerly, he put his weight on the ladder. It seemed to be holding. It was now or never, I thought, and almost as if to confirm this crucial decision, the cries and wails of those trapped on the roof rent the smoke-laden night once more.

Slowly transferring his weight, he ascended the slightly swaying ladder. He placed all his faith in the barbed teeth and bill somehow holding on to the brickwork, which, for all anyone knew, might have been in a structurally weakened state. At last, after a heart-pounding few minutes, he was close enough to grasp the brickwork of the parapet wall. He slowly inched up and over and on to the roof, from which some nasty looking yellow smoke was percolating through defective mortar joints and slates.

'What have you got, Ben?' asked ADO Tom Monsal, after locating the burly Station Officer halfway up the first-floor landing. Ben Tuke was of that old school who seldom asked his troops to go somewhere he wouldn't venture himself, hence his present location in the smoke and fierce heat of this fire fight.

'It's a bad one, Guv, I think that the place is crammed with a couple of Asian families. Just before you got here I was told that there are three trapped up on the roof. We've also had a jumper who's impaled on the railings,' he replied, his eyes glinting in the dim light of his box lamp, which cut a beam through the thick, acrid smoke.

'Yeah, it don't look good, mate, does it? What with that job near here not long back when we lost a few, I've had a gut feeling ever since Control told me about the multiple calls received.'

Tom Monsal turned to Staff Sub Officer George Marross, who

was in charge of the Command Unit automatically sent on to all 'make up' incidents, and who was at his side, clipboard and pencil in hand. 'Sub, send from me at this address a priority message – *Make Pumps six, one to be an escape, plus Turntable Ladder required.*' The short, burly Sub Officer scuttled off to transmit the message, which would bring on two extra Pumps, one of which would be another 50-foot escape ladder as well as the 100-foot Turntable Ladder.

'We'll be on the safe side, Ben, with these extras in case we have difficulties getting those off the roof.'

'Got it, Guv,' replied Ben Tuke as he stepped back into the smoke-filled hallway where two men were working a jet into the inferno on the ground floor.

Sevvy was now on the roof, his appearance causing both fear and salvation for the Asians clinging to the ridge plate or the side of a crumbling chimney-stack.

'English, does anyone speak English?' shouted Sevvy. A wrinkle-faced man, whose features reminded one of those soldiers on the sentry posts near the Khyber Pass, and was clinging on to the chimney-stack, answered in the affirmative. 'Right, listen closely please, and then tell the others what I have said,' coughed Sevvy, as a thick cloud of smoke and heat enveloped him. 'Tell them that they must try to keep as calm as they can. That the Brigade will get them down and that the fire in the house will soon be extinguished, and to hold tight on to the roof.'

Noting the speed and colour of the smoke percolating through the slates, he knew that there was terrific heat and pressure at the highest levels of the building. He knew that the roof on which they were all so precariously perched might be on the verge of collapse, but he also knew that the last thing he wanted was for them to realise this as it could lead to them all leaping off. 'How did you get up here?' shouted Sevvy to the man who spoke English.

'There is a small window in the attic roof through which we squeezed to escape the fire. It is the other side of the chimney,' he replied.

Sevvy could now see that behind the Asian a cloud of smoke was billowing out from this skylight, but the heat and conditions in there would be such that escape was impossible. He therefore decided to edge across the ridge to the chimney to secure the rescue line to the

231

chimney-stack. Then feed it to the three men clinging to the roof, to assist their security in this precarious position.

Slowly, he edged across and was able to grab the soot-blackened stack, pull himself up and carefully pull out the rescue line from its canvas bucket-like container. He made a running bowline knot and dropped the large loop over the stack and pulled it taught, then fed the line out and instructed them to take a hold with one hand whilst keeping their other grasping the ridge plates.

It seemed an eternity since he had reached the roof, but it was no more than ten or fifteen minutes and shortly the blare of two-tones and the staccato clamour of bells could be heard as the additional appliances approached. I had got the searchlight down from the escape and the powerful silver shaft of light suddenly illuminated the roof, its white beam reflecting against the still swirling clouds of smoke at roof level.

'Hang in there, there's another escape en route,' I shouted to Sevvy, some 40 odd feet above the ground, and I knew that, provided the roof didn't collapse, they ought to get off their deadly precarious perch in one piece after all.

In the meantime Ben Tuke and Tom Monsal had ensured that three BA teams were now totally committed to the searching and fire-suppressing operations. The intense heat of what appeared to be a suspicious fire indicated the use of accelerants, but the large diameter hose lines, although unwieldy and fiendishly heavy to manoeuvre, soon began to absorb this great heat in the volume of water delivered.

Tom Monsal had felt his strange foreboding about this fire from the outset, and I had felt my own premonition that we were in for a nasty job. Neither of us would be proven to be wrong as the incident unfolded.

High on the steep slopes of the roof, the precariousness of which was not helped by the freezing cold of the early hours, Sevvy managed to get all three holding the secured line, but it was a great relief to hear that the second escape ladder was being pitched. In a matter of seconds the helmeted head of Toby Belchering from Islington appeared above the parapet.

'Get 'em all to hold hands in line and link up to you. We'll take 'em on to the head of the escape one by one, but nice and easy, buddy, just nice and easy.'

Miraculously, and within ten minutes of the escape being pitched, we had managed to get all of the long-suffering Asian men down on the ground where each bowed down and kissed the freezing cold of the hard pavement where we could all have ended if things had taken a less fortunate turn.

The unfortunate man impaled on the railings had been certified dead on scene by a doctor from the Royal London Hospital, and crews had just finished extricating him as Sevvy and I got back to the front of the building where Ben Tuke, Tom Monsal and the duty Divisional Officer were standing in conversation, looking up at the building from which smoke was still issuing.

Seeing us, Ben excused himself and came across. 'You guys did a great job up there and if I've any say in it, it won't go unrecognised, but there's still a lot to be done. The main body of fire is knocked down but the BA crews took quite a hammering in the heat. There's still a number of persons unaccounted for so I want you two to assist with the searching. It's still bloody red-hot inside but it's breathable without BA so get to it, fellas, but don't disturb anything unduly because going by how well this fire was going, it may well have been deliberately ignited.'

The BA wearers had located four persons, two men and two women, unconscious in a rear room on the first floor, and had carried them down to the street and to the several ambulances that had been mobilised to this fire. It had been terrifically hot and extremely smoke-logged inside the house, and it looked as if it might be touch and go as to whether the rescued would survive.

The heat was still at a high level when we entered. It increased as we ascended the charred and blackened stairways. On those stairs and landings piles of spalled ceiling and wall plaster had amassed as a consequence of the fire's effect on the structure, along with the demolishing effect of the water jets on walls and ceilings.

It had been discovered that the four-storey Victorian house was occupied by three Bangladeshi families who were involved with a clothing business in the area, and that as many as twelve relatives occupied the property.

We had been successful in taking three from the roof, and along with the deceased male who had died on the street railings and the four rescued by the BA teams it was possible that a further four or five persons were still unaccounted for.

It was possible to work without the protection of BA, but only just. The main body of fire and smoke had ventilated earlier. But there was still a lot of smoke present from the still flaming and smouldering timber stairs, timber doors and skirting boards. Mingled with these pungent fumes there was that unique odour, which comes from only one source: the sweet, sickly smell of burned human flesh.

Given the extremely punishing and deteriorating conditions present in the initial stages of this inferno, the BA men had done an excellent job in locating and bringing out the four persons so rapidly.

They would have worked almost totally by touch as the smoke was so dense that seeing was virtually impossible. That almost impenetrable blanket of superheated smoke would have hidden the sad sight of the two badly burned bodies, which we located on the second-floor landing, half buried under collapsed ceiling debris.

Sevvy went straight down to inform the Guvnor that we had found two bodies on the second-floor landing, apparently dead, while my eyes took in yet again that hideous sight of charred human remains.

ADO Tom Monsal gave instructions for a further informative message to be transmitted, setting out the details of the latest casualties to be located, and then made his way up the stairs with Ben Tuke to witness the scene himself.

'Leave everything as it is, fellas, the Brigade photographer is on his way to record the scene, and I will need statements from whoever first located these two unfortunates,' said the ADO. 'Push on now up to the other floors as quick as you can,' he went on. 'I hope I'm wrong, but if there is anyone still inside I don't hold out much hope for them, I'm afraid, given the ferocity of this fire.'

It was only after we had forced open a heavy panelled door adjacent to the head of the stairs at the third floor, the highest and hottest point of the fire, that we wished the ADO had been wrong.

Inside what had been a small bedroom of about ten by twelve feet, with walls that were blackened by the fire's smoke, but with little evidence of direct burning, there was a double bed positioned underneath a sash window. Lying on her back was the lifeless form of a woman whose face had that high-cheekboned beauty so prevalent in those of her race. Her long black hair lay on the smoke-stained pillow, and from her left nostril a gossamer sphere of mucus had formed, which may have been the end product of the last breath she ever took.

As I took in the scene through the remnants of smoke, my gaze lowered down the crumpled sooty sheets of the bed and froze on an image that will be forever etched on my mind. Kneeling on the bedroom floor were two small girls, their frail arms encircling their Mother's thighs, and their Mother's right arm holding them both as if protecting and comforting from the horror that had befallen them. Other than a slight smoke-blackening of their natural dusky skin, their lifeless forms were undamaged. I could, at that precise moment, only consider that the heavy door had protected them from the worst heat, and that they had been asphyxiated by the smoke.

All of the experience in the world can never completely case-harden Firefighters against the loss of human life. Such feelings are intensified whenever children perish as was the case on that fateful early morning. No matter how effective the conscious mind might be at suppressing the unpleasant, there remains within the deepest subconscious a file of images that can resurface in future dreams or reflections. That particular image remains as clear in my mind today as it was on that icily cold morning in East London.

Thankfully, such sad scenes were far outnumbered by those many incidents where lives were saved. But perhaps it is the vividness of such sights, and the irreversible finality of death, which they so starkly illustrate, that creates a mental bedrock from which flows a powerful current of human tenacity and unwavering resolve. A strong current, which pulls Firefighters ever forward and onward in their unceasing vigil and unquestioning response when protecting communities from the danger of fire and other emergencies.

For my own part, and on reflection, I feel privileged to have been part of that vigil. A vigil both by day and by the long watches of the night within the capital in general, but within the East End in particular. For it was there, in that diverse, colourful, cosmopolitan environment, amidst the honest banter, warm camaraderie and silent tension, that my fellow firemen and I were able to gain such a fulsome experience of human life for so long.

Epilogue

When the news began to break of a very serious rush hour incident within the Underground rail network, deep below London's streets, on the morning of 7 July 2005, my thoughts flashed back 30 years.

Despite the passing of three decades, the memories and images of another morning during which death and terror descended on the city's underbelly, and on the Underground's rush hour passengers, remain deeply etched in my mind.

Some of those memories of the dreadful disaster at Moorgate on 28 February 1975 have been told in the preceding chapters. The clarity of my memory in relation to that incident bears testimony to the deep and lasting impressions that such fortunately rare occurrences can make upon the mind of both rescuer and rescued.

As clarity eventually emerged from the confused reports of what exactly had happened on 7 July, anyone who had been on the front line at Moorgate three decades earlier will have had their own memories triggered into a clear focus.

Similarly, on 11 September 2001, when the CNN breaking news flashed those unbelievable images of the heavily smoking Twin Towers in south Manhattan, my mind had returned at once to those memorable days spent with some of 'New York's Bravest' as the firefighters of that city have long been labelled. It had been my tremendous good fortune then to have been a guest of the Fire Department of New York.

The experience of riding out with Engine Company 82 and Ladder Company 31 in that ethnic melting-pot of the south Bronx, during the busiest periods for emergency responses ever experienced anywhere, has remained crystal clear in my memory.

The irrepressible spirit of New York's firefighters, their raw

237

courage and deep humanity, as illustrated in the citations read out during the annual gallantry medal presentation day, mark these people out as being special in a world where respect and consideration for others appear increasingly scarce.

Anyone who has spent a decent amount of time on a busy New York fire house cannot fail to notice their joking banter and the unadulterated pride and passion they hold for their daily work in protecting lives and properties within the city that never sleeps.

I found it difficult to believe, therefore, that more than 300 of these special characters were reported missing following the collapse of the Twin Towers, and that some of those who had made me so welcome during my memorable visit may well have been amongst those who had perished.

Those who were present in the carnage of Moorgate or at the terrible life-taking inferno of King's Cross in 1987 would have had a close empathy with the crew members who responded on 11 September 2001 and 7 July 2005.

When fire and rescue workers step into locations of such hazard that those fortunate to survive are fleeing from it in terror, they experience a strange amalgam of feeling: a stomach-churning apprehension mixed with a strong sense of disciplined resolve, drive and steely determination.

Such emotions are the by-product of experience, augmented by the conditioned response arising from rigorous training, and Firefighters need to draw on them when stepping into the unknown to help others.

In the 30 years since the Moorgate disaster, the London Fire Brigade, along with the rest of the UK service, has witnessed much change. The men and women within its ranks today benefit from levels of personal protection, improved communications and a range of other technological and system advancements that were not even on the drawing board three decades back.

Since the mid 1970s health and safety legislation has played no small part in the way in which fires are fought, and there are more than a few who believe that it has placed too firm a shackle on the time-proven and tested tactics of fire and rescue operations.

As has been seen, traditionally first attendance crews would 'get in' to a fire quickly, often without the protection of breathing apparatus and 'eat smoke'. This to effect a rescue or to knock down a small blaze to prevent it becoming an inferno, and examples of this raw and punishing approach have been recounted within this book.

238

If this wasn't done, the fire could take charge and not only destroy property, not only pollute the environment unnecessarily with toxic products, but place Firefighters at a greater overall risk from structural collapse and flashovers.

The developments in breathing apparatus and the provision of a set for all crew members has meant that smoke eating, which no doubt contributed to the early deaths of far too many, has become a thing of the past.

However, there were more than a few of the old 'fire dogs' who questioned the stringent application of health and safety laws to every facet of an occupation where personal risk has to be accepted if lives and properties are to be saved or damage limited.

However, the gradual development of a litigious society and a compensation seeking culture began to see the raw tactics of earlier years outlawed and what had rightly been an institutionalised sense of urgency diluted.

Increasingly the larger fires are now fought 'from the street', something that some of the old 'firedog' stalwarts of earlier years would have termed 'washing windows', rather than by that vital early penetration deep into a building. Indeed such has been the growth of health and safety that even the traditional sliding pole is under serious threat. This device, which for decades has played a noble part in saving those vital seconds when life is at stake by allowing crews to rapidly access appliances, rather than waste time and risk a nasty fall by racing down stairs, is increasingly becoming outlawed in spite of the fact that in over a hundred years only a minute number of casualties resulted from its use. And of course it is not always possible to site crew quarters at ground level next to the emergency appliances.

So, a great deal of change has taken place since the earliest accounts within this book were recorded. These changes have included a noticeable shift in most quarters, away from the militaristic, authoritarian approach. This 'direct' style of safety management, which has for decades been battleground tested within fields of conflict by our armed forces, and which better ensures personal safety in times of crisis and conflict, has been in most cases replaced by one in which a 'lighter touch' has become the order of the day and reflects a society in which firm instructions, delivered for altruistic reasons, are wrongly perceived as 'bullying' or 'harassment' in the eyes of some.

By the early 1980s, the wheeled escape, for decades the mainstay of London's front-line rescue ladders, had been replaced by the 13.5-metre alloy extension ladder. The lack of 'solidity' of the latter compared to its predecessor, was compensated by its ability to be carried to locations previously inaccessible to the much revered 'escape'. As we observed in Chapter 18, the London fireman's love/hate relationship with the hook ladder also ended in the early 1980s. There, a combination of maintenance issues, health and safety during training concerns and a reduction in non-domestic fire casualties as a consequence of the Brigade's effective policing of fire safety legislation, helped sound its death knell. Additionally, health and safety at work concerns have seen 'live' carry down drills (which required personnel to both carry a colleague down a ladder using the classic fireman's lift and also be carried down themselves, so as to be able to empathise with the feelings of a rescued person) become effectively outlawed. This vital operational rescue manoeuvre, which has been performed for years in thousands of drills with very few casualties, and which has been replicated in the saving of many lives in the harsh reality of fire and rescue work, was replaced by the use of an articulated joint dummy, which was itself secured into a safety harness.

Few, if any, of the characters around during the earlier periods of these accounts could have foreseen that within a decade or so women would be able to enter the male-dominated world of the front-line operational fire station. By the early 1980s, and as a consequence of laws relating to equality of opportunity and sexual discrimination, women were rightly able to enter the service and serve alongside male colleagues, and a few have progressed to the higher echelons of management. In the last decade of the millennium, the first female firefighter peacetime fatality occurred when a young woman, working side by side with colleagues, was caught by a flashover, which occurred during firefighting operations within a fire in a commercial premises in a provincial brigade.

In 2004, the National Fire Service discipline regulations, which reflected the extremely high standards required of personnel engaged in such a potentially hazardous occupation, and which resemble those employed in the uniformed military and police service, were repealed, to be replaced by the procedures, hearings and tribunals used within conventional industrial and commercial non-emergency organisations.

The national fire service practical and written promotion examinations, without which promotion to higher substantive ranks could not be achieved, and which were touched upon in Chapter 11, were disbanded in 2006. The earlier system by which a junior officer (who had passed the comprehensive technical written papers but had still to gain a wide practical experience) could at least call upon the time- and incident-tested theory to better carry out their command duties was replaced by a national scheme called the Integrated Personal Development System (IPDS). In this system, instead of a qualifying examination, an individual's career progression and competencies are scheduled to be personally tailored and monitored on the basis of performance and personal and psychological appraisal testing mechanisms. At about the same time as the introduction of IPDS, the traditional eleven ranks from firefighter to chief fire officer were removed and replaced by seven 'roles', with the term 'manager' introduced instead of that of 'officer'. The national Appointment and Promotion Regulations, by which a man or woman could enter the service as a raw recruit and attain the highest position, were also altered at this same time and the doors were opened for persons from without the fire service to directly enter and compete for the highest command positions against those staff who had entered by the traditional route.

In 2004, all UK fire authorities were required to produce what are termed Integrated Risk Management Plans. In essence, these exist to form a template by which individual fire and rescue services can best rationalise finite resources, and help focus on the highest life risk locations. One consequence of this is that the traditional dispatching of a multiple appliance attendance to known high risk non-domestic premises has been diluted in many quarters in order to produce a greater response to domestic fires in which most fire casualties occur. Such rationalisations have taken place alongside massive changes to fire safety legislation. As was touched upon in Chapter 16, it was the diligently applied fire safety expertise in effectively policing the fire authorities' prescribed requirements of the 1971 Fire Precautions Act that saw fire deaths in many non-domestic premises substantially reduced between 1971 and 2006.

In 2006 the Fire Precautions Act was repealed when the Regulatory Reform (Fire Safety) Order 2005 came into force and placed the onus for occupant safety squarely on the shoulders of employers and managers of virtually all non-domestic premises. Although the fire authority is still required to enforce this new law, the former prescriptive regime, itself based upon the use of fire service inspectors (the vast majority of whom had first-hand firefighting experience) was ended, and non-fire expert employers handed an unconditional responsibility.

There have been, therefore, substantial shifts, which the proponents of change have argued are necessary for an emergency service that has to compete in a world of tightening local authority purse strings, but still maintain operational effectiveness in a constantly changing world.

However, what has not changed, and what cannot ever be changed, is the fact that fire and rescue personnel, however well trained and equipped, are still human beings. They all, therefore, have the individual potential to experience the full gamut of thoughts and emotions peculiar to the human condition.

Because the prevention of tragedy, and the saving of human life, lies at the very heart of the Firefighter's ethos, there will always be a sense of urgency in the fire station when the signal for an emergency response sounds, and no amount of preventive and protective safety law, shifts from 'ranks' to 'roles', or direct entry promotion systems can stifle these emotions.

The adrenaline rush created when the turn out signal sounds is no less strong today than it was when the call bell clamoured for the sort of emergencies that have been recorded within this book.

No one riding on the gleaming red vehicles, responding to Moorgate (1975), King's Cross (1987), to those smoking skyscrapers in south Manhattan on 11 September 2001, or to the carnage of the 7 July 2005, can know for certain what situation lies behind the cryptic words on the call out slip.

What is certain now, in the aftermath of 9/11 and 7/7, is that a new dimension of terror has arrived to be added to the traditional hazards to which our Firefighters have responded so magnificently for well over a hundred and fifty years. No crew member, swaying like sailor on a rough sea, as the Pumps, ladders and other emergency units weave their way through dense city traffic, has ever been totally sure what they will be confronted with on arrival.

Now, and because of these atrocities, the deadly threat of the terrorist's bomb has arrived to worsen that uncertainty, and the heart will beat the faster, and the adrenaline will surge the stronger as the address of the incident comes closer. It is then that the cool

242

competence of the 'good hands' with their developed ability to hold a tight and steely rein over the inner emotions, has to come to the fore. That competence and control is born out of practical experience, regular meaningful training and, historically, from the firm but fair leadership employed by some of the characters described in this book.

It is a fitting testimony that the operations on 7 July 2005 were so effective, as was demonstrated by the way all of the emergency services involved brought order out of the initial confusion and chaos caused by this new form of terror.

Within this book mention has been made of the terror that rained from the skies on to and around those courageous men and women who were involved in fighting those conflagrations that arose from the blitz bombings on the capital. Out of the dreadful terror and human loss of those wartime incidents numerous lessons were learned. To those substantial foundations were added those building blocks of fire and rescue strategies that derived from the sorts of incidents depicted within this book.

This fine heritage, and established tradition of handing down hard-won skills, will hopefully never be diluted. For that self-same school of hard-won experience has proved to be a major strength and a vital ingredient where the safety of the public and Firefighters is concerned. Coupled with this is the fact that as welcome as the reduction in 'working jobs' has been in terms of reduced casualties and property loss, it can create a downside in terms of a diluted sense of urgency unless those who are promoted to the more influential management positions can ensure that they are exposed as far as possible to a first-hand experiencing of fire and smoke.

As we have learned, until crews are on scene, no one knows with certainty what fate awaits them and this uncertainty will now be magnified in a new era of lurking terrorism. However, what is certain is this: the public can take comfort in knowing that an unceasing vigilance is being kept and that calls for help will result in a swift and sure response. They can be sure in the knowledge that fire and rescue teams will deploy high courage, determined resolve and a unique brand of humanity. A humanity that is honest and unquestioning and which is the hallmark of dedicated Firefighters everywhere. Men and women who, in venturing into the unknown, place the safety of others before themselves, as the events described within this book have shown and which were so graphically and visibly illustrated to the world on 11 September 2001 in New York and 7 July 2005 in London.

Glossary of Abbreviations and Terms

ADO   Assistant Divisional Officer

AFA   Automatic fire alarm

BA   Breathing apparatus

Branch or branch pipe   Technical term for the hose nozzle

BHQ   Brigade Headquarters

Ceiling hook   A long wooden pole having a metal point and spur at its furthermost end. Used to pierce a ceiling laden with water on the floor above, or to pull down ceiling laths and plaster

Dewhurst ladder   A 30-foot (9-metre) timber extension ladder carried on the pump

DHQ   Divisional Headquarters

DO   Divisional Officer

ET   Emergency tender. A specially equipped appliance which carried gear for dealing with a range of larger fires and non-fire emergencies. Crewed by specially trained personnel who were competent in advanced BA and rescue procedures.

                        Strategically sited across the capital and mobilised to all fires requiring eight or more pumps, major incidents, or to any major emergency at the request of the officer in charge.

Fire Services Act 1947

Legislation introduced when the local authorities regained control of UK fire brigades after the nationalisation of the fire service (NFS). Placed a number of legal duties on fire authorities to provide efficient firefighting and fire prevention services. (Revised in 2004.)

Home Office Fire Risk Categories

A national system which graded all areas from inner cities to remote country hamlets into perceived levels of fire risk. These determined the number of fire appliances despatched to fire emergencies and the time in which they had to be on scene.

HP

Hydraulic platform. An extending aerial appliance fitted with a cage and a water monitor. Used to get above a large blaze to direct a large firefighting stream or to rescue persons from high/precarious situations. Strategically sited across Greater London.

Informative message

A radio message sent by the officer in charge from an incident and serving to inform senior supervisory officers of the details in relation to the size of fire, persons trapped, equipment in use, rescue operations etc.

Ladders

Fire brigade speak for the 100-foot (30-metre) steel extending Turntable Ladder used to rescue persons or to provide a large fire stream from its water monitor permanently attached at its head. Strategically sited across Greater London.

Leading Fireman

The first rank on the promotion ladder. Known today as a 'Crew Manager'.

London Building Acts

Fire protection legislation unique to inner London's major structures such as dockland warehouses, and major office and commercial buildings.

Make up

A priority prefixed radio message sent from the officer in charge of an incident requesting additional fire Pumps or specialist appliances or equipment. The term derives from the added numbers of appliances requested, and which 'make up' the total numbers already on scene or proceeding to it.

Mickey

Fire brigade speak for a malicious false alarm call. Said to derive from saying that someone is 'taking the Mickey'.

Mobilising Control

One of four control rooms across the brigade into which 999 emergency calls were received and nearest available fire appliances and crews mobilised, and where all radio messages were sent and received from the incident ground

One One D

The section of the 1947 Fire Services Act which placed a duty on every local authority fire brigade to obtain information on premises to make them familiar with the situation ahead of any fire emergency.

Operational Note

A document promulgated across the whole brigade which provided detailed technical information on premise layouts, fire and other hazards, water supplies and a range of other information designed to increase the brigade's operational efficiency and to help reduce dangers to firefighters.

Persons reported

A priority prefixed radio message sent from the officer in charge informing Mobilising Control that persons are reported to be trapped within a burning building. In London Fire Brigade the receipt of a 'persons reported' resulted in an ambulance being automatically sent on to the incident.

Principal Officer The highest ranks in the fire service ranging down from Chief Fire Officer (CFO), Deputy Chief Fire Officer (DCFO) to Assistant Chief Fire Officer (ACFO).

Pump One of the two front line pumping appliances housed on London fire stations. Capable of providing a powerful number of fire fighting jets from street hydrants or open water supplies. Equipped with an onboard water tank to supply a hose reel jet as an initial attack Normally carried the Dewhurst ladder plus two hook ladders, and normally crewed by four Firefighters. Equipped with brackets to enable the wheeled escape ladder to be carried and thus known as a dual purpose appliance.

Pump Escape Identical to the Pump but carried the 50-foot (15-metre) wheeled escape ladder which was hand wound to its working height of 50 feet. By lashing a 'first floor ladder' to its head, a further 10 feet (3 metres) of reach could be attained.

The 'escape' as it was known was the principal rescue ladder. It remained in front line service in London until the 1980s, and had then been serving London and saving its citizens for over a hundred years. Normally crewed by five Firefighters.

Pump Ladder Replaced the Pump Escape after the wheeled escape ladder was withdrawn. The ladder is of alloy construction known as the '135' which denotes its fully extended height of 13 and a half metres. It is extended by a hauling line.

Rising main Commonly termed a 'riser'. It is a vertical metal water main with valves provided at every floor to enable crews to get a jet to work inside a building without having to use as much hose, it thereby saves precious time. It is charged from street mains via a fire pump.

RTA Road traffic accident.

GLOSSARY OF ABBREVIATIONS AND TERMS

Special service A non-fire emergency call such as a road or rail incident, person under a train, collapsed building, persons shut in a lift etc.

Station Officer The third rank up the promotion scale and the officer normally in charge of a fire station watch and its appliances. In London the station officer is generally known as 'Guvnor' or 'Guv'. Today the rank is called Watch Manager 'B'.

Stop message A radio message sent from the officer in charge which literally means 'stop mobilising'. Its receipt indicates that the incident is under control and that no further emergency attendances are needed.

Sub Officer The second rank up the promotion scale. Normally the second in command of a two or more appliance fire station and known as 'Sub'. Known today a Watch Manager 'A'.

Watch The name for a shift of firefighters and their officers in charge. Prior to 1978 London's fire stations had Blue, Red and White watches, with a fourth watch, Green, being added after that time. The term is borrowed from the navy.

Water monitor A large diameter nozzle attached to the head of a turntable ladder or hydraulic platform to provide a large water stream at large blazes. Ground and appliance mounted monitors are also available.